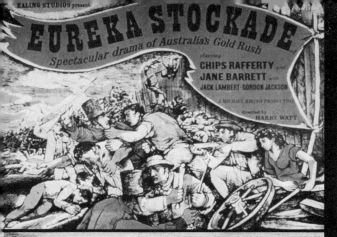

EALING STUDIOS present

EUREKA STOCKADE
Spectacular drama of Australia's Gold Rush

starring
CHIPS RAFFERTY and
JANE BARRETT with
JACK LAMBERT · GORDON JACKSON

A MICHAEL BALCON PRODUCTION

Directed by HARRY WATT

Ealing Studios present

JOHN CLEMENTS & GOOGIE WITHERS in

J.B.PRIESTLEY'S
THEY CAME TO A CITY

produced by MICHAEL BALCON

Ealing Studios present | **MICHAEL REDGRAVE · GOOGIE WITHERS**
MERVYN JOHNS · BASIL RADFORD
NAUNTON WAYNE · SALLY ANN HOWES
ROWLAND CULVER · FREDERICK VALK

DEAD of NIGHT

DISTRIBUTED BY EAGLE-LION

EALING STUDIOS present their first film in Technicolor

SARABAND

A Romance that rocked the Thrones of Kings

FROM THE NOVEL BY HELEN SIMPSON

starring

STEWART GRANGER
FRANÇOISE ROSAY
JOAN GREENWOOD
FLORA ROBSON

directed and designed by
BASIL DEARDEN & MICHAEL RELPH

A MICHAEL BALCON PRODUCTION

EALING STUDIOS present

Jenny Laird in
PAINTED BOATS

Directed by CHARLES CRICHTON   Produced by MICHAEL BALCON   Screen play by STEPHEN BLACK

A NEW SCREEN STAR IN A ROMANCE OF THE CANALS

Colour by TECHNICOLOR

Ealing Studios present
ANTHONY STEEL
DINAH SHERIDAN · HAROLD WARRENDER
WHERE NO VULTURES FLY

a MICHAEL BALCON production · Story and Direction HARRY WATT

An adventure story of savage Africa

EALING STUDIOS PRESENT
A Michael Balcon Production   **against THE WIND**

Robert Beatty
Simone Signoret
Jack Warner
Gisèle Préville
Paul Dupuis
Gordon Jackson

DIRECTED BY Charles Crichton
SCREENPLAY BY T. E. B. Clarke

They played macabre jokes - lively but deadly

EALING STUDIOS PRESENT

FRANÇOISE ROSAY
TOM WALLS · PATRICIA ROC in
JOHNNY Frenchman

PRODUCED BY MICHAEL BALCON   DIRECTED BY CHARLES FREND   SCREENPLAY T · E · B · CLARKE

£8.95
SA82

The eight faces of Alec Guinness in *Kind Hearts and Coronets*. 'His demure, understated genius . . . was a faithful reflection of the studio itself.' [From Peter Ustinov's Foreword]

GEORGE PERRY
presents

Forever
EALING

*A CELEBRATION OF THE GREAT
BRITISH FILM STUDIO*

with a foreword by
PETER USTINOV

PAVILION
MICHAEL JOSEPH

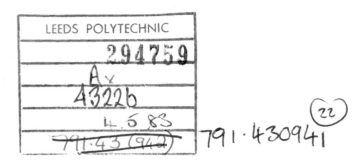

791.430941 (22)

First published in Great Britain in 1981 by
Pavilion Books Limited
8 Cork Street London W1X 2HA
in association with Michael Joseph Limited
44 Bedford Square London WC1B 3DU

Designed by Lawrence Edwards

Set, printed and bound in Great Britain by
Fakenham Press Limited, Fakenham, Norfolk

76 020743 -1

Perry, George
    Forever Ealing.
    1. Ealing Studios – History
    I. Title
    384′.8′06542184   PN1999.E/

ISBN 0–907516–06–8

Contents

Acknowledgments

The stills from Ealing films in this book are the copyright of EMI Films Limited – a Member of the THORN-EMI Group, and were obtained from EMI Films and the National Film Archive.

My special thanks are due to members of the British Film Institute, particularly Brenda Davies, former head of the Information Department, and Michelle Snapes, the head of the Stills Department who, with ever-willing help from their teams, supplied their special skills and knowledge whenever requested. Colin Lord, the Stills Department Administrator at Elstree, also worked hard on my behalf to seek out long-forgotten visual treasures. Christine Walker gave many hours of assistance on general research and in the mammoth task of collating the filmographies. My old friend Margaret Gardner was immensely helpful. Especial thanks are due to Peter Ustinov, who while filming as Hercule Poirot took time to write his apt foreword. Brigid Avison and Rose Bean of Pavilion Books were unstintingly dedicated in seeing the book into production, and, above all, Colin Webb inspired it, encouraged it and ensured that it was published. Lawrence Edwards supplied his talent and skill to the design and layout. My wife, Frances, gave me all the patience, support and practical assistance I required at every step.

The book is dedicated to the memory of Mick Balcon, in the spirit in which he accepted his knighthood, as the personification of Ealing and of all the men and women who made it what it was.

Foreword

The American tradition decrees that Big is Beautiful, for reasons which are evident. The British tradition, until the confusion produced by technological advances in a shrinking world, has always held that Small is Superior.

When Drake and Raleigh were busy singeing the King of Spain's beard and Shakespeare was equally busy forming and writing his transcendant works, Britain was a taut and unpredictable place, filled with the arrogance of smallness, and with but scant respect for the visibly greater power of some other nations. This jaunty, disrespectful attitude hibernated during the somnolent splendours of the Victorian era, when the growth in wealth was inevitably accompanied by a loss of both efficiency and sensibility, to re-emerge in the Second World War in the form of Chindits, Popski's Private Army, and the plethora of romantic units which once more glorified the small by mocking the big and seemingly all-powerful.

The films of Ealing were the accurate, and often inspired reflection of this side of the British character. Everything about Ealing was defiantly small, and glorified the small at the expense of the big, the conventional, the pompous.

One thinks of *Passport to Pimlico*, for instance, in which Pimlico, an area in London near enough to Victoria Station to capture occasional whiffs of foreignness, discovered in some ancient documents that it was independent of the British Isles, and exercised its prerogatives by becoming a jewel of paradoxical smallness in the heart of a Britain

rendered vast and impotent by this sudden emergence, like a stubborn pimple on an elephant's hide.

Or again, *Whisky Galore!*, a title evidently deemed
too dangerous in America, which had always had an
alcoholic problem and even espoused prohibition,
and where it became *Tight Little Island*. This title
was a more accurate description of the film's character than the original one, since it made delicious fun
of a neglected island in the Hebrides upon which a
ship with a cargo of whisky is wrecked, and it
forestalls the effect of the later discovery of North
Sea oil on Scots and English alike.

In terms of what is still called the Film Industry,
if the Americans turned out the symphonic works
with mammoth 'production values', Ealing stuck
doggedly and defiantly to chamber music, with
emphasis on individual contributions. Alec Guinness was the actor most firmly identified with this
golden era, and his demure, understated genius,
brimful of subtle ironies, was a faithful reflection of
the studio itself. It too was demure, being extremely
difficult to find, and with no trace of the florid
Hollywood palladian style, evocative of both industrial power and eternal rest. Ealing Studios hide
behind a green sward in a suburban street, and the
humble gates seem to give on to cottage industries.

Perhaps its most perfect achievement was *Kind
Hearts and Coronets*, a film of exquisite construction
and literary quality. There are not many films which
make one wish to read the text. Alec Guinness
appeared in a variety of roles, ranging from an
admiral to a spinster, all of them remarkably alike
while being totally dissimilar, a masterpiece of self-
assurance in an intimate stratosphere of the actor's
art.

In the nature of things, Ealing was too good to
last. Even Drake and Raleigh had to grow old and
less adventurous. But then, their opposition was
merely the floating altarpieces which constituted the
Invincible Armada, monuments to the True Faith
rather than to maritime technique. Ealing was up
against much more pernicious problems. The Rank
group at that time was striving to break into the
American market, evolving a mid-Atlantic accent
for its actors, and searching for a style which would
be easily comprehended in Peoria.

How useless this exercise was was subsequently

proved by the Beatles, who imposed their personal
style everywhere. By being stubbornly themselves,
they triumphed, and it is a fitting irony that Ealing,
which could never have survived the compromises
of a furtive and pusillanimous period in British
film-making, has since become the object of cult-
worship in that very part of the world where it had
been deemed too English and too parochial to stand
any chance of penetrating.

The mini-mogul of this quaint little Empire was
one Sir Michael Balcon, as different from his richly
vulgar and malaproper transatlantic counterparts as
it is possible to imagine. There was something about
his authority as secret, as exclusive, as that of a chief
of MI5, or of a Minister of Intelligence, if such a
thing is conceivable.

He and his Ealing may have gone, but their
memory retain the fresh fragrance of immortality.

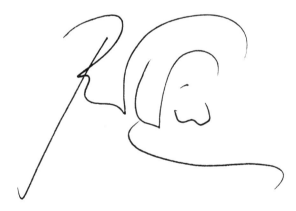

Previous page: Peter Ustinov's only
Ealing appearance in *The Goose Steps Out*,
1942

Introduction

A newly-hired nineteen-year-old secretary at *The Sunday Times* was exploring my filing cabinet. She came across a fat folder labelled Ealing. 'What's this?' she asked. 'It's a book I'm doing,' I answered. 'Great!' she said. I beamed. And then she spoilt it. 'But why Ealing? Why not, say, Clapham?'

It serves as a reminder of how rapidly time buries the past. It is fifty years since Ealing Studios opened for business, and twenty-five since they passed into the hands of the BBC. The last film bearing the discreet Ealing logo was released in 1959. But unlike many other old British film studios that are now furniture warehouses, factories, housing estates and shopping centres, the buildings on their compact site between Walpole Park and Ealing Green retain their pristine appearance, and moreover, cameras still turn on the stages.

Nor does Ealing's cinema output languish forgotten. The medium of television, as well as preserving the Studios intact, also provides air time for the old films, and shows them frequently. It is not merely the middle-aged and elderly who relish the antics of the Pimlico Burgundians, the Titfield railwayfolk, the inebriated Todday islanders. Younger audiences (excepting Sarah-Jane, the secretary) have discovered the films, coming on them at first as quaint period pieces, but then appreciating the freshness of their appeal, decades after they were made.

The Forties, the quintessential Ealing era, do not inspire much nostalgia. The frivolous Twenties, the glamorous Thirties, even the rebellious Fifties and the freewheeling, anarchic Sixties, are the simplistic images that have a pull on the imagination. But the Forties had no flappers, no bright young things, no beatniks, no flower children, no hippies. I can testify that it was a rotten time in which to be a child – a drab, serious age of deprivation and diminished aspirations. It is true that for many adults the war was the most exciting thing that had ever happened to them, delivering risk, thrills, involvement and conviviality, a set of circumstances that was bound to make post-war readjustment all the more difficult. But for the women and children who stayed at home, the pleasures were for the most part few. I remember my childhood as one of constant upheaval, paternal absence, perpetual deficiences of those items normally regarded as juvenile staples – sweets, comics, toys, rubber balls. The cinema was one of the few consolations and, usually in the company of a responsible adult, I would visit the local Odeon, its gleaming white faience-tiled façade temporarily muddied by grey-green camouflage paint, to see such Ealing films as *The Black Sheep of Whitehall*, *The Goose Steps Out* and the moving *San Demetrio London*, although to be fair it was their content rather than their provenance which interested me.

But it was during the early post-war period that Ealing reached its apogee. The mirror sequence in *Dead of Night* haunted me for weeks. The open spaces of *The Overlanders* seemed every bit as enticing as Ford's Arizona in *My Darling Clementine*. Cavalcanti's discursive *Nicholas Nickleby* sent me at once to read the book. *Hue and Cry* seemed to me to be the perfect schoolboy fantasy, with a comic paper coming to life. I still have my inky diary for 1949, the greatest year for Ealing in which three of their best films were released. The war had been over for four years, but everyone was still obliged to have identity cards and ration books. Britain's streets still bore the gaping evidence of bombing, new building was strictly controlled, and even the most modest improvement to one's home required a building permit. The basic petrol ration left little for private motoring, and new cars were only for export, as were luxury goods, a category that included washing machines and vacuum cleaners. 'Export or Die' read a slogan plastered up in Piccadilly Circus. Even electric advertising signs were rigidly banned until the middle of that year when crowds gathered in thousands around the statue of Eros to watch the word 'BOVRIL' erupt into coloured lights after ten years of extinction.

I note that on 2 May, two days after Wolverhampton beat Leicester 3–1 in the Cup Final, I went to the long-vanished Marble Arch Pavilion to see a new Ealing comedy 'acclaimed by the Press' called *Passport to Pimlico*, which was accompanied by 'This Modern Age No. 27 – Education for Living', an episode of J. Arthur Rank's expensive answer to the American *March of Time* series of documentary magazines. I was a young teenager then, but I remember the occasion well. Nowadays the film seems to be a lively social satire based on an original and enterprising idea. Then it seemed an astonishing lampoon of the government and the mandarins of Whitehall who were at the time busily devaluing the pound, tightening Britain's belt, festooning its citizenry with forms and red tape, while spending taxpayers' millions on such lunatic projects as the Bristol Brabazon and the groundnuts scheme, and generally seeing to it that collective national misery was a worthy condition.

That same year, during what was to be a scorching summer for once, came the next great Ealing film, the most successful black comedy made in Britain and in my view Ealing's best film. The cinema where I saw *Kind Hearts and Coronets*, a film which mercifully had nothing to do with contemporary life, and which was accompanied by an earlier Ealing comedy, *Fiddlers Three*, has long since been replaced by

an office block, just as the Odeon at which I first saw *Whisky Galore!* is now a supermarket. Virtually all of the great art deco temples that formed the major landmarks of my rising years have gone, and the one or two that remain have been mutilated by shoddy conversion into small multi-screen theatres. Ealing's day was done when the first big wave of closures took place in the mid-Fifties, and the new ITV channel beckoned the public to stay at home and watch television.

In its heyday Ealing Studios had an institutional value that transcended the accepted notion of the place of cinema in society. The extravagant behaviour of Alexander Korda and the evangelistic tycoonery of J. Arthur Rank attacted the headlines and the misapprobation. Ealing, however, was looked on as acceptable, modest, quality-conscious and culturally responsible. Even Ealing posters were markedly different from those generally associated with the film industry. During Sir Michael Balcon's tenure, efforts were made to encourage well-known artists to try their hand; thus John Piper, Edward Bawden, James Fitton, John Minton, James Boswell and Edward Ardizzone, among others, produced posters for tube stations, street hoardings and cinema fronts. Their work may have lacked the eye-catching hard-sell technique of their Hollywood counterparts, but they advertised not only the film but something of Ealing's steadfast seriousness of purpose. Ealing was the one part of the British film industry which fitted into the prevailing tradition of left-of-centre, middle-class cultural earnestness that was then apparent in such institutions as Penguin Books; *Picture Post*; much of the BBC and especially William Haley's brave creation of 1946, the Third Programme; the *Manchester Guardian*, as it was still known; London Transport's publicity department; the *News Chronicle*; and, perhaps its largest but least enduring manifestation, the Festival of Britain. This trait could be called Balconry, for want of a better term.

Ealing's character was mainly determined by that of its celebrated production chief from 1938 onwards, Sir Michael Balcon, a legendary figure in the history of the British film industry. His background was that of the Birmingham Jewish middle classes, and his family had many South African connections.

Balcon had begun producing films in the early Twenties and had co-founded Gainsborough. He reached Ealing with years of successful pictures behind him, and had been responsible for the output of Gaumont-British in the Thirties. Balcon ran a tight ship and his style did not suit everyone. He was a great believer in the cross-fertilization of ideas, and very little of Ealing's creation took place behind closed doors. Rushes, or 'dailies', were not private affairs, but open to anyone in the Studios' employ, and everyone there was encouraged to keep an eye on each other's work and to discuss it freely. It was a place in which the editor was highly regarded, and nearly all Ealing's directors had served earlier in the cutting-rooms – Charles Crichton, Charles Frend, Henry Cornelius, Thorold Dickinson, Robert Hamer, Leslie Norman, Michael Truman and Seth Holt were all former film editors. A much smaller number had graduated from screenwriting – this group included Basil Dearden, Harry Watt and Alexander Mackendrick. But significantly no actors were ever elevated to a directorial role. Balcon was less than awed by their creative capabilities. 'I was often far from happy', Sir Alec Guinness, the greatest of Ealing players, told me, 'in an atmosphere which resented actors and their necessity.'

In many respects the film business has undergone a volte-face since those days, and it is perfectly normal at the present time to find the actors having a major say in the creative control of a production, including the choice of director, but it is a power only acquired on the strength of their 'bankability', or their potential to attract finance. Ealing, however, operated almost on a repertory basis, with a number of reliable performers appearing again and again, no doubt attracted as much by the idea of regular work as of contributing to the product of a much-favoured British studio. But Ealing, good as it was for reputations, was no place in which to get rich.

In the Studios' early days, when Basil Dean was in command, the main source of screen material for films other than the comedies of Gracie Fields and George Formby was the West End stage; the theatre remained Dean's main interest throughout his time at Ealing, and he regarded film merely as an extension of the medium. On his arrival at Ealing, Balcon had to go along with the established production programme, but the start of the Second World War a year later hastened his conversion of the majority of the Studios' output to films based on original screenplays. One by one the old guard of directors from the Dean era faded away, and new opportunities arose to be fulfilled by the young men of talent on whom Balcon had cast an eye, such as Pen Tennyson, Basil Dearden and Charles Frend. At the same time the comic films of George Formby and his successor, Will Hay, ensured an Ealing pull at the box office.

One of Balcon's shrewdest moves during this period was to bring in Alberto Cavalcanti, who exacted a creative influence on Ealing output as massive as his own. It was Cavalcanti who pioneered the use of documentary techniques in the making of fiction features, stamping them with the mark of authenticity. Some of Ealing's wartime films were overt propaganda, their effectiveness heightened by the professional skill of the film-makers; *Next of Kin*, an anti-'careless talk' film, expressed its message so graphically that Churchill wanted to ban it as he felt that it would demoralize audiences.

By the end of the war Ealing had found and developed a recognizable style which it was then able to apply to an eclectic range of subject matter. One of the persistent Ealing myths is that only two kinds of film were made there – comedies and war films. But almost every film genre was tackled, with the exception of the musical (*Champagne Charlie* was the closest approach to that area) and the Western, although many familiar ingredients of the latter could be found in the films Balcon made in Australia. The use of real locations was something which the studio was particularly good at, even when recording sound out-of-doors was still a difficult operation. Romney Marsh was used for the filming of *The Loves of Joanna Godden*, a love story set amidst the sheep and long grass. The streets and bombsites of London form the backdrop for *Hue and Cry*, a comedy with a climax involving hundreds of young boys. *It Always Rains on Sunday*, a drama set in the East End, shows the teeming markets and shabby streets of Bethnal Green and Whitechapel, as if in a documentary.

It is the great Ealing comedies, which must

include *Passport to Pimlico*, *Whisky Galore!*, *Kind Hearts and Coronets*, *The Man in the White Suit*, *The Lavender Hill Mob* and *The Ladykillers*, that are the legacy for which the Studios are best remembered, although they were only a small proportion of the whole. Perhaps against his better judgment, Balcon was persuaded by J. Arthur Rank himself to make the expensive and financially unsuccessful historic drama, *Saraband for Dead Lovers*; its failure was mitigated by the acclaim in the same year given to the similarly costly and prestigious production, *Scott of the Antarctic*, an epic story of British heroism on the one hand, the downfall of gentlemanly amateurs on the other. Many other Ealing films should be remembered for their quality, among them *The Blue Lamp*, which, for all its naïvety in present-day terms, was the first conscious attempt to portray police work in London in realistic close-up; *Mandy*, a small-scale, touching story of the problems besetting a deaf child, which made the long-standing actor Jack Hawkins into a major star; *The Cruel Sea*, Hawkins' most famous film, a sombre and restrained adaptation of a celebrated bestseller of life in the wartime navy; and *Nowhere to Go*, the penultimate film to bear the Ealing mark, a dark thriller revealing the tragically short-lived talent of its director, Seth Holt.

Of the ninety-six films made under the Balcon aegis, inevitably there are a number of failures, and even one or two embarrassments. But the average Ealing film met a number of criteria that gave it an edge over the rest of British output of the time. Ealing is often sneered at for its cosiness and paternalism, for its fail-safe method of working, and for being a sort of cottage industry of film-making. The predominance of men among the production staff (Diana Morgan and Janet Green were the only female writers of any consequence, and during the war, possibly as a result of a manpower shortage, Mary Habberfield and Eileen Boland received editing credits, initially under Sidney Cole's supervision) undoubtedly led to Ealing's deficiencies in handling women and women's subjects, but there were a few exceptions; Robert Hamer in particular showed skill in his direction of Googie Withers in *Pink String and Sealing Wax* and of Valerie Hobson and Joan Greenwood in *Kind Hearts and Coronets*.

Another canard is that Ealing never took any chances and always played safe. The record shows that Ealing often exposed itself to the risk of failure, and when it occurred Balcon wasted little time on recriminations. By its nature, the film business is one in which temperament and ego abound, and in which bitter rivalries can damage careers and work. Under his firm grip such things were not allowed to get out of hand. Proof of the success with which Balcon kept things together lay in the consistency and loyalty of the Ealing team. Some who had joined him near the beginning or had even, as in Basil Dearden's case, worked at the Studios in Dean's time, were still with Balcon at the end, twenty years later.

It was Balcon's mission to present the British character, or his idea of it. He regarded the British as individualists who were not averse to joining up with each other to battle against a common cause. He saw a nation tolerant of harmless eccentricities, but determinedly opposed to anti-social behaviour. He venerated initiative and spirit, personal achievement rather than reliance on some higher authority. He was of the 'small is beautiful' persuasion, not caring for large organizations or the bureaucratic powers of civil servants. Ealing's values were decent, virtuous and simplistic, and finite of ambition. Balcon ran the Studios much as would be expected in the plot of a typical Ealing film, with him as a Jack Hawkins figure galvanizing a motley collection of disparate people into an efficient, cohesive force, capable of outsmarting and taking advantage of the faceless corporation (Rank) which would otherwise swallow them up, and of keeping their identity intact. The pity is that there could be no happy ending, only a slow fade-out. It was not really that the money men eventually won, but that the times changed and the special qualities of Ealing no longer seemed appropriate.

The Ealing story, however, is one that deserves to be told. It was an aspect of the British film industry in which some national pride is not misplaced.

London   May 1981

CHAPTER 1

Life before Balcon

When the twentieth century began, Ealing was a prosperous middle-class suburb on the western edge of London. Beyond it lay the yet undeveloped fields of Greenford and Heston, still unmistakably country villages with farms, cows and muddy lanes under the oaks and elms of rural Middlesex. The prevailing wind blows from the south-west, and in those days of coal fires the thick smoke pall which usually hung over the dense inner London districts and the East End rarely offended the residents of the pleasant western suburbs. Ealing's prosperity derived from the railway, Brunel's Great Western providing a fast service to Paddington, a mere five miles up the track, while the District Railway, electrified as early as 1905, offered a direct link with the City. The town was an attractive dormitory for the professional classes, who lived in the Victorian villas surrounding Ealing Common and in the tree-lined avenues leading from it.

South of the busy Uxbridge Road, which linked London with Oxford, is Ealing Green, the historic nucleus of the neighbourhood. It was here in 1902 that Will Barker, a pioneer of the British film industry, bought two houses facing the Green: West Lodge, which had nearly four acres of grounds, and The Lodge. Barker had begun as an amateur in 1896, the year that the Lumière Brothers exhibited their moving pictures in London for the first time. He had obtained one of their cameras for £40, and for the next five years had amused himself and his friends with displays. In 1901 he became a professional, and started making films on an open-air stage

at Stamford Hill. In the early days films were only fifty feet in length, the capacity of the magazine in the Lumière camera, and were sold outright to showmen and 'penny gaff' (converted shop) owners at a guinea a time. When he moved to Ealing, Barker continued to film out-of-doors, until in 1907 he built his first covered stage, a glass construction like a greenhouse. The first Ealing Studios eventually consisted of three such stages.

Barker, a colourful, energetic pragmatist and former commercial salesman, became the managing director of Warwick, one of the most famous of the early British film companies, but later, as the industry developed and films grew in length and ambition, he branched out on his own. He had considerable flair and showmanship, and many of his pictures were adventurous for their time. In 1912 he made the first screen version of *Hamlet*, taking all of one day to film the twenty-two scenes. The sets were built one inside the other, and as each scene was shot its set was peeled away to reveal the next. The film cost £180, but its satisfactory profit was £600. Barker's film of *Henry VIII* created a sensation. According to Dr Rachael Low, in her definitive history of the early British cinema, 'It could with justification be described as the first really important British film.' In the first place, it brought Sir Herbert Beerbohm Tree and his company to the screen. Tree demanded and was paid £1,000 for his appearance, money Barker had to borrow. Secondly, it caused an uproar in the trade when the entrepreneurial producer announced that he was

Will Barker, Ealing's pioneer film-maker

released in 1915, was *Jane Shore*, starring his chief leading lady, Blanche Forsythe. It was the most spectacular British production to that date, employing thousands of extras in some of the set-piece scenes, and, because it dealt with a period of English history in which internal conflict prevailed (the Wars of the Roses), it was seen in some quarters as the British answer to D. W. Griffith's contemporary masterpiece set in the American Civil War, *The Birth of a Nation*.

Barker's contribution to British film history which established Ealing as an important production centre was relatively brief. In common with many other British producers, he was badly affected by the First World War. Although at first he was kept busy producing recruiting films for Kitchener's army, his output later dwindled away. When the war ended he decided to retire from the industry. In 1920 Ealing Studios were sold to General Film Renters, who leased them out to anyone who wanted to use them. During the Twenties the old place underwent hard times, and the only people interested in it were producers of short subjects. In 1929, with the advent of talking pictures, it was bought by Union Studios, who re-equipped it at a cost of £250,000. But they were unable to make it successful and went into receivership. So ended the first Ealing Studios.

The period was one of uncomfortable transition for the film industry. It did not take long for the effects of the 1929 Wall Street crash to be felt in Britain. Nevertheless, the City had begun to take an interest in the burgeoning world of talking pictures. It is hard, more than half a century after the event, to grasp the extent of the upheaval in the film industry brought about by the advent of sound. It took more than two years from the New York premiere of *The Jazz Singer* in October 1927 for manufacturers to reach a joint agreement standardizing sound equipment, so that all films could be shown regardless of how they were recorded. Inevitably, the Vitaphone system, using synchronized discs, was jettisoned, and in 1930, Western Electric, a Bell Telephone subsidiary, and RCA (the Radio Corporation of America), came to terms with the German Tobis Klangfilm company, and with a compatible sound-on-film process divided the world into territories.

going to burn publicly all twenty prints six weeks after its release. Barker was trying to stamp out the practice whereby worn-out, tattered prints continued to circulate, to the public's discontent; his move did succeed in forcing exhibitors to mend some of their ways – and it also sent the rental price rocketing.

Like his more famous successors at Ealing, Barker was very conscious of the Britishness of his output. As the American star system took root and pre-First World War audiences were avidly awaiting every fresh Mary Pickford import, Barker built up an Ealing stock company of home-grown players, hoping that the public would recognize and follow them. His films tended to have a patriotic tone, none more so than his epic on Queen Victoria, *Sixty Years a Queen*, an economical production – the white horses drawing the royal coach were whitewashed – which is said to have made its begetter £35,000. His most famous film, directed by Martin Thornton and

Below: Barker's 1913 epic, *Sixty Years a Queen*
Right and bottom: *Jane Shore,* with Blanche Forsythe

A cinema owner might have to spend as much as £4,000 on wiring his theatre for sound, but the alternative was closure, for not only did the supply of silent films dry up but audiences were no longer interested anyway. Until harmony was achieved there were something like two hundred sound systems to choose from, most destined for rapid oblivion, and the wrong decision could mean ownership of useless, obsolete equipment. The arrival of the 'talkies' brought about changes in exhibition practice, such as the introduction of second features to enable the backlog of silent films to get a screening, coupled with talkies at the top of the bill. When the silents were all used up, audiences still demanded a second film, which meant the arrival of the 'B' picture, or the dreaded British variant, the 'quota quickie', so-called because the Cinematograph Act of 1927 had introduced a minimum percentage of British programming to protect the home industry. The outcome in the Thirties was minimal films in every sense, just to fulfil the law. There was also a change in renting methods. Bookings had always been at a flat rate, which would vary according to the importance of the film. The distributor did not share the exhibitor's risk, but on the other hand did not benefit from his success either. With the talkies came a sliding scale, with 'break points', stages at which the percentage increased when takings reached certain levels.

The new owners of the Ealing site were Associated Talking Pictures (ATP), a company formed by Basil Dean, a prominent theatrical producer, with the distinguished actor-manager, Sir Gerald du Maurier, as his chairman. ATP had already made three films on rented stages at Beaconsfield Studios. The first, a talkie of John Galsworthy's celebrated play, *Escape*, was made with the RCA sound system, and was released in Britain through a distribution company set up by the Radio-Keith-Orpheum Corporation of America (better known as RKO). Dean was then joined by Stephen Courtauld, of the rayon manufacturing family, and Reginald Baker, a senior partner in a firm of chartered accountants with many clients in the film industry. After the third film had been shot at Beaconsfield it became clear to the company that it would be better to have a home of its own, and space was found at Ealing, in the gardens and apple orchard to the south of the stages constructed by Will Barker, large enough to contain a modern complex totally purpose-built for the new medium of sound films. Basil Dean, in his autobiography, described how his enthusiasm for Ealing was confirmed when he received a report from the Meteorological Office that the district had the best record of freedom from fog for anywhere within the Greater London area, including Elstree, where

Opposite: aerial view of Basil Dean's newly-built Ealing Studios

Escape, ATP's first film, from Galsworthy's play: (right) Gerald du Maurier, Edna Best, (below) Phyllis Konstam, Eric Cowley, Gerald du Maurier. Much was shot on location in Devon.

Basil Dean with early 'talkie' microphone,
directing *Looking on the Bright Side* in
1932, shortly after Ealing's opening

there was the biggest concentration of rival sound
stages. They decided to go ahead, and briefed
Robert Atkinson, the architect who had been
involved in Union Studios' attempt to bring talkies
to Ealing Green, to start working on fresh designs.
Meanwhile, Dean and Baker set sail for the United
States to reinforce their agreement with RKO.

The outcome was not quite as hoped. The terms
agreed with the Americans turned out to be less
favourable than those that had been in operation
before, where production costs had been matched
dollar by dollar. Now RKO expected ATP to carry all
the initial expense, with the American company contributing its share of the negative cost on delivery.
Fortunately, Baker and Courtauld were able to
secure the finance to go ahead with the building
work from sources in London, using a skilful blend
of bank guarantees and insurance policies. Construction of the first two of the planned four stages
began in March 1931; they were respectively the
small Stage 1 of 1,972 square feet and the big Stage 2
of 9,576 square feet. (Stages 3A and 3B, completed
in 1934, were paired, each giving 6,035 square feet,
and the last one to be built, which opened in 1944,
was the Model Stage, used for special effects, which
was 4,819 square feet in extent.)

The new Ealing Studios were the first to be built
in Britain with talkies in mind, and Dean and Baker
had gained much wisdom during their visit to Los
Angeles on how that could be best achieved. They
planned to fit RCA Photophone equipment, and to
take advantage of the company's new Noiseless
Recording system which had eliminated much of the
unpleasant background hiss that marred early
soundtracks. The house facing Ealing Green, The
Lodge, became the administration building, but
retained its pleasantly domestic Regency character.
The adjacent main entrance provided a charming
way into the more prosaic, factory-style area behind
it. Dean's pine-panelled office, later Michael Balcon's, was on the ground floor at the rear, with
french windows looking out on to a small lawn on
which were eventually placed a couple of beehives.
The site at Ealing Green, less than four acres in
extent, was absurdly small in comparison with most
Hollywood studio lots, but nevertheless Dean was
determined to have everything as up-to-date as pos-

sible. The core of the studio was the power house, where all the electricity needed was generated independently of the public supply. Dean resisted engineering arguments that it should be located in a corner, away from the stages, in order that the whine and vibration of the machinery would not disturb filming, and instead insisted that means be found to insulate the generators with cavity walls and rubber foundations. His solution worked.

But other, potentially more fatal problems arose. For Britain, 1931 was not a happy year. The great slump took hold, and in August a financial crisis gripped the City, precipitating the resignation of the Labour government and the election of the National coalition under Ramsay MacDonald. Unemployment soared towards the three-million mark and Britain went off the Gold Standard. The government cut the salaries of civil servants, teachers, the police and the services, and raised taxation. Whole industries came to a standstill as men were laid off indefinitely. The greatest impact of the depression was felt in the north, where London and the Home Counties were looked on with a certain contempt, understandably in view of the decisions taken in Whitehall and Threadneedle Street. It was a terrible climate in which to be halfway through the construction of a film studio, and among the consequences of the slump were a severe increase in the liabilities of ATP, and a withdrawal of support by the insurance companies during the building programme. Estimates for the cost (about £70,000) were found to be hopelessly wrong, and only by considerable personal support from Stephen Courtauld, who brought his brother Jack, a Member of Parliament, on to the board, was completion made possible. Another headache that the directors faced during this period was the non-delivery of the sound equipment from RCA. The demand throughout the film industry had been so great that the company was having difficulty meeting orders. It was essential, if ATP was to continue trading, that it started operating from Ealing as quickly as possible. Luckily, Basil Dean, in New York to discuss a Broadway play project, was able to lean heavily on the top men at RCA, and on 25 October Reg Baker received a cable from him that the *Aquitania* would shortly set sail, carrying all the vital equipment.

Elizabeth Allan and Hilda Simms in *Nine Till Six*, the first film to be made at the new Ealing Studios

Thus at the end of November 1931 a modest opening ceremony was performed at Ealing Studios, with the tape being cut by Mrs Stephen Courtauld. And a few days later, on 2 December, with the plaster and paint still damp and workmen applying the last touches, Basil Dean went on the studio floor with *Nine Till Six*, an adaptation of a play by Aimée and Philip Stuart, which had featured an all-female cast and was now enlarged with the addition of one man, Richard Bird. Elizabeth Allan, its comeliest star, was simultaneously appearing in another film, *The Chinese Puzzle*, being made by Julius Hagen at Twickenham, with a dovetailed schedule and weekend shooting. Not surprisingly, her exhaustion eventually caught up with her. The film itself was a box-office disaster, following the pattern already established in the handful of pre-Ealing pictures that they had produced and distributed through RKO. Even *Escape*, the first wholly-talking British film to feature the English countryside, was not a success.

Below: the Prince of Wales examines 'the organ' during his visit to Ealing when *The Impassive Footman* was being made

Right and opposite: Ealing's brightest early star, Gracie Fields, in *Looking on the Bright Side.* Her co-star was Richard Dolman

During the shooting of *The Impassive Footman*, Ealing Studios were honoured by a royal visit. The Prince of Wales, still four years from his accession to the throne, had been invited by Jack Courtauld, and was particularly fascinated by one of Ealing's best-known technical innovations, the mobile control board nicknamed 'the organ' which at the beginning of a take could start the camera turning, mark the film for synchronization, shut down the noisy air-conditioning or heating system, sound the bell, light up the 'Silence' sign outside the stage, turn on the red light, switch off the telephones and lock the doors. In 1932 it was a very impressive piece of apparatus. The Prince visited the cutting rooms, and then went on to 'The Inn', as the studio restaurant was known. Dean later recalled how, once ensconced in the directors' dining room, he offered the Prince some tea, but was somewhat abashed when his royal guest demanded a whisky and soda, as alcohol was not consumed on the premises. Luck-

ily a bottle was found in somebody's office.

The salvation of Dean's reputation as a film producer came with his introduction of Gracie Fields to the screen. The Lancashire comedienne had been on the music-hall stage since the age of thirteen and had become a popular star in the provincial theatre in the Twenties. Her bright optimism and vitality, together with the uninhibited gusto of her singing style, proved to be just what audiences needed to counter the gloom of the depression years. Her first film, *Sally in Our Alley*, was made at Beaconsfield while ATP were still using the British Lion stages there, and was directed by Maurice Elvey. When it opened in July 1931 it was an instant hit, securely establishing her as an important box-office star. Her second film, *Looking on the Bright Side*, was made at Ealing, the direction being shared by Graham Cutts and Basil Dean himself, and in spite of irritating interference from her current husband, Archie Pitt, who regarded himself as Gracie's Svengali, it turned

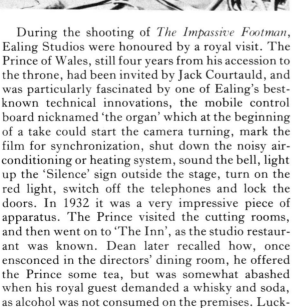

out well, and helped to overcome Gracie's earlier apprehension at embarking on a film career.

The parting of the ways between ATP and RKO began to seem inevitable. At the start of the relationship, before ATP's own studios were in operation, Dean had been appointed RKO's European representative with the responsibility to find potential material, and to examine the possibilities of acquiring cinemas in Britain. Consequently, the recently-built Leicester Square Theatre was bought, with the intention of becoming the West End showcase for RKO product, and it was there that *Sally in Our Alley* opened, meeting the quota demands for British films. But for the most part the American controllers expected them to play in the bottom halves of double bills, and were incensed if even a palpably indifferent American film – as many of RKO's were at the time – was relegated to that position. Not surprisingly, the development of Ealing meant that Dean was unable to give RKO the time and energies

they expected. Nor was the arrangement working from ATP's point of view. In spite of their distribution agreement in America, not a single dollar was returned on nine pictures delivered to RKO. Such screenings that had been arranged were in art houses, the excuse being that general audiences would not understand the British accent. Such an argument should not have applied to Australasia, however, and ATP withdrew *Looking on the Bright Side* from that market, giving it to another distributor, with the expectation of a showdown. It seemed that RKO was having troubles on its own doorstep, as a result of a Federal order divorcing General Electric from RCA, and was having to meet a foreclosed bank loan of $2 million. RKO withheld payments due to Ealing, pending a breach of contract action; this in turn led the banks controlling Ealing's financial destiny to call for an end to the company's own production, and the leasing of the studios to other producers.

Arthur Wontner as Sherlock Holmes
in *The Sign of Four*

Opposite: *Perfect Understanding*, Gloria
Swanson and Laurence Olivier.
Note the early mike boom

Below, top: Rosemary Ames, Richard
Dolman, *Love on the Spot*
Middle: Billy Milton, Edmond Breon,
William Austin, *Three Men in a Boat*
Bottom: *Loyalties*, Heather Thatcher,
Philip Strange, unknown, Basil Rathbone,
Joan Wyndham and Griffith Humphreys
overacting

Their attitude was perhaps understandable, given the poor performance of the first films emerging from the new studios. There had been a feeble adaptation of Conan Doyle's *The Sign of Four* with Arthur Wontner repeating his stage Sherlock Holmes; two Sapper stories, *The Impassive Footman* and *Love on the Spot*; a version, directed by Graham Cutts, of Jerome K. Jerome's *Three Men in a Boat*; and an adaptation of Galsworthy's play, *Loyalties*, directed by Basil Dean. During this period of low ebb, less than a year after the studios had opened, the American star Gloria Swanson helped the financial situation by producing and appearing in *Perfect Understanding*, directed by Cyril Gardner, with a screenplay by a young director of quota quickies, Michael Powell, and co-starring Laurence Olivier. In 1933 no other productions needed rented space, and rather than become a quickie factory Ealing closed down, with even its office staff working only alternate weeks on half salary during the crisis. Finally, there was a settlement with RKO, and an agreement to end the relationship.

A new company was now formed by ATP to handle the distribution of Ealing films. It was called Associated British Film Distributors (ABFD), although the lacklustre returns on its first wares, *Three Men in a Boat* and *Loyalties*, were a disappointment. Dean, meanwhile, decided that he wanted to direct a sound version of Margaret Kennedy's novel, *The Constant Nymph*; his first experience of films had been six years earlier when he supervised and adapted Adrian Brunel's silent version. Because of the situation regarding the screen rights, the film could not be made by ATP. Dean had to direct it at Gaumont-British, in their studios at Lime Grove, with the man responsible for the 1927 Gainsborough production, Michael Balcon, as his producer. The young

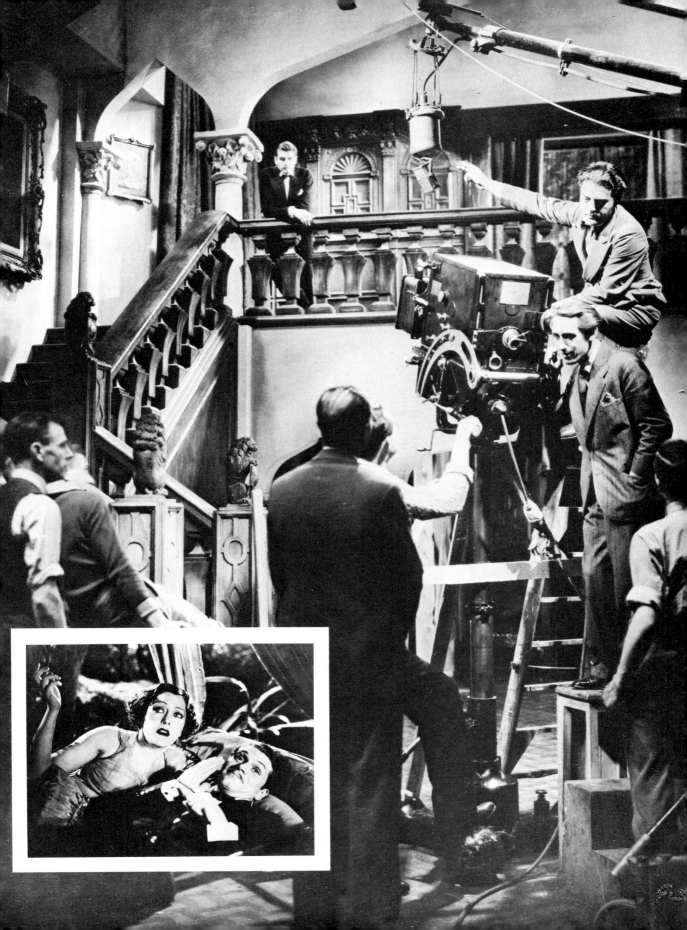

Matinee idol Ivor Novello with Fay
Compton in *Autumn Crocus*, a Tyrolean
romance directed by Basil Dean

actress, Victoria Hopper, selected to play the hero-
ine, later became the third Mrs Dean.

By coincidence, another film which was set, like
The Constant Nymph, in the Austrian Tyrol, started
production at almost the same time. *Autumn Crocus*,
from a play by Dodie Smith, concerned a romance
between a holidaying English schoolmistress and an
innkeeper. Dean was anxious to direct it because
he had staged the play in London and New York.
To make two films on the same location for two
different companies called for a certain legerdemain,
but Dean achieved it by throwing a considerable
burden on his young assistant director, Carol Reed,
who was put in charge of the location unit.

The career of Gracie Fields continued to ex-
pand, *Looking on the Bright Side* being followed by
This Week of Grace and *Love, Life and Laughter*, both
directed by Maurice Elvey, the latter film set in
Ruritania. Her next, *Sing As We Go*, was directed by
Dean, who had shrewdly pulled in the popular
author, J. B. Priestley, to write the film, which with
its realistic view of summer life in Blackpool
revealed how much of Britain's industrial population spent its holidays. It also marked Stanley
Holloway's introduction to Ealing, in the role of a
comic policeman. Priestley also wrote the succeeding work, *Look Up and Laugh* and, although the
star's and the author's roots were on opposite sides of
the Pennines, it turned out to be a happy partnership, resulting in the two most satisfactory films of
pre-Balcon Ealing output. Gracie became the most
important British box-office star, eventually reaching a dizzy salary, for the day, of £40,000 a picture:
more than the entire budget for many films at that
time. When Hollywood made an offer of £50,000 a
film, which she accepted, Dean realized that their
valuable star had moved out of the Ealing league,
and in 1937 he directed her last film there, with what
seemed like an autobiographical plot, the ironically-
titled *The Show Goes On*. Gracie had parted in the
meantime from the irascible Archie Pitt, and had
become romantically attached to the diminutive
Italian, Monty Banks, who directed her penultimate
Ealing picture, *Queen of Hearts*. Three years later, as
a result of her marriage to Banks, an unnaturalized
alien, she was forced to leave Britain for America, in
order to save him from internment, and in so doing
incurred public wrath from those who felt that she
had deserted her country in its hour of need.

Gracie Fields in (above) *This Week of Grace* and (left) *Love, Life and Laughter*, both directed by Maurice Elvey

Left: Gracie warbles a number in *Love, Life and Laughter*
Below, left: the finale from *Sing As We Go* as the mill reopens for business

Right: Alfred Drayton appeared with Gracie Fields in *Look Up and Laugh*

Below: also *Look Up and Laugh*, an automotive contretemps

Opposite: Gracie's last two Ealing films,
(top) *The Show Goes On*, with Owen
Nares, and (bottom) *Queen of Hearts*

Gracie Fields' successor as Ealing's
biggest box-office draw was to be George
Formby, here in *I See Ice*

Luckily, there was a suitable 'star' replacement for
Gracie Fields on the Ealing payroll. George Formby
was the son of a famous Lancashire music-hall comedian, and made his screen debut in 1934 in *Boots,
Boots*, which was made in Manchester. It enjoyed
great success in the north of England, and Dean sent
for a print. It was an unremarkable film, but Dean
felt that the personality of the gormless, well-
meaning, disastrously inept character played by
Formby could be usefully built up. He made haste to
sign him up, having heard that John Maxwell, the
head of British International at Elstree, was also
after him. He found that just as Gracie had been
dominated by Archie Pitt, so George was firmly
under the thumb of his formidable wife Beryl, who
dictated the terms of the contract.

The new Ealing star's tastes were simple and
unsophisticated, his education minimal. He had a
love of speed, which Dean immediately exploited by
putting him in a film about a youth whose passionate
ambition is to win the Isle of Man Tourist Trophy
on his motor cycle. He assigned the playwright Walter Greenwood, author of the realist drama, *Love on
the Dole*, to write the screenplay, and Monty Banks
to direct. The end product, *No Limit*, was one of the
most commercially successful films ever produced at
Ealing, the first of eleven George Formby was to
make there, and which were to establish him as the
top male box-office attraction for several years in
succession.

Monty Banks also directed the second Formby
film for Ealing, *Keep Your Seats Please*, which, like
No Limit, co-starred Florence Desmond, who
needed some persuasion to appear as she had been
disturbed by the toothy comic's desire to upstage all
his co-performers. The next, *Feather Your Nest*, was
directed by William Beaudine, and then Dean established a Formby unit with Anthony Kimmins, a
retired Fleet Air Arm lieutenant-commander and
auuthor of a successful West End farce, *While
Parents Sleep*, as director. *Keep Fit*, *I See Ice* and *It's
in the Air*, the last with a setting in the Royal Air
Force, were quickly produced in 1937 and 1938.
The formula for all the Formby films had him trying
to keep his job in the face of all kinds of unexpected
catastrophes, while at the same time attempting to
woo the girl, who was invariably being won over by a
polished and handsome rival. There was a mandatory pause in the action for a song or two in which
Formby accompanied himself on a ukelele (later a
hybrid instrument known as a 'banjulele') with
occasional lyrics so rich in *doubles entendres* that they
have the power to amaze even forty years later, and
titles like 'With My Little Stick of Blackpool Rock'
or 'Me Auntie Maggie's Remedy'. There was much
slapstick and invariably a comic chase. Audiences
loved them, except in the West End where there was
no market at all. But Formby's instinctive timing
and accomplished physical agility earn him a place
among the great clowns of the screen from either
side of the Atlantic.

Opposite, top: Florence Desmond, George Formby and ukelele in *Keep Your Seats Please*

Opposite, bottom: with Kay Walsh in *Keep Fit*

Left and below: riding in the TT Races and in blackface make-up in *No Limit*

Right: George Formby with Cyril Ritchard and Kay Walsh in *I See Ice*

Below: conferring with director Anthony Kimmins during filming of *It's in the Air*

Meanwhile Dean had been pursuing prestige with films such as *Lorna Doone*, in which his wife, Victoria Hopper, starred opposite the Old Etonian actor John Loder, the same teaming used for a pretentious life of Mozart, *Whom the Gods Love*, both films proving to be costly flops. While ABFD was making headway, thanks to the Fields and Formby pictures, the complicated nature of film finances meant that ATP was still an unviable concern. An attempt by Jack Courtauld to forge a link with the new John Corfield–Lady Yule company, British National, came to nothing, as one of the conditions of a merger was that both Reg Baker and Basil Dean should resign from their posts as joint managing directors, and Dean from the chairmanship. Jack Courtauld then withdrew on account of an illness which was soon to prove fatal. Lady Yule, with an immense fortune ready to bestow on the film industry, meanwhile went into partnership with the evangelistic scion of a Yorkshire flour-milling family. It was the beginning of J. Arthur Rank's involvement in films.

After the death of his brother, Stephen Courtauld became increasingly disturbed by the poor accountability of Ealing Studios. He felt that Basil Dean had to take a large share of the blame, since he was still actively pursuing a career in the theatre as well as taking on the production and even direction of many films at Ealing. Courtauld felt that there was insufficient creative management, and attempted to impose a new regime for production control, which Dean resisted. In April 1938 Courtauld demanded Dean's resignation from his company posts. Dean, tired and defeated by the film industry and aware that war was likely to occur within the next eighteen months, was not unhappy to retreat back to the theatre, which had always been his first love. His finest hour was to come when he ran ENSA (Entertainments National Service Association), the organization responsible for bringing drama and variety shows to the troops on active service during the war years.

Dean's resignation was a turning point for Ealing, for the man invited to fill his place as head of production was an old colleague and friend of Reg Baker, Michael Balcon. It was one of the most fortunate occurrences in the history of the British film industry that he was available at the time.

Michael Balcon was born in Birmingham in 1896, the year that Will Barker began experimenting with moving pictures. His background was respectable, but not prosperous, and after leaving school at seventeen Balcon worked as an apprentice for a jewellery manufacturer. Prevented from enlisting during the First World War because of an eye deficiency, he went instead to work for the Dunlop Rubber Company, at first on the shop floor, helping to shrink solid tyres on to truck wheels, then as personal assistant to the managing director. His desire to get into the film business was inspired by the enthusiasm of Victor Saville, a friend who had been invalided out of the army, and who had worked on the sales side of a London film company. Together, they acquired the rights of distribution in the Midlands for certain American films, including those controlled by C. M. Woolf, who had set up a renting company in London called W. and F. Film Services. Balcon and Saville named their company Victory Motion Pictures, and its chairman was another young Birmingham businessman, Oscar Deutsch, who in the Thirties was to create the Odeon circuit of cinemas.

Saville and Balcon really wanted to get into production, rather than distribution, and leaving their Midlands company in the hands of Balcon's elder brother, Shan, they took off for London, and with a joint capital of £200 opened an office in Cranbourn Street, near Leicester Square. British production was in the doldrums; it was difficult for an impoverished industry that had been virtually wiped out by the First World War to take on the mighty output of Hollywood, which included the films of Mary Pickford, Charlie Chaplin and the blockbusting epics of D. W. Griffith. Balcon saw that their best hope for breaking into production lay in making sponsored shorts, and they signed their first contract with the help of Sidney Bernstein, the son of a suburban cinema owner, later an important circuit chief and later still the founder and chairman of Granada Television.

Then Graham Cutts arrived on the scene. He also came from Birmingham, where he had managed the Sol Levy group of cinemas, but since reaching London he had actually managed to direct films for Herbert Wilcox. Cutts had obtained an option on

the rights of a play by Michael Morton called *Woman to Woman*, which had enjoyed a satisfactory run in the West End. He asked Balcon to produce the film, which he would direct. With backing from Woolf, Deutsch and others, Balcon rented Islington Studios, which had been opened by Famous Players-Lasky, the forerunner of Paramount, during a period when they had dabbled in British production. It was decided that a Hollywood star was needed to give *Woman to Woman* box-office appeal; Saville set off for America and came back with Betty Compson, Lon Chaney's leading lady in *The Miracle Man*, whom he signed for £1,000 a week. It was an enormous gamble, but one which the success of the film seemed to justify. Unfortunately, the expensive lady star had been hired on a two-picture deal, and the second one, *The White Shadow*, was cobbled together too quickly, absorbing the profits of the first. But it consolidated the reputation of her co-star in both, Clive Brook, who was rewarded with a Hollywood contract, and it marked an early stage in the career of Britain's greatest director, Alfred Hitchcock, then Cutts' first assistant and set designer.

In 1924 Cutts and Balcon set up a company called Gainsborough Pictures, while Saville went off to

Left, top: Basil Dean shooting *Lorna Doone* on location on Exmoor

Bottom: Margaret Lockwood, John Loder, Victoria Hopper and Roger Livesey on a set in the film

Below: Basil Dean's costly flop, *Whom the Gods Love*. Stephen Haggard (top, with Dean's wife, Victoria Hopper) played Mozart in a biographical farrago

Michael Balcon in the Thirties –
the man to succeed Basil Dean

join Gaumont at Shepherds Bush. They bought Islington Studios, a deal that was clinched by Reg Baker, later Dean's associate in ATP, and then a young chartered accountant. During the Twenties, Gainsborough launched not only Hitchcock (whose first two films were made in Germany in a collaboration between Balcon and Erich Pommer of the mighty UFA company) but also Ivor Novello, whose career as a film star flourished after he appeared in Hitchcock's third film, *The Lodger*, and in *The Rat*, directed by Cutts. Towards the end of the decade W. and F. Film Services were acquired by Isidore Ostrer, who was in partnership with his brother Mark, and merged with the Gaumont company which owned the Shepherds Bush studios and a few cinemas. The new organization, the Gaumont-British Picture Corporation, handled production, distribution and exhibition: an example, in the language of the industry, of vertical integration, a most desirable condition. The Ostrers and Woolf then relaunched Gainsborough as a public company in association with Gaumont-British, with a third Ostrer brother, Maurice, on the board. Unfortunately, the development of the sound film gave Gainsborough a rough passage for the next two years. Balcon had to go to Hollywood to help pro-

duce the sound film of R. C. Sherriff's celebrated war play, *Journey's End*, with Welsh-Pearson. Sound facilities were eventually installed at Islington in 1930, but almost immediately a major fire nearly destroyed the studios.

In 1931, Balcon was invited by Isidore Ostrer to take charge of production at Gaumont-British's newly rebuilt Lime Grove Studios at Shepherds Bush, while still retaining production control of Gainsborough at Islington. During the next five years he built up an association with many directors, writers and designers who would eventually follow him to Ealing, among them Walter Forde, who directed *Rome Express*, Frank Launder and Sidney Gilliat, who began as writers for Balcon, and Michael Relph, who was a design assistant to Alfred Junge. Among the outstanding range of films produced by the two studios during the Balcon Gaumont-British period are the great series of Hitchcock thrillers, beginning with *The Man Who Knew Too Much*, with Nova Pilbeam as a kidnapped child, and including Robert Donat and Madeleine Carroll in *The Thirty-Nine Steps*. There were a number of musicals with Jessie Matthews, such as *Evergreen*, and a series of Jack Hulbert–Cicely Courtneidge comedies, including *Jack's the Boy* and *Falling for You*. Among other diverse films were Flaherty's documentary, *Man of Aran*, Saville's *I Was a Spy*, with Madeleine Carroll, *Jew Süss* with Conrad Veidt, *The Iron Duke* with George Arliss, and *Tudor Rose*, directed by Robert Stevenson.

But by late 1936 the British film industry was heading for one of its worst crises, the result of over-confidence and over-production. The industry ran itself inefficiently, and there was no middle path between the big hits and the flops. Gaumont-British lost £100,000 in 1936, and production at Shepherds Bush was closed down. But before that happened, Balcon had already decided to leave, at the end of his five-year contract. He had accepted an offer from Louis B. Mayer, the head of Metro-Goldwyn-Mayer, to head production of a new MGM British wing, set up as a result of the quality test that had been recommended for insertion in the new Cinematograph Films Act as a way of combatting the quota quickies.

Balcon produced *A Yank at Oxford* for MGM at

Denham Studios, but after many traumatic incidents felt that he could not go on working for a Hollywood corporation headquartered 6,000 miles away. Leaving Victor Saville to produce the next two MGM pictures, *The Citadel* and *Goodbye Mr Chips*, Balcon managed to extricate himself from his contract, with the intention of going into independent production with Walter Forde, beginning with a film version of the Edgar Wallace story, *The Ringer*. It was at this point that Reg Baker suggested to Balcon that he make the film at Ealing. Balcon agreed, and Baker arranged a parking space nameplate to be put up for him, where it was seen on a visit, with some surprise, by the MGM-British managing director Ben Goetz.

Although Balcon was to impose his stamp on Ealing from that point onwards, he followed a path already beaten out by Basil Dean, a debt that he was ready to acknowledge. When the BBC bought Ealing Studios in 1955 they offered to put up a plaque recording its history to that date and Sir George Barnes, the Controller of Television, invited Balcon to choose the wording. Part of the inscription reads: 'These studios were built in 1931 and occupied by Ealing Studios Limited until January 1956. During a quarter of a century many films were made project-

Top: in Dean's time nearly half the films made at Ealing were by other companies. Balcon changed all that, although John Corfield's 1946 production, *Bedelia*, with Ian Hunter and a murderous Margaret Lockwood, was one of the rare exceptions

Above: Hollywood import Anna May Wong, about to strangle Elizabeth Allan in *Java Head*, a Dean production

Top: Carol Reed's first film as director was *Midshipman Easy* with a young Hughie Green (second from left)

Middle: the cast also included Margaret Lockwood (in white nightdress)

Bottom: Reed went on to make *Laburnum Grove*, from the J. B. Priestley play, with Victoria Hopper and Cedric Hardwicke

ing Britain and the British character.' It is true that of the sixty films shot there during Basil Dean's reign, nearly half were made by other companies who had rented space (in Balcon's time this was the case with only one or two Flanagan and Allen films and John Corfield's *Bedelia*) and so most of the films had no identity with Ealing as such, and could have been produced at any of a score of studios then in existence. But to Basil Dean's credit he managed for the most part to keep the quota quickies away, and he also made several, more positive contributions to Ealing's development. He was not afraid of technical innovation and was among the first British film producers to embrace the medium of sound. He encouraged the adoption of streamlined methods and, apart from the 'organ' described earlier, a new type of camera crane was also pioneered there during his time. He launched the careers of many important figures in British film history, among them Carol Reed, who began as an assistant on Dean's *Java Head*, and directed *Midshipman Easy* and *Laburnum Grove* there; Margaret Lockwood, who was to be the top female box-office star in the mid-Forties, and had her first film part in *Lorna Doone*; and Ronald Neame, who photographed some of the George Formby pictures.

Not least, there were the Gracie Fields and George Formby films which went right against the genteel Shaftesbury Avenue side of Dean's character, and presented a robust, northern view of life, with pleasing results at the box office. Although the working classes formed the mass audience for British films of the Thirties, it was rare indeed for the industry to pay them any attention. Most films of the time featured people who lived in panelled french-windowed interiors, dressed for dinner, and were surrounded by butlers and maids. Such people in reality would not have gone near the cinema. But Gracie Fields and George Formby established the Ealing comedy – admittedly of a different order from that which was to come. Nevertheless, in the minds of many thousands of filmgoers, by the time Dean left the Studios Ealing had become associated with laughter and a jolly night out at the pictures.

CHAPTER 2

Getting into gear

Balcon arrived at Ealing with ten years of corporate experience behind him, first with the Ostrer brothers, and latterly with Louis B. Mayer. He had seen the work of the Gaumont-British period come apart as a result of the 1937 crisis, and now he had fallen victim to the ways of Hollywood tycoons. He had no stomach for the politics of the big corporation, and had found that the kind of production programme which had developed at Gaumont-British did not allow him to give the attention to individual projects that he would have liked. The scale of Ealing was to be different – manageable and creative. He and Walter Forde formed a company, called Balford, to work with Reg Baker and ATP.

Forde had made various films for Balcon at Shepherds Bush, including the notable *Rome Express*. Originally a music-hall slapstick comedian who had graduated to the silent cinema and become the leading British screen comedian, he made the transition to sound with ease. The best films that he directed tended to be comedies, as might be expected, but he made several thrillers as well, including *The Gaunt Stranger*, the first film to be produced by Balcon at Ealing. It had been made twice before as *The Ringer*, the title of the Edgar Wallace story on which it was based, first as a silent version directed by Arthur Maude in 1928, and then as a talkie three years later, produced by Balcon and directed by Forde at Islington. (There was even a fourth, directed by Guy Hamilton in 1952.) It is one of those crime stories where virtually the entire cast is suspect until the real killer is unmasked. An unpretentious, averagely competent film, it was released as a 'programmer', that is to say, the lesser film in a double bill but not quite a B picture.

The Gaunt Stranger was nearing completion when Reg Baker asked Balcon to produce *The Ware Case* which was to be a vehicle for Clive Brook (who had starred in Balcon's first film, *Woman to Woman*, in 1922) and to be directed by Robert Stevenson, who had made films at Gaumont-British, including *Tudor Rose*. *The Ware Case*, a successful play by G. P. Bancroft, had also been filmed twice before in silent days, first in 1927 by Walter West, with Matheson Lang as the unhappy baronet who after his acquittal admits killing his wealthy brother-in-law and then kills himself, and again in 1928 with Stewart Rome. The point of the film was really that even the most dissolute of aristocrats, after having charmed his way out of a murder conviction, could do the right thing in the end. In spite of the technical gloss of the Old Bailey courtroom set (most of the story is told in flashback at the trial), *The Ware Case* is a stagey, melodramatic piece. But it was made on schedule within its budget, and was thus able to go into profit.

Balcon was now asked by Stephen Courtauld and Reg Baker to join the board of ATP and its associated companies, and to take control of the production programme. As if to indicate that things were going to follow a different course, the name Associated Talking Pictures, while still applied to the parent company, became supplanted by the title Ealing Studios, and from then on all films produced there

by Balcon were so designated. Eventually a logo was designed with the studio name flanked by sprigs of symbolic laurel leaves, but in the early days the Union Jack was the background for the end title.

The first few films of the Balcon era were hangovers from the previous regime. The George Formby series continued with *Trouble Brewing* under Anthony Kimmins' direction. George played a newspaper compositor who unmasks a gang of counterfeiters, the brains of which was the news editor. Much to the delight of the film magazine *Picturegoer,* the machine room scenes were filmed at Odhams, Watford, where their weekly was printed. For some reason (perhaps the title had been thought up first) the denouement took place in a brewery, which gave all the crooks an opportunity to fall into the giant vats of fermenting, foamy liquid. The girl was played by the young actress Googie Withers who had earlier been seen in a bit part in Hitchcock's

Opposite, top: Sonnie Hale (centre) in *The Gaunt Stranger,* the first Ealing film under Balcon

Bottom: Clive Brook, Jane Baxter and Barry K. Barnes tight-lipped and tense in *The Ware Case*

Below: Googie Withers and George Formby in *Trouble Brewing*, a formula vehicle in his usual style

The Lady Vanishes. She made several more films at Ealing and became probably the most successful actress to work there. The producer of the Formby films, a Canadian called Jack Kitchin, had started his career as an extra in Hollywood at the age of nineteen, and had later become a film editor.

Let's Be Famous, a comedy directed by Walter Forde, was embellished with songs by Noel Gay, and used the then current craze for radio spelling bees as its peg. The Irish comedian Jimmy O'Dea was teamed with Sonnie Hale, with Betty Driver as a stagestruck girl in a role that was reminiscent of those played by Gracie Fields. Forde returned to the thriller genre for his next film, another Edgar Wallace story, *The Four Just Men*, originally made as a silent by George Ridgway in 1921. Apart from the opening sequence of the new version, in which a man is snatched from a foreign jail just as he is on the verge of execution, the excitement followed a pre-dictable path, with the tall, patrician-looking Alan Napier making a plausible villain. Made in the uneasy interim period following Munich, it is larded with jingoistic sentiments, and stressed the vulnerability of Great Britain to the whim of foreign megalomaniacs, as well as the skills of the gentlemanly amateurs defending (and inevitably saving) the British Empire. For a scene in Parliament a set of the House of Commons was built at Ealing, and a young MP, Aneurin Bevan, was enlisted as a technical adviser on parliamentary procedure.

Forde was to make three more films at Ealing before moving on. *Cheer Boys Cheer*, the last to be released from the Studios before the outbreak of the Second World War in September 1939, was about rivalry between two brewing factions. Greenleaf stands for good old-fashioned English ale and traditional pubs, Ironside for chromium-plated efficiency and ruthless marketing policies. Greenleaf

Jimmy O'Dea and Sonnie Hale in *Let's Be Famous*

Top: *Cheer Boys Cheer,* with Peter Coke and Nova Pilbeam

Bottom: *The Four Just Men,* Griffith Jones, Francis L. Sullivan, Frank Lawton and Hugh Sinclair, setting the Empire to rights, an Edgar Wallace story made topical

resist a takeover and so an Ironside scion joins the old family firm incognito with the intention of finding a way to undermine it. Instead he falls for the Greenleaf daughter, and is gradually won round to the virtues of the old-fashioned way of doing things. The film ends with harmony all round, the families united in matrimony and business partnership. Charles Barr, in his thoughtful critical survey of Ealing films, quite rightly identifies *Cheer Boys Cheer* as the prototype of the Ealing comedies of a decade later, albeit much more broad in approach, with sequences such as those involving Moore Marriott and Graham Moffatt bordering on slapstick; but his suggestion that Ironside and Greenleaf are metaphors for Nazi Germany and England cannot be taken too literally without the conclusion becoming unpalatable. One of the screenwriters was Roger Macdougall, who would be responsible for *The Man in the White Suit* eleven years later.

Opposite, top: climax of the comedy,
Sailors Three, directed by Walter Forde

Below: *Saloon Bar*, with Gordon Harker
and Anna Konstam

Bottom: title trio, Michael Wilding,
Tommy Trinder, Claude Hulbert

Forde's next film, *Saloon Bar*, again had a beery background. A film version of a stage whodunit by Frank Harvey Jr, it suffered from a verbose script by Angus MacPhail and John Dighton, and a pedestrian pace. The leading character is portrayed by Gordon Harker, the ultimate stage cockney, who plays a bookmaker with a penchant for amateur detective work. The atmosphere of the pub in which much of the action is confined is reasonably well-drawn, with its gallery of regular customers including the habitué glued to his chair (Mervyn Johns). As if echoing Forde's previous film, there is another pub in the neighbourhood which has been facelifted by its owners into an art deco orgy of chrome and mirrors. But the film is very obviously a lift from a stage play.

Forde's last film at Ealing, released in October 1940, was *Sailors Three*, a broad comedy which included a couple of song-and-dance numbers, in which three shipmates (Tommy Trinder, Claude Hulbert and Michael Wilding) get drunk in a South American neutral port and inadvertently join the wrong ship, which turns out to be a German pocket battleship, the *Ludendorff*, which they subsequently capture. Forde's music-hall training enabled him to see that the gags were well-timed.

Robert Stevenson was to make two films for Ealing after *The Ware Case* before taking himself off to Hollywood, where he had received an offer from David Selznick. The first was *Young Man's Fancy*, a romantic comedy set in the 1870s with Griffith Jones as a young lord who is being forced into a loveless marriage by his autocratic mother. Seeking solace at a music hall, he meets a pretty human cannonball (Anna Lee, Stevenson's wife) who quite literally drops into his lap. He runs off to Paris with her, where the couple are caught in the siege but, in spite of the privations, find themselves deeply in love. After a return to England it looks as though the hero will still have to go through with his enforced marriage, until his father, the Duke, played by Seymour Hicks, somewhat implausibly sends him away from the church door back to the arms of his beloved lady 'cannonologist'. As in many of the early Ealing films – *Cheer Boys Cheer* was another – the younger generation is pushed around and manipulated by its selfish elders.

Stevenson's ultimate Ealing film was *Return to Yesterday*, an adaptation of a play by the actor–playwright Robert Morley, *Goodness How Sad*. Clive Brook played a famous actor who returns from success in America to the seaside town in which he started, for a nostalgic examination of his roots. He falls in love with a struggling young actress, and then, in order to enable her to leave him for a younger man, acts the part of the cad in the traditional self-sacrificing manner. For Clive Brook the part was scarcely a challenge and Anna Lee was regarded as somewhat colourless as the actress. When the film was finished Stevenson and his wife left for a Canadian holiday, and from there went on to Hollywood. Meanwhile the war began, and as Stevenson was a pacifist he did not return, staying in America to make *Tom Brown's Schooldays* and *Back Street*. In more recent years he has worked exclusively for the Walt Disney Organization, and made what is probably their last classic film, *Mary Poppins*, released in 1965.

The third noteworthy director at Ealing in this period was Penrose Tennyson, a great-grandson of the poet. Besotted by film while at Eton, he left Oxford University in 1932, after less than a year there, to work in the scenario department of

Gaumont-British. Aged only nineteen, he became an assistant on *The Good Companions*, and quickly received attention and respect from his senior colleagues, particularly Michael Balcon and the associate producer on the film, George Pearson. Later he worked on *Farewell Again*, and as Alfred Hitchcock's assistant on *The Man Who Knew Too Much*. The little girl who was kidnapped in the latter film was played by Nova Pilbeam, then only fifteen. A friendship developed and some years later she became Mrs Pen Tennyson. Quickly graduating to Hitchcock's first assistant, he even doubled for a back view of Madeleine Carroll in *The Thirty-Nine Steps*. When Gaumont-British ceased production, Tennyson went with Balcon to MGM and worked as Jack Conway's assistant director on *A Yank at Oxford*. Later, Conway wrote to Balcon from MGM's headquarters at Culver City to invite Tennyson to work in Hollywood, but the opportunity never arose. With Balcon's departure his protégé soon found that the big freeze was operating against him, and he was laid off. Balcon asked him to join Ealing, and decided with Reg Baker's agreement that Pen Tennyson, still only twenty-five, should be given a chance to direct his first picture.

The subject assigned to him was *There Ain't No Justice*, a boxing story set firmly in a working-class milieu. On the face of it, it might have seemed a strange choice for an Old Etonian from a wealthy background. There are parallels with the case of Anthony Asquith, whose film career began more than ten years before Tennyson's. He, too, was from a distinguished family (his father was the first Earl of Oxford and Asquith) and, obsessed by films, had left Oxford as soon as he could enter the industry, directing his first picture at twenty-five. And like Tennyson, Asquith involved himself heavily in the activities of the leading technical trade union, ACT (the Association of Cine and Allied Technicians), which today incorporates an extra T for television. The significant difference is that whereas Asquith went on to make films until he was in his sixties, Tennyson was dead before he was thirty.

There Ain't No Justice was a modest film, a 'programmer' on a low budget. Its hero, played by Jimmy Hanley, is a young mechanic drawn into the fight game by a crooked promoter. When he learns

Below: Griffith Jones and Anna Lee in
Young Man's Fancy

Right: Elliot Mason as seaside landlady
and Clive Brook in *Return to Yesterday*

Bottom: Nan Hopkins, Jimmy Hanley,
Michael Hogarth and Edward Chapman
in *There Ain't No Justice*

Simon Lack, Paul Robeson in *The Proud Valley*

that he is being duped he wins the fight he is meant to lose, after a near-riot has broken out in the arena, instigated by the disgruntled promoter. Hanley was taught to box by the British Empire champion, Bombardier Billy Wells, who was the first man to beat the gong for the trademark of the Rank Organisation (then General Film Distributors). Romantic interest was supplied by Jill Furse, an actress whose career ended prematurely with an early death through illness. Tennyson had boxed at Eton and took a great interest in the sport, although there would have been a world of difference between the well-conducted bouts at a public school and the sweaty, smoke-laden atmosphere of an East End ringside. The low-life aspects of the film were put across without patronage, although at this distance of time the working classes seem somewhat overdrawn, with their pigeon-fancying and 'Knees Up Mother Brown' routines. But it should be remembered that British films for the most part steered away from realistic portrayals of the masses, normally only showing them in a comic context, as in some of the George Formby films. And although it got no nearer the West End than the far end of Tottenham Court Road, and secured the scant release reserved for so many lesser British films in the Thirties, *There Ain't No Justice* was noted by some of the more perceptive critics as the debut of a young director of promise. 'A slice of Cockney life,' said *Picturegoer*.

Balcon had selected a White Russian, Sergei Nolbandov, who had formerly been a lawyer before reaching England and marrying a Scottish wife, as the associate producer for Tennyson's film. Like many in the new Ealing team, he had worked at Gaumont-British, where he had been an editor. He gave Tennyson strong support and encouraged him to involve his social conscience more firmly in his second film, *The Proud Valley*, a story set in a Welsh mining village. In casting the villagers Tennyson began an Ealing tradition of using people who had not appeared before a camera before; among his happy discoveries was Rachel Thomas, who played a miner's wife. The film starred the black American singer, Paul Robeson, as a ship's stoker who, not least on account of his singing voice, gets a job in the local pit, which is closed after an accident, throwing the whole village on to the dole. The miners march on London to urge the owners to reopen the colliery, but war is declared as they get there, and they agree to resume work in the national interest. There is a further underground disaster, and the newcomer to the community dies saving the lives of others. The prosperity that returns to the valley comes about as a consequence of war.

The film's ending was changed during shooting. Originally the miners were to have taken charge of the pit themselves with the intention of running it as a co-operative; but filming was overtaken by the declaration of war and Balcon shied away from the leftish notion of the workers succeeding where the owners had failed, feeling that it would seem like unhelpful propaganda. As it was, there had been great difficulty finding a pit that would allow location filming, and it was only after studio shooting had begun that a colliery company at Stoke gave permission for their pit-head to be used. Then within a week of commencement of principal photography several members of the crew and one of the leading actors received their call-up papers, added to which the disruption of transport and the imposition of the blackout caused considerable logistical difficulties. Nevertheless, the film finished only three days over schedule.

The Proud Valley appeared in 1940, around the same time as Carol Reed's film of A. J. Cronin's mildly socialistic best-seller, *The Stars Look Down*, which had Michael Redgrave as a miner's son who struggles to become an MP and to end the oppressive practices of the mine-owners. Inevitably the two films were compared. Both had disaster scenes, and it was generally noted that *The Proud Valley*, in spite of its smaller budget, had achieved greater realism. There was another handicap that the Ealing film had to face. Paul Robeson had been giving interviews on his return to America that were heavily pro-Russian. Had he said the same things less than two years later he would have been applauded, but at that time in the war, close on the heels of the signing of the German–Soviet Pact and the attack on Finland, the Russians were tainted with as much opprobrium as the Germans. A large section of the public was incensed, including the autocratic press baron, Lord Beaverbrook, who instantly banned all mention of

---

Robeson and his film in the newspapers that he controlled. Such petty spitefulness was one of Beaverbrook's traits, and many notable people went on his 'black list'.

Having finished *The Proud Valley*, Pen Tennyson married Nova Pilbeam, and then embarked on preparations for a film showing life in the Royal Navy during wartime. He was a member of the Royal Naval Volunteer Reserve, called the 'wavy navy' on account of the zig-zag stripes worn as officers' insignia of rank, but had been granted an exemption so that he could move ahead with the film, which was called *Convoy*. Clive Brook, in his last Ealing work, played the captain of a cruiser whose job was to protect a convoy of merchant ships sailing towards England across the North Sea. In order to experience such an assignment, Tennyson made a voyage on HMS *Valorous* on convoy duty in waters off the east Scottish coast, with deadly minefields and marauding U-boats a constant menace.

Convoy is the first of many distinguished films about the war made at Ealing. It attempted to show how war is conducted, but also that the men involved are human beings. There is a somewhat banal subplot which has John Clements as a sporty young lieutenant who seems to have run off with the captain's wife. By the end, as he dies heroically for his ship and his country, he is revealed to be not such a cad after all. But the main issue is the plight of the convoy when it is attacked by a supposedly invincible German pocket battleship. The British cruiser fights a delaying action to enable the destroyers to get the merchantmen to safety and, although heavily outgunned and almost sunk, holds on long enough for help to arrive.

Although there was a great deal of work with miniatures, the battle scenes were impressively shot. Apart from Judy Campbell in the superfluous and thankless role of the captain's wife, the acting style was one of calm, earnest underplaying that was to be the standard for this kind of film (ridiculed mercilessly in 1961 by the satirists of *Beyond the Fringe*). Not all the dialogue took place on the bridge and in the ward room. There was even an affecting view of life below decks, with Edward Chapman as the gruff, sly master of a tramp steamer in the convoy and Edward Rigby as his cockney mate. They too

have their moment of heroism and glory. *Convoy* was not only highly regarded by the critics – 'the most exciting, lifelike and rational account of the Navy's work in wartime yet seen on the screen', wrote one – but was also a huge box-office success, and received an American release with good returns, the holy grail of the British film industry. Balcon urged Tennyson to make another war picture, but he had decided that his deferment from the Navy could no longer be continued. He was posted to an anti-submarine trawler, and later worked on Admiralty training films. Returning from Scapa Flow to Rosyth in a Fleet Air Arm aircraft, after shooting footage, he died as the plane crashed, and a career of great promise came to a premature end.

Pen Tennyson's last film was also the most significant, for it marked the beginning of an official awareness of the importance of the cinema in creating useful propaganda to help the war effort. At the start of the war the attitude of the authorities was wholly negative. Cinema screens were blacked-out along with the streetlights. In the initial panicky

Below: John Clements, Clive Brook and a young Stewart Granger on the bridge in Pen Tennyson's *Convoy*

Bottom: an enemy shell hits a gun position in a battle scene

reaction all places of entertainment were closed and the BBC radio services merged into one dreary emergency programme. After a fortnight the nation was at the end of its tether, and the cinemas were allowed to reopen. But the government was unconvinced of the worth of the film industry in disseminating a point of view. There were even moves to halt production totally, as being of no value to the national war effort. Many studios were commandeered and turned into shadow factories, as the *ad hoc* and often secret assembly plants were known. Part of Pinewood became an outstation of the Royal Mint, the first time, said the wags, that J. Arthur Rank's big Buckinghamshire studios were making money. Denham, however, escaped seizure because the ebullient Hungarian, Gabriel Pascal, was making *Major Barbara* there and, whether by accident or cunning, managed to extend his shooting schedule until the panic was over. Balcon spent anxious weeks persuading Whitehall not to requisition Ealing, and eventually got his way. A film studio in such a densely-populated area of West London offered less of a target of military importance to enemy bombers than a factory turning out war materials.

Having won that battle, Balcon next had to get official recognition that film could play its part in the war. Alexander Korda, the most celebrated of the film industry's expatriate Hungarians, had quickly leapt on to the propaganda bandwagon with *The Lion Has Wings*, a film intended to assure audiences of the state of readiness of the Royal Air Force. It had been commissioned just before the outbreak of war, and was directed jointly by Adrian Brunel, Brian Desmond Hurst and Michael Powell, with a starry cast that included Ralph Richardson, Merle Oberon and June Duprez. The film was in the cinemas by early November but suffered noticeably from its hasty assembly, an awkward mixture of documentary realism, tritely-staged fiction scenes, obvious modelwork and gratuitous clips from earlier Korda films, especially *Fire Over England* in which Flora Robson played Queen Elizabeth. With his characteristic flair for charming money from unpromising sources, Korda had managed to get the Ministry of Information to foot the bill, but as a consequence the film was interfered with by civil servants anxious not to exacerbate the 'phoney war', the period after the invasion of Poland which ended abruptly in May 1940 with the Nazi *Blitzkrieg* on the Low Countries. *The Lion Has Wings* had a large audience, but it was by no means a satisfied one, as was revealed by a Mass Observation survey of the time: 43% criticized the lack of story, 27% the propaganda element. At best, the case for official sponsorship was not proven.

Another difficulty faced by Balcon was the loss of many valuable technicians into the services. By the end of 1940, Ealing, which operated with a relatively small workforce of a couple of hundred people, had fifty employees in uniform and away on active service; Balcon, in a New Year message published in *Picturegoer,* differentiated them as eleven officers and thirty-nine men. Eventually two-thirds of the technicians employed in the British film industry were called up. In order to keep going, Balcon was forced to look in other directions. The one that attracted him most was the Crown Film Unit, formerly the GPO Film Unit, a group of documentary makers now under the aegis of the Ministry of Information. In his autobiography Balcon says: 'The documentary movement, as symbolized by the Crown Film Unit, was in my view the greatest single influence on British film production and more than anything else helped to establish a national style.' Alberto Cavalcanti, who at the start of the war had produced *The First Days* (directed by Humphrey Jennings, Pat Jackson and Harry Watt) and who in the Thirties was a mainstay, with John Grierson, of the British documentary movement, was invited to join Ealing as an associate producer and director. Born in Brazil, from 1920 to 1933 Cavalcanti had worked in Paris as a film writer, art director and later film-maker, directing *Rien Que Les Heures* and *En Rade*. He came to Britain at Grierson's invitation in 1933, and directed *Pett and Pott, Glorious Sixth of June, Coalface* and several other documentaries. One of his first actions at Ealing was to make a propaganda documentary attacking the Italian fascist dictator, called *Yellow Caesar*. But his principal contribution would be towards the feature film, and he, more than any man other than Balcon, would determine an Ealing style.

Among the directors lost to war service was

Opposite: Coral Browne raids George
Formby's pocket in *Let George Do It*
watched by a startled Phyllis Calvert

Below: George separates his wife (Peggy
Bryan) and domineering mother (Elliot
Mason) in *Turned Out Nice Again*

Anthony Kimmins, who rejoined the Royal Navy, becoming a captain on the staff of the Director of Naval Intelligence. His last Ealing film, just completed by the outbreak of war, was the George Formby comedy, *Come On George*, in which the hare-brained hero finds himself as a jockey with a terrible mount that has already savaged three former riders, and only gets over his fear by recourse to a quack brain specialist. Characteristically, the fearless Formby, who had once been a stable apprentice, eschewed doubles and did the riding himself. (His little-known debut in films had been as a child, twenty years before *Boots, Boots*, in *By the Shortest of Heads*, a racing drama made by Ealing's pioneer, Will Barker.) Kimmins never returned to Ealing. After the war he took up an offer from Korda and was responsible for several films of integrity, such as *Mine Own Executioner*, and also the legendarily abysmal *Bonnie Prince Charlie*, for which débâcle the producer was more responsible than the hapless director.

Meanwhile, George Formby's Ealing films fell into other hands. Two were directed by Marcel Varnel who, although French-born, had a remarkable talent for British comedy, and had made films for Will Hay, the Crazy Gang, and the very popular radio comedy team of Arthur Askey and Richard Murdoch. His lasting masterpiece was the film he made with Will Hay in 1937, *Oh Mr Porter!*. *Let George Do It*, Varnel's first Formby film which opened in July 1940, was also the first Ealing comedy to use the war as a background. George, a member of the Dinkie Doo Concert Party, finds himself on a boat to Bergen, Norway, by mistake, in order to replace a British intelligence man. Unmasking a spy ring (it is still Norway's pre-invasion period), he escapes, aided by Phyllis Calvert as a British spy. *Spare a Copper* followed, directed by John Paddy Carstairs, in which Formby played a Merseyside special constable on the trail of Nazi saboteurs, with a pompous theatre owner and a shipyard managing director's assistant as fifth

columnists. The notion of unsuspected German spies in respectable positions was to recur in more serious Ealing films such as *The Foreman Went to France* and *Went the Day Well?*. Finally, Formby's last film at Ealing eschewed the war. *Turned Out Nice Again,* with its title based on a familiar Formby catchphrase, was again directed by Marcel Varnel. In it, George plays an assistant in a Lancashire women's underwear firm who is tricked into buying the rights for an apparently worthless yarn. He is fired, but the yarn turns out to be revolutionary, ensuring a happy ending. The Greenleaf–Ironside conflict is reprised, with George's traditional firm clinging to whalebone and flannelette, while its up-to-date rivals favour lightweight scanties, but this time it is the old-fashioned way that is condemned. The plot had rather more substance than was normal in a Formby film, breaking new ground in enabling him to marry the girl (Peggy Bryan) early in the picture, although through the intrusion of his possessive mother he temporarily loses his devoted wife.

After Kimmins and Jack Kitchin had left, Balcon found that he had to take over many of the duties of running the Formby unit himself. He had never found much common ground with the comedian, and shed no tears when Formby signed a contract with Columbia after finishing his eleventh film at Ealing, the last five during the Balcon period. Balcon felt, however, that he had a more than adequate replacement to hand.

Will Hay was quite different from the uncultured Formby. He was a keen amateur astronomer, for example, and in 1933 had discovered a white spot on Saturn. He was also an air fanatic, and had been a middleweight boxer. A reticent man, his private life was little-known to the public and he rarely gave newspaper interviews. As a performer he was much more to Balcon's taste. Although the films that Hay had made during the Thirties, mostly for Gainsborough, had not been anything like the money-spinners starring Formby, they had maintained a consistent standard, and he was listed among the top ten British box-office stars by the *Motion Picture Herald*. Marcel Varnel, who had directed six out of the seven previous Hay films, also directed the first of his pictures under his new Ealing contract. *The*

Ghost of St Michael's, which opened in April 1941, was a disappointment to some of Hay's fans because of the absence of the old back-up team of Moore Marriott and Graham Moffatt, but in compensation there was Claude Hulbert, who specialized in silly-ass characterizations. Hay usually played a seedy, fraudulent and incompetent schoolmaster, prison governor, stationmaster, solicitor, and so on, and in this film he reappeared in his most familiar role as a pedagogue, called out of retirement because of the war to join the staff of a school that has been evacuated to a remote Scottish castle, with the formidable matron (Elliot Mason) as a German spy, and John Laurie as a dour caretaker given to telling the fearsome story of the castle's ancient curse.

Will Hay himself directed his remaining features in association with Basil Dearden, who had joined Basil Dean at Ealing in 1937 as a writer. Dearden's real name was Basil Dear, but he changed it, not because of its overtones but to avoid confusion with Dean. *The Black Sheep of Whitehall* had Hay as the

Master comedian Will Hay in (left)
My Learned Friend and (above) with
Charles Hawtrey and Claude Hulbert
in *The Ghost of St Michael's*

Below: Will Hay with John Mills and Margaret Halstan as matron in *The Black Sheep of Whitehall*

Opposite: with Anne Firth as a friendly German in *The Goose Steps Out*

head of a correspondence college with only one pupil who is refusing to pay his fees. The plot centres on mistaken identities and during its course Hay appears in six different disguises, twice as a woman. The film was some way short of his best work, and John Mills, who earlier had been invalided out of the Royal Engineers where he had been a junior subaltern, was wasted in the part of the pupil.

Hay's next film, *The Goose Steps Out*, used a war theme more broadly. Once again a plot device of mistaken identity is used, this time when an arrested German spy turns out to be Hay's *doppelgänger*, with British intelligence taking advantage. Hay's biographers, Ray Seaton and Roy Martin, are dismissive of the film, which they feel is crude, jingoistic and laboured, 'best excused as Hay's contribution to the war effort'. It is certainly true that the Germans are pathetic caricatures, humourless idiots lacking the

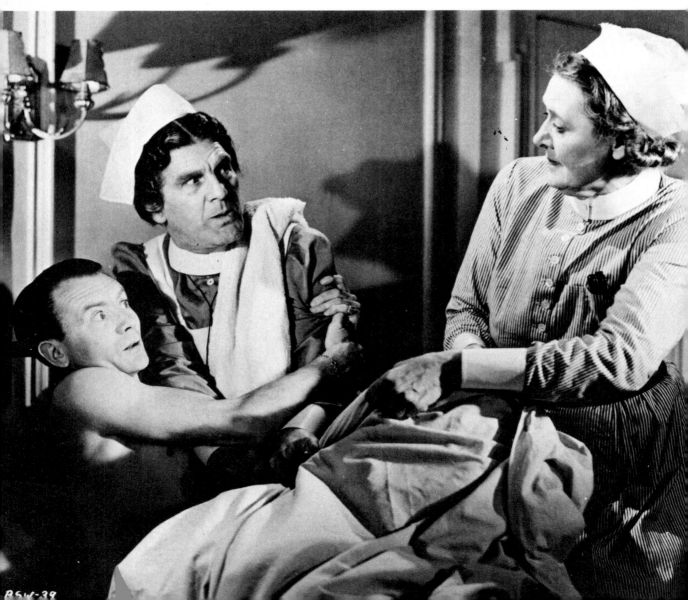

intelligence even to guard their secret weapons properly, but for that matter the British, represented by Hay, are muddlers and amateurs, achieving their aims by accident. The most remembered scene in the film has Hay in his familiar role of a teacher before his class, but he is in Nazi uniform, masquerading as a German masterspy and his pupils are young brownshirts, embrionic agents learning how to behave in England. His class, which includes Charles Hawtrey and Peter Ustinov, is taught that the correct form of respectable salutation is a V-sign with the knuckles facing outwards, and shortly they are all practising assiduously before the portrait of the Führer. In the climate of 1942, when British morale was at its lowest, what may now seem jingoistic acted as an innocent safety valve, and the film was popularly received.

Unfortunately, Hay's next film, *My Learned Friend*, was to be his last. During shooting in 1943 early stages of cancer were diagnosed, and in the remaining years before his death in 1949 his talents were almost entirely confined to the radio. *My Learned Friend* was his most interesting film at Ealing, and reunited him with Claude Hulbert. The action was set in what had become the mythical world of 'pre-war', with Hay as a disbarred solicitor who ties up the prosecution and wins an acquittal from a charge of writing begging letters – a rare burst of competence, this, from a man whose legend was built on his bungling ineptitude, but then the prosecuting counsel was Claude Hulbert, whose capacity for muddying the waters could make Hay seem a genius of clarity. The two of them embark on a frantic chase in pursuit of a psychopathic murderer newly released from prison, who is working through a vengeance list with Hulbert's name near the top. The climax of the film takes place on the clockface of Big Ben, our heroes endeavouring to stop the minute hand reaching noon, which will trigger a bomb. Exactly the same ludicrous situation occurs in the third screen version of *The Thirty-Nine Steps,* made in 1978, where it was not meant to be funny, although any member of the audience familiar with the Hay picture would have been amused. In a curious way *My Learned Friend* anticipates *Kind Hearts and Coronets*, which also has a murderer working through a list of people he feels wronged by, and planning appropriately specific fates for them. This is not entirely coincidental. One of Ealing's strengths was the remarkable continuity of its personnel, and John Dighton worked on the screenplays of both films.

Hay's last film stands apart from all his others in that the tone is sharper, more callous, more cynical. And while in general his Gainsborough films must be regarded as more satisfactory than the later Ealing ones, *My Learned Friend* is a worthy fadeout.

In some ways Balcon felt a certain bitterness as the war progressed. Undoubtedly he nursed a sense of betrayal by some of his former colleagues who had decamped to America at the outset, and who in some cases had made special pleas in the Press. For most of them there was nothing of which to be ashamed. Alfred Hitchcock, for example, had gone to Hollywood just before the war, having signed a contract with David Selznick. His *Rebecca* won the Academy Award as the best picture of 1940, and Hitchcock was quickly at work on a next, *Foreign Correspondent*, part of which was set in wartime Britain. He claimed that there was no work forthcoming at Gaumont-British for him, except at a salary less than his former one, although the Ostrers issued a vigorous denial. Shortly afterwards, Hitchcock and his wife, Alma Reville, became American citizens. Similarly Victor Saville, who had stayed with MGM after Balcon's departure to produce *The Citadel* and *Goodbye Mr Chips*, went off to Hollywood to produce a Nelson Eddy–Jeannette Macdonald musical, *Bitter Sweet*. Herbert Wilcox also went there to produce and direct four films, beginning with *Nurse Edith Cavell* in which Anna Neagle uttered the famous words, 'Patriotism is not enough!'. And Alexander Korda based himself in Hollywood to

Some of the footage of *Ships with Wings* was shot on the carrier HMS Ark Royal. Here a Swordfish is armed with a torpedo

film his tribute to the stirring days of Britain's past, *Lady Hamilton*. There was a long list of actors and actresses who had suddenly found the prospect of work on the other side of the Atlantic irresistible; the Press coined the phrase 'Gone with the wind up' to describe them. Balcon wrote frequent denunciations during 1940, and he rejected the defence that some of the people concerned were doing a better job promoting Britain's cause by making films in the then neutral United States than by staying at home. He felt that the proper place to make films about Britain was Britain, and that the best film-makers had a duty to do so.

Having been hit by the collapse of the 'prestige' film before the war, when large-scale movies with an international tone had failed to capture world markets, Balcon's philosophy was now turned firmly inwards. He wrote in the Winter 1940 number of *Sight and Sound*: 'For far too long the American market has been a mirage which has filled the British film traveller with false hopes and inspired the British producer with wishful producing. The British producer can make no greater mistake than to have the American market in mind when planning and creating a picture.... I have found that the essential English films like *Tudor Rose*, *Owd Bob* and *Convoy* are the ones that score success in America, not films made with the American market in mind.'

At least with *Convoy* he had achieved a measure of official co-operation. Moreover, the Studios had been busy making Ministry of Information shorts and other government-sponsored filmlets, such as the Food Flashes, which would be sandwiched between the newsreel and the trailers, advising people how to collect their ration books or dig for victory. Even Will Hay was featured in a short describing how to deal with incendiary bombs. Walter Forde directed this little film, *Go to Blazes*, which ran less than ten minutes.

Ealing's pathway towards finding a form for its war films veered off course with Sergei Nolbandov's *Ships with Wings*, premiered in November 1941. The mixing of commercial entertainment values with documentary-like realism was not easy to accomplish. Hollywood, with America still neutral, was providing plenty of escapist fare, and the films that used the war as a background did so with a calculated regard for the box office – the dashing Tyrone Power as *A Yank in the RAF*, for instance, in which the ending was changed so that he could fly back from his bombing raid on Berlin into the arms of Betty Grable. *Ships with Wings* had excellent opportunities for a realistic portrayal of the war – one of the cameramen, Roy Kellino, had sailed on the aircraft carrier, HMS *Ark Royal*, and obtained some fine actuality footage – but it suffered from a storyline that was every bit as novelettish and absurd as the worst that Hollywood could produce.

The plot centred on John Clements, who once again played a young officer under a cloud who redeems himself by volunteering for a dangerous mission and dies a hero, crashing his aircraft into a dam that must be destroyed. Much unconvincing modelwork marred the battle sequences, particularly the raid on the dam, but a real life carrier-based action against the Italian naval base at Taranto occurred between the completion of the film and its release, which offered an opportunity for the publicists to make something from little. The suicidal heroics of Clements and his colleagues, played by Michael Wilding and Michael Rennie, with Leslie Banks and Basil Sydney as senior officers (Cecil Parker, of all people, was cast as a German commander), worried Winston Churchill, who felt that the poor showing by the Fleet Air Arm in the raid at the end of the film would cause alarm and despondency, for they only achieved their objective after losing an entire squadron. He attempted to delay the release, and get the film shelved. This official reaction was conveyed to Balcon while he was hosting a lunch party at the Savoy for several senior naval officers, including Lord Mountbatten, to launch the film. Luckily for Balcon, Churchill allowed the First Sea Lord, Admiral Sir Dudley Pound, to make the final decision, and he permitted the film to go out; but it was not to be the last time that Churchill, whose favourite film was Korda's lushly romantic evocation of the Nelson era, *Lady Hamilton*, would attempt to interfere with a picture's release.

There was another footnote to the *Ships with Wings* affair. During shooting Stage 2 was hit and badly damaged by German bombs – a warning, some said, that this was not the type of film Ealing should be engaged in producing.

CHAPTER 3

Propaganda and truth

It was more than just bombs that wreaked havoc on the British film industry in wartime. In the last year of peace there had been twenty-two different studios with sixty-five sound stages between them. By 1942 this number had fallen by more than half, to nine studios with thirty stages. With only a third of the pre-war technical workforce remaining out of uniform there was a dearth of skill. Materials normally used for set construction were diverted elsewhere, and so ingenious improvisation became necessary. Not surprisingly, there was a startling drop in output. In 1940, 108 'long' British films had been registered; by 1942, the number had shrunk to forty-two. In order to fulfil the quota many older films had to be reissued. Yet in spite of the fact that some cinemas were destroyed in the Blitz, film-going became an increasingly popular diversion. Audiences steadily rose from nineteen million a week in 1939 to more than thirty million by 1945, the all-time record. Other forms of entertainment suffered severe restriction – in the blackout there could be no floodlit football matches or greyhound racing – and at home there was only the BBC 'wireless' with its Home and Forces programmes. The cinema provided a night out, a temporary respite from rationing, war work, fire-watching and austerity. It was a great opportunity for British films, but ironically, it was a hard time in which to grasp it. Costs had risen hugely – by 1944 a production budget would be three times its pre-war equivalent. Entertainments Tax bit hard into the box-office takings, and there was also an Excess Profits Tax which helped to raise budgets, necessary, it was argued in Wardour Street, if British films were to compete in the same market place as the glossy, star-studded films, often in Technicolor, that flowed from Hollywood.

In spite of all the difficulties, the British cinema in wartime found its voice. There was a brief, brave period in the Forties when it actually looked as though an indigenous style was beginning to emerge. It would not be until around 1958–60 that another momentary flowering would take place, and that would be on a more limited scale and for very different cultural reasons. In the middle years of the war there was a strong sense of national unity, and sufficient change from the old order to diminish the rigidities of the class structure. No such phrase as 'temporary gentlemen' was levelled at ranker officers as it had been in the 1914–1918 conflict. Shopgirls and debutantes might find themselves working side by side in the same tank component factory. Bombs rained down on rich and poor alike. It was a great morale booster for East Enders to see the King and Queen walking round the rubble of their devastated terraces, knowing that Buckingham Palace had also suffered a direct hit, albeit on the swimming pool. It was a time of hope. People looked towards a better future beyond the war. The Beveridge Report paved the way for the creation of a welfare state; the Abercrombie Report showed how London could be rebuilt to give everyone decent housing and a share of green space. The momentum that would result in a Labour landslide in 1945 was already under way.

In spite or even because of adversity, the British cinema flourished. Quantity was supplanted by quality. Better writers were attracted into films. Extravagant practices for the most part disappeared; even film stock was scarce, and footage was made to count. Basil Dearden, who began directing films in wartime, would for the rest of his career shoot with amazing economy, usually getting it in one take.

The entry of America into the war at the end of 1941 encouraged a greater receptivity for British films across the Atlantic, particularly those that offered an insight into the way Britain was facing the struggle. *In Which We Serve*, Noël Coward's tribute to the Royal Navy based on the story of Mountbatten's ship, the destroyer HMS *Kelly*, received rave reviews from American critics. Harry Watt's *Target for Tonight*, a feature-length documentary made for the Crown Film Unit about an RAF Wellington bomber, 'F for Freddie', taking part in a raid on Germany, was shown in twelve thousand cinemas in the Americas, and seen by fifty million people. It was not long before Watt was working at Ealing, drawn there by Cavalcanti, whose influence was now beginning to show.

Under 'Cav', a new group of directors was emerging. It was soon a matter of policy that Ealing directors came from Ealing staff, and were thus automatically inculcated with the Ealing philosophy. Monja Danischewsky, known as Danny, who from 1938 to 1948 was Ealing's director of publicity, said of Cavalcanti in his memoirs, *White Russian, Red Face*: 'If Mick [Balcon] was the father figure, Cavalcanti was the Nanny who brought us up.' On the wall of a stage a painted inscription read: 'The Studio with the Team Spirit.' Watt was rather surprised to find that, in spite of the democratic way in which the place was run, there were no less than three segregated eating places for those who worked at Ealing: the main canteen for the majority, including the artisan foremen; a restaurant for the departmental heads and the middle management; and at the top end of the scale, the Directors' dining room for Balcon, Baker, Courtauld if he happened to be there, and distinguished visitors. In Dean's time this room was called the Deanery. During Baker's interregnum it became the Bakery, and when Balcon took over it inevitably became the Balcony. The irrepressible Danny remembered a Norwegian theatrical producer called Stein Bugge, and fervently hoped that he would not develop an ambition to usurp Balcon.

The Directors' dining room was the setting for Balcon's famous studio conferences of senior people, production executives, film directors and writers who sat around a huge circular table, big enough to seat a dozen people comfortably, which had been built *in situ* as there was no way of getting it through the door. Many a film idea was hatched at these meetings. More than any other British production company, Ealing worked on the team principle – the cross-pollination of ideas, the weekly Round Table conferences, the convivial overlap of interests. It was a close group, as anyone who worked there will testify, and many a conference would continue for hours afterwards in the Red Lion across the Green. A far higher proportion of the Ealing output, compared with other studios, consisted of original screenplays, rather than adapted novels and plays, and Balcon was wont to encourage anybody in the studio to produce film ideas. The Ealing team held together remarkably well at a time when there was great dissatisfaction elsewhere in the industry, and film-makers constantly moved around. Many of the Ealing stalwarts who began their careers in wartime under Cavalcanti advanced up the Ealing ladder when they had shown their worth. Even the director of publicity, Monja Danischewsky, bored after some years in the job, was given the chance to produce *Whisky Galore!* Balcon wrote in his autobiography: 'Later critics were inclined to say we were becoming "inbred", that we had a middle-class point of view, and that we were a kind of exclusive school with me as Headmaster. There may be some validity in these arguments, but working this way certainly produced for a number of years those films which had some sense of national pride. . . .'

Charles Frend had been a film editor, and had worked with Balcon at both Gaumont-British and MGM. With Cavalcanti as associate producer he made a film which started off as a Ministry of Information two-reeler intended to spell out the principles of economic warfare. Ealing injected additional finance into it and built it up into a full-length feature mixing actuality with fictionalized material.

Will Hay as a ship's master with Bernard
Miles as his mate in the overt propaganda
film *The Big Blockade*, directed by Charles
Frend

A strong cast was provided, which even had Will Hay playing a comparatively straight part as a trawler skipper explaining to his mate (Bernard Miles) how the navicert system, one of wartime's lesser mysteries, worked. Made with the co-operation of the Ministry of Economic Warfare, the War Office, the Navy and the Royal Air Force, *The Big Blockade* was heavily propagandist and didactic in tone, perhaps an inevitability given the brief it was to fulfil. 'Fighting is one side of war,' explained the commentary by a celebrated Fleet Street figure, Frank Owen. 'There is another side – that is, stopping the enemy from fighting.' As well as actors other public figures appeared, such as the American journalist Quentin Reynolds and politician Hugh Dalton. The Germans are caricatures, serving only to spell out the lesson that is being taught. Did people really pay money to go and see a film so overtly educational in purpose? It is true that in wartime there was usually an audience for anything unless it was labelled 'highbrow' and possibly the public did want to see Robert Morley posturing in Nazi uniform. For Charles Frend it was an opportunity to get his directorial feet wet, but in many respects it was a much less satisfying work than his next film. It is an interesting side-note that the two editors of *The Big Blockade*, Charles Crichton and Compton Bennett, were both to become directors shortly afterwards, the former as one of the pillars of Ealing, and the latter making only one more film there, a documentary called *Find, Fix and Strike*.

Frend's second film was *The Foreman Went to France*, which was based on the real experiences of one Melbourne Johns, who managed to retrieve some vital machinery from under the noses of the advancing Germans. Clifford Evans played the foreman, renamed Ted Carrick for the film, who surmounts the obstacles of red tape to reach France,

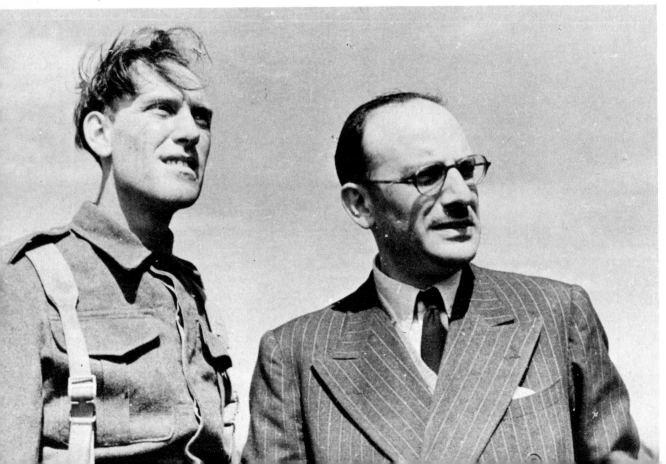

From *The Foreman Went to France:*
(opposite) Michael Balcon with Tommy
Trinder on location, (below) refugees
cowering from an air attack, and (bottom)
Clifford Evans, Gordon Jackson and
Tommy Trinder at an *estaminet*

and then faces dive-bombers, refugee-clogged
roads, spies disguised as British soldiers and the
ever-advancing enemy. He falls in with a pair of
tommies separated from their unit, one played by
the comedian Tommy Trinder, the other by the
Scottish actor Gordon Jackson, who was suggested
for the part by the playwright James Bridie. Their
adventures are shared by an American girl (Constance Cummings). The French sea captain who
eventually brings the group back to Britain was identified in the credits as François Sully, although he is
easily recognized as the corpulent British character
actor, Francis L. Sullivan, an example of Ealing's
occasional whimsicality.

The film portrayed a small group of people from
different walks of life beset by great odds, but win-
ning through together, and it was the most satisfying
Ealing war film to date, establishing what was to be a
formula for many serious films and several of the

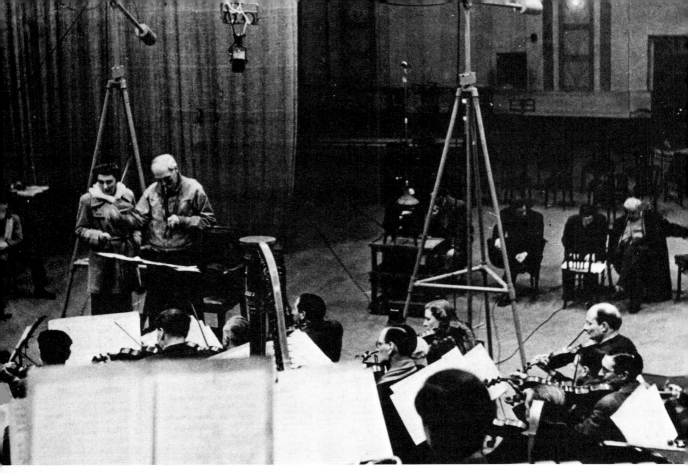

post-war comedies. Frend's approach, following a narrative storyline that was written by J. B. Priestley, and scripted by John Dighton, Angus MacPhail and Leslie Arliss, was steady and careful. The only palpable directorial flaw was the casting of Trinder, who was allowed to play in a much broader vein than the others, and undoubtedly many people were lured into the cinema expecting an entertainment in the 'You Lucky People!' vein.

The music for *The Foreman Went to France* was composed by William Walton, the first of three Ealing scores by him, the others being for *Next of Kin* and *Went the Day Well?*, although none achieved the popular acclaim for his work on a contemporary film, Leslie Howard's *The First of the Few*, and for Laurence Olivier's *Henry V* which followed. The musical direction at Ealing was in the hands of Ernest Irving, a scholarly composer who had spent many years working in the theatre before turning to films. He joined Ealing at the beginning of the Dean era, and was not only responsible for many scores himself but introduced other composers from a broad spectrum to Ealing films, including Walton, Vaughan Williams, John Ireland, Alan Rawsthorne, Richard Addinsell, Benjamin Frankel, John Greenwood, Lord Berners and Georges Auric. His home was a large house on Ealing Green next to the

Studios, and his imposing, if waspish, presence was one of the staple sights. Monja Danischewsky tells the story of how Irving declined to arrange the music for Pen Tennyson's memorial service because John Clements wanted to recite Cory's translation of the Alexandrian poet Callimachus's epigram on Heraclitus, 'They told me, Heraclitus, they told me you were dead', on the grounds that it was a homosexual's lament for his boy friend. 'We don't want anything to do with fellows like that in Ealing Studios,' he said.

Next of Kin brought Thorold Dickinson to Ealing on a special assignment. He had produced *Midshipman Easy* and directed *High Command* in Basil Dean's day, and some years later was to make *Secret People*, his last film, there before retreating to academe. But in 1942 he was a rarity, a non-Ealing director making an Ealing film. It started as a training short, and to make it Dickinson had to be seconded from the army, although there had been a slight security hitch when it was discovered that he had been on the anti-Franco side of the Spanish Civil War. Captain Sir Basil Bartlett drafted a storyline designed to point out the dangers of careless talk, a subject which Balcon felt deserved a far wider audience than a purely service one. He got Dighton, MacPhail and Dickinson to build it up into

Opposite: Ealing's musical director,
Ernest Irving, in action. The overcoats
indicate the spartan conditions of a
wartime winter without heating

Below: realistic battle scenes in Thorold
Dickinson's *Next of Kin* bothered
Churchill, and the release of the film was
held up. It became a big hit

a full-length commercial feature, and more than
doubled the production budget with an injection of
Ealing money. Mervyn Johns was cast as a Nazi
agent at large in Britain with the brief to discover the
details of a planned commando raid on a French
port. With horrifying ease he is able to fit the jigsaw
together without attracting suspicion. The raid
takes place and, although it achieves its purpose, it is
devastating in terms of casualties, because the
enemy is prepared for the attack. 'Careless talk costs
lives' was the wartime slogan that formed the message of the film; and at the end the spy is still free,
eavesdropping in a railway compartment on the
indiscreet conversation of two officers, played by
Basil Radford and Naunton Wayne. Besides many
familiar actors, a few serving officers were also given
small parts without ill effect.

The raid, shown in graphic detail, was staged on
the Cornish fishing village of Mevagissey, standing
in for France. Fact overtook fiction, and before the
film could be released the disastrous raid on Dieppe
took place, which claimed the lives of thousands of
troops. Once again Churchill tried to stop a film
from being shown, this time on the grounds that it
would cause great distress to the next-of-kin of those
lost at Dieppe. But as with *Ships with Wings* he
allowed a military opinion to override his own. In
the Press it was known as the 'hush-hush' film
because it had been shot in secrecy, the details of its
story kept under wraps. The news that there was a
chance that the public would not be permitted to see
it caused a small storm in a teacup. The controversy
had undoubtedly helped the film's chances, and it
made a very handsome profit. But Ealing's deal with
the government meant that their return was limited
to their investment, plus a very small percentage,

Opposite and below: Cavalcanti's *Went the Day Well?* asked what would happen if the Germans invaded an English village disguised as Tommies. The two intimidated women are Muriel George and Patricia Hayes

the rest going into the coffers of the Treasury.

Cavalcanti, who had been associate producer on *The Foreman Went to France*, now directed his first Ealing feature. The story was by Graham Greene who worked on the script with Dighton, MacPhail and Diana Morgan. *Went the Day Well?*, a mysterious title from some anonymous lines, 'Went the Day Well? We died and never knew, But well or ill, For freedom we died for you,' began in the future, a view of an English churchyard after the war. We are then told of the events that occurred in the village of Bramley Green in the spring of 1942. It is an idyllic rural setting, ancient cottages and a church surrounded by fields tilled since the Domesday Book, spring flowers in the hedgerows, old oaks and elms bursting into full leaf. The life of the village is self-contained, and war seems a long way away. Suddenly there is an eruption of military vehicles and the place is swarming with khaki uniforms. The villagers are told that it is an exercise for the Royal Engineers, and mum's the word. They respond by billeting the soldiers, while the officers are entertained by the gentry. Gradually odd things are noticed. Why do the visitors write the figure seven with a cross stroke? Why has one of them got a bar of chocolate made in Vienna? Why are they so impatient with a small boy? Can it be ...? And slowly and horrifyingly the placid community realizes that the enemy is in its midst, German paratroops disguised as British soldiers. As the Germans declare themselves the hitherto supposedly pukka British major (Basil Sydney) allows himself an 'Ach, so?'. The villagers are rounded up and locked in the church, and attempts to summon help are brutally frustrated. The vicar rings a peal on the church bells and is shot; patrolling Home Guards some way off hear the bells and assume it is a mistake, because it is a signal for the arrival of enemy parachutists, and obviously nothing like that could have happened. They are then ambushed by the Germans and wiped out. The village squire is a traitor, a notion so improbable that it has not occurred to the villagers, who look on him as their natural leader. When the vicar's daughter realizes, she shoots him down with a service revolver, a shocking act for a well brought-up young Englishwoman. But there is no gentility left – the defenders fight as though possessed, rejoicing at

every invader's death. Finally, word reaches the outside world through a small boy (Harry Fowler), a friend of the poacher (Edward Rigby) who has died in the attempt, and the British army moves in and mops up the enemy. The only piece of England that the Germans have gained is the section of the churchyard where their bodies rest.

The story has an affinity with *An Englishman's Home*, a patriotic play that attempted to sound the bugle call to arms before the First World War. More recently a similar theme was used for the film of Jack Higgins' novel, *The Eagle Has Landed*, the plot of which concerned an assassination attempt on Churchill during a stay in Norfolk. Even the device of the graveyard, with German names on the headstones, was used. *Went the Day Well?* is regarded by Cavalcanti as the best of his Ealing films, with a pacifist idea behind it. In an interview with Elizabeth Sussex in *Sight and Sound* (Autumn 1975), he said: 'People of the kindest character, such as the people in that small English village, as soon as the war touches them, become absolute monsters.' But the more obvious lesson, the appropriate one for the time that the film was shown, is to be alert and prepared at all times to distrust even the familiar.

Opposite, top: Grant Sutherland and Jack
Lambert in Harry Watt's *Nine Men*, set in
the Western Desert, but shot on a sandy
coastline in South Wales
Bottom: Philip Friend, Tommy Trinder,
Mervyn Johns and Billy Hartnell as
auxiliary firemen in Basil Dearden's *The
Bells Go Down*, set in the London Blitz

Your neighbour could be an enemy; the battle could be on *your* doorstep. It is a theme already touched on in the two previous films, and for that matter in the humbler George Formby vehicle of two years earlier, *Spare a Copper*.

Although the film still has the capacity to shock, largely due to the way Cavalcanti establishes the setting with its agreeably evocative early scenes of rural stasis, the matter-of-fact treatment of the first appearance of the soldiers, their procedures shot with the literal, documentary style of a training film, then the explosion of violence in the most peaceful of situations and the subsequent bloodbath, it seems that the reaction in its own time was more blasé. 'The scripting is indifferent, banal at times, and the direction lacks cohesion,' said the *Monthly Film Bulletin*. 'Artificial ... trite melodrama,' said *Picturegoer*. It is salutary to remember that how a film is seen depends as much on the context of the time as the mood of the viewer.

Harry Watt's first film at Ealing was a relatively straightforward war film about a lost patrol in the desert. *Nine Men* is an incident from the North African war, although Watt, whose background experience was in the Crown Film Unit on a mere £15 a week, was able to shoot it on a stretch of sand dunes at Margam on the South Wales coast for only £20,000, which even at Ealing must have been a minuscule budget, and yet still produced a convincing result. Major Jack Lambert was given leave to play a resourceful sergeant faced with the responsibility of getting his own men to safety after their officer is killed. They hide out in a desert tomb and hold it against a fierce enemy onslaught for a day and a night before they are relieved. The story originated from Gerald Kersh, author of a book about the Guards in wartime called *They Died with Their Boots Clean*, and is deliberately low key and uncomplicated. The dialogue is spare and understated, the men accepting their hardship courageously and without rancour. The borderline between the true documentary of Watt's earlier work, *Target for Tonight*, is crossed imperceptibly, as he uses many of the same skills in creating the tensions of their plight. Like so many of the wartime documentary films, it is a close-up of men doing a job.

For *The Bells Go Down*, released in April 1943, three months after *Nine Men*, and directed by Basil Dearden, the scene changes from the Western Desert to the East End of London, where we follow the experiences of an assorted group of Auxiliary Fire Service (AFS) volunteers facing the Blitz of 1940. Once again, the film explores the way in which ordinary people, plunged into war, find within themselves the capacity for bravery and dedication. The crook in the group (Mervyn Johns) rescues the policeman who in peacetime has arrested him. Tommy Trinder, whose personality to some extent unbalances the cohesion of the group, is allowed to die heroically, trying to save the life of his hated commander (Finlay Currie). It was unfortunate for the Ealing film that it was released in the same week as Humphrey Jennings' Crown documentary, *Fires Were Started*, which again told a story of the AFS in London three years earlier. Jennings was already moving from 'pure' documentary towards fiction film techniques and, although his actors were all seconded firemen, they were given lines to speak, albeit improvised on the set rather than formally scripted in advance. By comparison with Jennings' film however, Dearden's looks like a polished studio work, an entertainment with a serious theme. Yet it amounted to hyper-realism when compared with the standard Hollywood view of Britain at war, exemplified by William Wyler's *Mrs Miniver*, with Greer Garson as a well-coiffed British wife in a Beverly Hills-type mansion somewhere in the Home Counties coping with class distinctions, rationing and a German aviator who arrives by parachute, or by Anatole Litvak's *This Above All*, with Tyrone Power as a conscientious objector and Joan Fontaine as the girl who inspires him to heroism by gushing amazing sentiments on what England means to *her*.

Sergei Nolbandov, of *Ships with Wings*, directed one more Ealing film before devoting his career to government films, and after the war to the monthly Rank series *This Modern Age*, which was intended to be Britain's answer to the popular American two-reelers made by Time-Life, *The March of Time*. *Undercover* was originally to have been called *Chetnic*, after the Yugoslav resistance movement under the command of General Mihailović. But politics overtook the situation, Mihailović and the Royalists were out, and the new leader was Tito.

Michael Wilding as a Yugoslav guerilla in
Undercover, with Wales once again
providing the foreign location, then
unavailable for filming

The screenplay, by John Dighton and Monja Danis-chewsky, was accordingly amended. It was a straightforward war drama following a Belgrade family. One brother (John Clements) becomes a partisan and takes to the mountains, while the other (Stephen Murray) stays in the city as a doctor and is regarded as a quisling, enabling him to pick up much useful information from a German general (Godfrey Tearle). The climax of the film is a pitched battle between the Germans and the guerrillas, with the ending a tribute to the fervent patriotism of the Yugoslav people. The film was shot in Wales, using the hills of Brecon as the mountains of Yugoslavia, and Rachel Thomas, who had performed so success-fully in *The Proud Valley*, played the part of the mother of the Petrovitch family, with Tom Walls somewhat miscast as her husband. The film is unconvincing and cliché-ridden, and not for a moment are its players believable Yugoslavs. The only notable thing about it was that it marked the screen debut of the fourteen-year-old Stanley Baker, whose acting had been limited hitherto to the school dramatic society.

Ealing's last film to be presented in 1943 was another war film in which a small group of men face incredible hardship with unquestioning courage, submerging individual and national differences so that the team can win through. It was a true story, the reconstruction of an epic voyage of an oil tanker which, although so badly damaged it is abandoned, is reboarded later by its crew and brought home to port. *San Demetrio London* was directed by Charles Frend, with Robert Hamer as the associate pro-ducer, and they both wrote the screenplay from the official narrative of the original exploit by F. Tenny-son Jesse.

After drifting in a lifeboat for three days, several members of the crew decide that their chances are better on their old ship, which is floundering in mid-Atlantic. They succeed in putting the fires out, patching up the engines sufficiently to limp on to their port of destination, Greenock. As they make their way up the Clyde they proudly refuse the offer of a tow. Without realizing it, they have made them-selves eligible for salvage money, and the last scene shows them in court receiving a shared award of £14,000 for their efforts. The judge says: 'It has given me the best working day of my life in listening to the very modest recital of some gallant gentlemen concerning a memorable achievement.'

The earlier common assumption of leadership and superiority that distinguishes the officers from the lower decks in *Convoy* and *Ships with Wings* has been replaced by a democratic consensus – the big decisions of whether to board the tanker or not and whether to attempt to get it back to England are reached collectively. It is almost as if Ealing is saying that the officer class has let Britain down, and that it is amongst them that the spies (*The Foreman Went to France*), the quislings (*Went the Day Well?*) and the pompous stuffed shirts (*Ships with Wings*) can be found.

Balcon regarded *San Demetrio London* not only as an epic story of endeavour but also as a way of reminding the public of the perils of Merchant Navy service. Petrol was desperately short, yet a black market flourished, enabling some people to evade rationing. It was in this climate that a Philip Zec cartoon in the *Daily Mirror*, which showed a tor-pedoed seaman alone on a raft with the caption '"The price of petrol has been increased by One Penny" – Official', was interpreted by the Cabinet as

From *San Demetrio London:* (below)
crewmen on an Atlantic tanker below
decks, and aboard the burnt-out hulk after
a Nazi attack; (bottom) Gordon Jackson
in centre and Robert Beatty, right, fight
the elements after abandoning ship

Opposite, top: Mervyn Johns and Glynis Johns in *Halfway House*, Ealing's first foray into the occult

Bottom: socialist allegory – the film of J. B. Priestley's tract, *They Came to a City*

David Farrar tests his skill in *For Those in Peril*, Ealing's air-sea rescue tribute

unpatriotic and nearly caused the paper's closure. On another level, the matinee idol of the musical stage and erstwhile Gainsborough star, Ivor Novello, was hauled off to Wormwood Scrubs for fiddling his petrol ration.

Following *San Demetrio London*, Charles Frend made a documentary, *The Return of the Vikings*, writing the screenplay with Sidney Cole. It had been commissioned by the Norwegian government in exile, and followed the story of a whaler skipper who becomes a paratrooper. Meanwhile, Charles Crichton, who was an editor on *The Big Blockade* and associate producer and editor of *Nine Men*, received his first directorial assignment with *For Those in Peril*, a story about the Air-Sea Rescue service which patrolled the Channel and North Sea in high-speed launches ready to pick up airmen who had been shot down. Ralph Michael played a new man who resents joining David Farrar's boat because he would rather be where the action is – in the air. During a mission they run into an enemy minefield and an armed trawler, are shelled by shore batteries and strafed by Focke-Wulf 190s. Farrar is killed and Michael has to take over and bring the craft and rescued aircrew safely home. He will never complain of dullness again. The story had been written by Richard Hillary, a fighter pilot in the Battle of Britain whose experiences inspired his fine book, *The Last Enemy*. After spending time at Ealing during his recuperation from burns received when he was shot down, he rejoined the RAF and a few weeks later was killed. *For Those in Peril*, in presenting the work of the Air-Sea Rescue crews in documentary terms, provided the public with another glimpse of an aspect of war that tended to be overlooked. It was also the closest Crichton got to documentary realism during his long Ealing career.

Basil Dearden's two films in 1944 were curiosities, neither really quite achieving what it set out to do, although the ideas were intriguing. The first, the more successful one, was *Halfway House*. A group of travellers, each with a personal problem, comes to a remote country inn in Wales. There is an indefinable strangeness in the atmosphere and in the conversation of the proprietor and his daughter (Mervyn Johns and his real daughter, Glynis Johns). Why are the only available newspapers a year old? Why does

the landlord's daughter not throw a shadow when she walks in the sun? It is because none of it is real, the Halfway House was bombed a year earlier and both were killed. As a result of their visit to the spectral hostelry, the assorted characters learn much about themselves, and their problems begin to fall away. The couple driven apart by grief over the death of their son are reunited, the embezzler and the black marketeer mend their ways, the sweethearts at odds with each other reconcile their differences. The film ends with a repetition of the conflagration, and the guests go their ways back to the real world with only a subconscious recollection of what has happened, but with a new strength to cope with their lives. Based on a play by Denis Ogden, *The Peaceful Inn*, Angus MacPhail, Diana Morgan and T. E. B. Clarke (Tibby to everyone at Ealing) did a satisfactory job in opening it up for the screen and, although one or two speeches sound stagey, the film's main weakness lies in the absolute falsity of its premise. No matter how well-acted, the fantasy is hard to sustain and never develops beyond a theatrical morality tale. There are points of comparison with Roy Boulting's version of Robert Ardrey's play, *Thunder Rock*, released eighteen months earlier, in which a writer, living in retreat in a lighthouse, peoples it in his imagination with the victims of a shipwreck nearly a century earlier. The

theme of the supernatural was explored much more satisfactorily by a British film in the following year with Bernard Knowles' *A Place of One's Own*, from an Osbert Sitwell story, and better still in the justly celebrated Ealing film, *Dead of Night*.

Dearden's next film was a great deal more theatrical than *Halfway House*, a more or less literal screen interpretation of a J. B. Priestley play, *They Came to a City*, which even used the same West End stage cast. It is a tract for socialism, presented in allegorical form, with a motley group of people drawn to the gates of a city wherein poverty, exploitation, slums, class distinctions and the profit motive have all been abolished. The trick is to guess which of those present will accept this Utopia. Certainly not the upper-class Lady Loxfield (Mabel Terry Lewis) or the irascible aristocrat Sir George Gedney (A. E. Matthews). A hen-pecked bank clerk (Raymond Huntley) would like to stay there, but his selfish wife (Renée Gadd) will not allow him. There is nothing there for Cudworth, the businessman (Norman Shelley). Joe, a seaman (John Clements) and Alice, a waitress (Googie Withers) might fit in but, having met and fallen in love, they feel their role is to go back and extol the virtues of Utopia to the rest of the world. Only Lady Loxfield's repressed daughter (Frances Rowe) and Mrs Batley, a charwoman (Ada Reeve), eventually stay. The sole concession to the cinema was the addition of a prologue and epilogue featuring J. B. Priestley himself talking to a young couple (Ralph Michael and Brenda Bruce) on a hillside overlooking some British industrial city. Otherwise, the film's action – if that is not a misnomer – is confined to stylistic sets. It is one of Ealing's most unsatisfactory films, a venture into an area that would be fairly difficult for any filmmaker, but one which for this studio, with its tradition of realism and a view of ordinary lives, was a disaster. Priestley's radicalism was based on the concept of universal friendship, but this play failed to offer any ideas as to how his Utopia could be achieved. And because we are never given a chance to see *inside* the city we have no way of knowing whether its idealism works or not. Priestley took strong exception to John Clements playing the hero, a reaction that turned out to be mutual when the actor was denied the opportunity of speaking the last

lines of the play, which came from Whitman and provided the title: 'I dreamed in a dream I saw a City, invisible to the attack of the whole of the rest of the Earth. I dreamed that it was a new city of Friends.' Instead, the last shot is of Priestley himself.

What seems to be apparent in the later years of the war is that Ealing was prepared to seek out fresh material, to attempt to make different kinds of film than the realistic, documentary-style features which had characterized so much of its output. Certainly after several unrelieved years the cinema audience was demanding more escapist entertainment, and from Hollywood there were plenty of Technicolor costume pictures, musicals and fantasies to satisfy the appetite. The British cinema, too, retreated into costume melodrama, following the successful box-office returns on Anthony Asquith's version of a Michael Sadleir novel, *Fanny by Gaslight*, a Victorian extravaganza with James Mason as a wicked nobleman. It sparked off a brief period later to be known as 'Gainsborough Gothic' and provided opportunities for James Mason (whose only appearance at Balcon's Ealing was as a volunteer fireman in *The Bells Go Down*), Margaret Lockwood, Phyllis Calvert, Jean Kent, Stewart Granger and Patricia Roc. It was not a field into which Ealing would venture, except tentatively. But Cavalcanti, fascinated by the possibilities of Victorian England, directed *Champagne Charlie*, which was set in the music halls of the 1860s. Tommy Trinder played George Leybourne, a popular performer of the day, and Stanley Holloway his rival, the Great Vance. Each tries to outdo the other with drinking songs and the feud culminates in an absurd duel. But the very existence of the halls is under threat from the theatre owners who try to have them shut down as disorderly houses. The rivals unite and succeed in satisfying the inspectors that there is nothing wrong with the robust music-hall tradition, which becomes established as part of the folk culture of the time.

Cavalcanti's film, laying on the smoke-laden, beer-swilling atmosphere with relish, managed to capture the boistrousness of a less-restrained age, as well as giving both Tommy Trinder and Stanley Holloway a chance to deliver several songs, some of them contemporary, such as the title number which

Mid-Victorian music-hall history as seen by Cavalcanti in *Champagne Charlie*, with Tommy Trinder. The middle dancing girl is Jean Kent, soon to be a Gainsborough star

was a Victorian favourite, others specially written for the film by Lord Berners and Tibby Clarke. While the Leybourne–Vance feud had its basis in fact, the film was not entirely accurate in its portrayal of the mid-Victorian halls, which were really large ale houses – it was only later in the nineteenth century that the variety theatres emerged, with greater respectability. Yet in the film the daughter (Jean Kent) of a proprietress (Betty Warren) ends up engaged to a scion of the nobility. Experts who

had studied Victorian music hall felt that the Ealing version was far too jolly and genteel, missing the Dickensian poverty and sordidness of the period. Had it not been so, however, the film would have been a lot less entertaining.

Another attempt to break out of the wartime rut, *Fiddlers Three*, again starred Tommy Trinder, this time teamed with Sonnie Hale, not seen in a film since Ealing's *Let's Be Famous* in 1939. They played two servicemen on leave who take shelter during a thunderstorm under the altarstone of Stonehenge, accompanied by a Wren (Diana Decker). In a flash they are transported back to Ancient Rome where they undergo numerous absurd adventures and fall foul of Nero (Francis L. Sullivan) who throws them to the lions. Fortunately for them, at this juncture they return to modern times. Essentially a comedy fantasy for Trinder, the film is not of great consequence. The script, by Harry Watt and Diana Morgan, was thick with laboured gags likening aspects of Roman times to wartime Britain. There were also several songs, sung by Frances Day and Elizabeth Welch. In format it was a British equivalent of the Abbott and Costello films of the Forties. A strange place in which to find Harry Watt, perhaps, but he had endeavoured to move away from the sincere war films for which he was known. His associate producer Robert Hamer shot many scenes and, although it was not well-regarded at the studio, its box-office performance was satisfactory, and it was even reissued in 1949 in a double bill with *Kind Hearts and Coronets*.

There were also two Flanagan and Allen films made at Ealing, produced not by Balcon but by John Baxter, who also directed. The first, *Dreaming*, was virtually plotless, so inconsequential was the storyline, but it exploited the attractive comic personalities of the two Crazy Gang members adequately as well as providing opportunities for celebrities and performers of the day to appear as themselves. The second, *Here Comes the Sun*, released in 1945, had a background of racing, prison and Fleet Street. Although distributed by Ealing they formed no part of the mainstream output.

Far left: Sonnie Hale and Tommy Trinder starred in
Fiddlers Three, which transplanted them back in
Ancient Rome

Centre: Bud Flanagan is cross-examined by a bewigged
Chesney Allen in *Here Comes the Sun*
Above: the other Flanagan and Allen film made by John
Baxter in the last year of the war was *Dreaming*

Ealing's last film made in wartime was *Johnny Frenchman*
which dealt with the rivalry of Cornish and Breton fisherfolk

With *Johnny Frenchman* there was a return to a more orthodox Ealing story. It concerned the rivalry before and during the war of the Breton and Cornish fishermen, who are eventually united by the threat of disaster. It is a simple hands-across-the-Channel story, directed by Charles Frend and scripted by Tibby Clarke in an admirably competent manner. The war was in its final year when the film was made, and part of France already liberated. Nevertheless it was impossible to take a film crew there, and so once again Mevagissey in Cornwall had to become gallicized. Tibby Clarke has recalled with delight his impression of Françoise Rosay adapting herself to the part of a French matriarch. Very much the *grande dame* of the French cinema, she had already appeared in *Halfway House* during her enforced English exile, playing opposite Tom Walls, cast in *Johnny Frenchman* as the Cornish harbourmaster. On arriving early at the location she looked round at the women on the quayside. When she spotted one she thought interesting she followed her, noting her every movement, every detail of her gait, and then adapted it for her own performance. 'I have known only one other artist who gave such careful application to the character,' recalled Clarke; 'Sir Alec Guinness!' Rosay was unable to talk to the crew of the boat she skippered in the film, as they spoke Breton, rather than French. Michael Balcon was delighted to find that the real Breton skipper was called Balcon, although pronounced with a short 'a'.

By the time the film was ready for screening, world events had moved startlingly forward. Not only had the war in Europe been concluded but a few days before the London opening the atomic bombs had terminated the war with Japan. There was just time to update the ending to refer to the victory.

Painted Boats had also been in production in the summer of 1944, yet did not get shown to the public until after the war had ended in the following year. It was set on the Midland canals and told the story of two families, the Smiths and the Stoners, who ply their narrow boats on the waterway. The Stoners are the progressives, with a motor, whereas the Smiths rely on a horse. In the typical Ealing fashion the two sides are united by both romantic involvement and the need to pool forces to overcome adversity.

Charles Crichton directed the film, which followed the Ealing documentary style even to the extent of having a voice-over narration written by Louis MacNeice and spoken by James McKechnie. A pleasant pastoral study of English life, it suffers from over-abrupt shifts between reality in the shape of statistical information and the fictional lives of the Smiths and the Stoners. But it marks the transition from war to peace for Ealing, and is also the last of the Studios' small films, running only sixty-three minutes. Henceforth everything produced was of full feature length.

Great changes had taken place in the British film industry during the six hard years of war, the most significant of which had been the emergence of J. Arthur Rank as the most formidable figure within it. By 1944 he controlled two of the three main exhibition circuits – Gaumont and Odeon – the studios of Denham and Pinewood plus Shepherds Bush and Islington, the biggest British distribution company – General Film Distributors – and some eighty subsidiaries which included production companies, equipment suppliers and radio manufacturers. Rank had 619 cinemas as opposed to his rivals, ABC, who had 442, and he controlled more than half the available studio space. Balcon watched the growth of the Rank empire with apprehension, and successfully lobbied for an official committee to be set up to look into 'tendencies to monopoly in the cinematograph film industry' as the subsequent Palache Report (named after its chairman, Albert Palache) was designated. It was an important report, recognizing the danger that the film industry might effectively dwindle to a 'duopoly', and it contained a prescient warning of what would happen if Rank pursued the American market with extravagant 'prestige' productions. It foresaw the demise of the independent producer, and asked that the government intervene directly in film finance to prevent them from being squeezed out.

The Palache recommendations were generally ignored, although the report influenced much of the 1945 Labour government's attitude, and led to the setting up of the National Film Finance Corporation in 1948. But no curbs were put on the further accretion of Rank interests and, by the time that the Monopolies' Commission looked into it twenty years

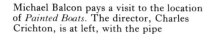

Michael Balcon pays a visit to the location
of *Painted Boats*. The director, Charles
Crichton, is at left, with the pipe

later, the situation was considered irreversible.

Balcon had realized that Ealing's survival was at stake for, without a release on one of the three main circuits of which two were controlled by the same group, there was no chance of a British film recouping its costs, let alone making a profit, as the booking power of the independent cinemas was inadequate. Balcon applied the 'if you can't beat them, join them' philosophy and, swallowing all his dislike of the Rank megalith, concluded a deal which gave Ealing a distribution guarantee in Rank cinemas under favourable terms and a fifty per cent (later raised to seventy-five per cent) stake in Ealing films, plus representation on the Rank board, yet with Ealing retaining total autonomy in production, choice and treatment of subjects, actors and so on. In other words, Ealing was to retain its full independence, but with the strength of the Rank Organisation behind it. The contract, a masterpiece of business skill by Reg Baker, was described by Balcon in his autobiography: 'This was a model contract, leaning if anything, to the generous side on the part of the Rank Organisation. It would be ridiculous to suggest that in the course of the eleven years the contract operated there were no moments of strain, but although on occasions it proved onerous to Rank, the contract was fulfilled by them meticulously and honourably. The contract certainly cushioned Ealing against the possibility of financial disaster, and in terms of achievement those years proved to be the most rewarding of my life, as it was during them that the best Ealing films were made.'

CHAPTER 4

Post-war ambition

There can be little doubt that Ealing Studios reached their peak during the first post-war years. The era lasted from the end of the war until the Festival of Britain in 1951. It is almost exactly the period of the post-war Labour government which was elected by a landslide vote in 1945, and then all but rejected in the General Election of 1950, hanging on until October 1951 by a tiny majority. The Attlee government carried out the greatest social revolution of the century, taking into public ownership the mines, the gas and electricity industries, the railways, the canals, road transport and the steel industry, and setting up the National Health Service, which was to be the foundation of the Welfare State. But the immediate post-war period was a time of considerable hardship. The British people, having endured six hard years of war, found that peacetime did not diminish their problems. In some respects things were worse than in the darkest days of the war, because at least then there had been a sense of national purpose, a target on which the anger of a public subjected to hardship and deprivation could be properly focused, a sharing of common goals, and the excitement of being witness to great events. Nothing caused the adrenalin to flow so freely as being under fire, and during the period of the Blitz and the VI and V2 attacks on London the atmosphere was filled with a strange, vicarious excitement.

In peacetime there could be nothing to compare. Some commodities were rationed even more stringently than before, such as bread which was not on coupons until 1946. The consumer revolution was a long way off. Not only was there little money available for what were then luxury goods like washing machines and refrigerators, but such things were difficult to obtain, owing to the scarcity of raw materials. Many products eagerly awaited by the public were still denied them, and designated 'export only'. Petrol was strictly rationed and new cars were almost unobtainable, so there was very little private motoring. At the same time the public transportation systems, having somehow kept going through the war, were now decrepit, antiquated and inadequate. Coal stocks on which the nation depended for its fuel were at a minimum level, and during the severe winter of 1947 became so depleted that all electric power had to be shut off for large parts of the day.

In spite of, or perhaps because of, national problems, in 1945 British film-going was at its peak, with thirty million attendances *a week*. For the first time the majority of Members of Parliament came from those sections of the populace that regularly went to the cinema. It seems scarcely conceivable that three out of every five people in the country should go to the pictures every week, but obviously there must have been many people who went several times. There was, after all, no television (BBC transmissions resumed in June 1946, but there were fewer than 30,000 sets – it would not be until the Fifties that television would become a popular medium in Britain). The cinema was still relatively cheap and, although Entertainments Tax was removing 36%

from the average one shilling and ninepence of a cinema seat, the huge audiences were keeping takings at a reasonable level. It is ironic that at the time of its greatest popularity the British film industry was unable to take full advantage of the situation. Housing was scarce, and priority was given to replenishing stock destroyed by bombing, often infilling bombsites with 'prefabs'. No new places of entertainment could be built, as licences were not granted for non-essential construction. Even modernization was forbidden unless it fell within the definition of war-damage repair. The derequisitioning of government-held studio space at least meant that it was possible to raise output. First features, of which twenty-eight were made in 1945, increased to sixty-five by 1948. The Board of Trade defined a first feature as having a length of at least 6,500 feet, although the industry itself regarded one or two films longer than this arbitrary figure as 'seconds'.

Ealing's first post-war film, that is to say the first film released after the end of the war which did not, unlike *Painted Boats* and *Johnny Frenchman*, use the war as the basis for the story, was *Dead of Night*, one of the best films ever made about the supernatural. It was the first 'portmanteau' film made at Ealing, wherein a number of different directors were able to contribute an individual story without unbalancing the unity. An architect (Mervyn Johns) arrives at a house party in the country where a number of other guests are assembled. Immediately he feels a sense of *déja vu*, that he has been through it all before. He realizes that a recurrent dream has suddenly come to life, and he knows, but cannot quite remember, that there is an evil climax. His revelation provides a talking point for the gathering, and by one the others relate various supernatural experiences they have heard about, or have actually witnessed, which are then shown in flashback to provide several films-within-a-film.

The first story is a simple haunting. During a Christmas party in an old house, a teenage girl finds a small boy sobbing alone in a room at the top of a hidden, narrow flight of stairs. He tells of unspeakable cruelties that are being enacted and she comforts him. Later there is no trace of him or the room. It seems that she has stepped into the previous century. This sequence was directed by Cavalcanti,

and was taken from a story by Angus MacPhail.

The next tale, the first official directing credit for Robert Hamer, came from a chilling story by John V. Baines. It follows the progress of an engaged couple. The girl (Googie Withers) sees an early Victorian mirror in an antique shop and buys it for her fiancé. As he is using it, he suddenly has an impression that the room reflected is not his own dressing-room. The couple marry, but the husband becomes sullen and morose, with bursts of sharp temper. The mirror is now dominating him; in it he sees himself in a large, heavily-furnished Victorian bedroom with a four-poster bed and a fire in the grate, though his wife sees only a normal reflection. He goes to a doctor, who suggests that it is a psychiatric problem, but when the man becomes violent and jealous his wife goes back to the antique dealer to find out the provenance of the mirror, and discovers that it came from a house where in early Victorian times the owner had been confined to his bedroom after an accident. He had then killed his wife and himself before the mirror in frustration and madness. After that, the contents of the house were put away until the present. Returning to her husband with this knowledge, she is attacked by him before she can reveal the mirror's secret. As he begins to strangle her, she, too, sees the hideous room in the mirror. She is able to smash it, whereupon her husband becomes normal again, unable to recollect what had happened.

This was followed by a short tale of premonition, directed by Basil Dearden from a story by E. F. Benson. Recovering in hospital from a car crash, a man (Anthony Baird) wakes up in the middle of the night to find that it is broad daylight outside. He looks down and sees a horse-drawn hearse. The driver looks up at him, nods towards the coffin and says 'Room for one inside.' The man gets back into bed, realizes that it is the middle of the night and that he must have been dreaming, and goes back to sleep. When he is discharged from the hospital he waits at a bus stop to go home. A loaded vehicle pulls up and the conductor says to him, 'Room for one inside.' It is, of course, the man in the dream. He steps back from the bus stupefied, the conductor shrugs and rings the bell, and the bus goes off without him. Suddenly, it is involved in a collision with a

Opposite, top: Basil Radford and
Naunton Wayne in the humorous
golfing story in *Dead of Night*

Bottom: Michael Redgrave with the
ventriloquist's dummy he cannot control
in the film's climactic episode

truck, goes out of control and crashes over the para-
pet of a bridge, falling on to a railway line and
presumably killing all aboard.

Light relief follows with a tall golfing story, a
version of a tale by H. G. Wells, somewhat modified
by Charles Crichton, who also directed the piece. It
featured Basil Radford and Naunton Wayne as golf
chums in love with the same girl (Peggy Bryan).
They decide that the only way to solve the problem
is to play for her, the loser to commit suicide. Naunton Wayne drowns himself as a result, and Basil
Radford marries her. But the spectre of his old
friend keeps turning up to ruin the proceedings. It
seems that Radford won by cheating and is therefore
not entitled to his prize.

The last of the stories, another directed by Cavalcanti, was to become the most celebrated. It concerned a ventriloquist (Michael Redgrave) who is
becoming possessed by his dummy, which has a
repugnant persona. The dummy leads its host to
degradation, murder, a prison cell and madness.
The possession motif is one that has been revived in
the cinema in recent years, and Richard Attenborough's *Magic* (1979) even used the idea of an
apparently animate dummy inspiring murder.

After the stories have been told, the film reaches
its climax and in a bewildering nightmare they all
intermingle with bizarre horror erupting to a point
at which the man in the centre of the action awakes at
home in bed. His wife reminds him that he has to go
down to the country about a commission. The film
ends with him approaching the same farmhouse,
and meeting the same host that we saw at the beginning. It is without doubt one of the most satisfying
entertainments ever offered by Ealing, brilliantly
conceived and wrought by a fusion of creative talent,
in the spirit of teamwork and the cross-fertilization
of ideas for which it was renowned.

Robert Hamer followed his *Dead of Night* episode
with a full-length film, a melodramatic view of
Brighton in the Nineties, *Pink String and Sealing
Wax*, which was adapted by Hamer himself and
Diana Morgan from a play by Roland Pertwee.
Mervyn Johns plays a chemist and public analyst, an
autocratic father who holds his children in close
restraint. His son (Gordon Jackson), whose romantic attempts are thwarted by his father, rebels and

seeks solace in a local public house, where he
becomes besotted by the landlord's wife (Googie
Withers). She uses the young man in a plot to kill off
her husband, obtaining the poison from the chemist's shop. When the public analyst is asked by the
suspicious police to inspect the exhumed body, the
woman tries to blackmail him by threatening to
implicate his son. He refuses to be diverted from his
stern path of duty, and the woman throws herself
into the sea, allowing a sort of happy ending, for the
son is at last allowed by his father to pursue his
original romantic intentions. The pacing of the film
led to a very slow build-up, with a lot of attention
paid to a sub-plot in which, just as the son is frustrated by his father, so the daughter is faced with
impossible difficulties in attempting a singing
career. The publican's wife, for all her flirtatious-
ness and open sensuality, is as much a prisoner of her
situation as the young man; her passions are kept in
restraint by a dreary husband, and her actions arise
from a desperate last attempt to escape rather than
from cold, calculated wickedness. The film, like
much of Hamer's work, is elegantly conceived, with
the starch and bombazine of the era faithfully repro-
duced, and Googie Withers is excellent, drawing
considerable sympathy to the part of a murderess.

Miss Withers, whose first name is in reality
Georgette, although she adhered to the comical
diminutive even when she had proved herself as a
serious actress, made no less than six films at Ealing,
the first as the girl in a George Formby picture,
Trouble Brewing. During the making of one of them,
The Loves of Joanna Godden, she met and married her
Australian co-star, John McCallum, who later
became the head of an important theatre group in his
native country. Gordon Jackson, the young man in
Pink String and Sealing Wax, also proved to be an
Ealing stalwart, beginning his film career there with
The Foreman Went to France, and making a total of
ten films for the Studios. In his early days he worked
only with special government permission as he was
engaged on what was considered to be more vital
war-work in the drawing office of a Scottish aircraft
factory. But Balcon had given him a deal that
enabled him to work part-time in films until his
Essential Work Order expired, when the Ealing contract would come into full force. Years later he

Googie Withers reaches for the poison in
Pink String and Sealing Wax

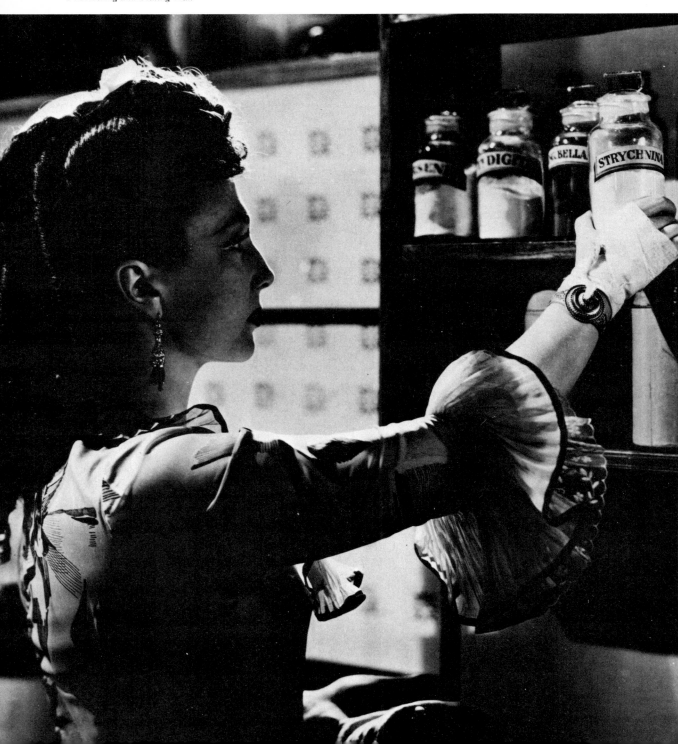

achieved international fame, not through films but by his television role of the all-knowing Scottish butler Hudson in the long-running series, *Upstairs, Downstairs*. In the lesser roles there were a number of performers who constantly cropped up – Edie Martin, for instance, who was a perennial old lady – and there was a sort of unofficial repertory system which kept actors working, and provided directors with consistent and untroublesome players.

Because Balcon's wife, Aileen, who was South-African born, had devoted the war years to working for the British Red Cross and had been closely involved in helping repatriated prisoners-of-war, he felt that there was good subject matter in a story about a group of Britons following their experiences from capture through to release. Originally, *The Captive Heart* was to have been called *Lover's Meeting*, but the novelist Lady Eleanor Smith instituted a passing-off action, as one of her works bore the same title. Ordinarily there would have been no chance of it succeeding as there was no similarity between the stories, but, as the aged novelist was on her death-bed, Balcon gallantly relented and ordered his title to be changed. The original story by Patrick Kirwan was scripted by Angus MacPhail and Guy Morgan, the latter an ex-journalist who had himself been confined in the prisoner-of-war camp, Marlag Milag Nord, which the British Army of Occupation permitted to be used for filming. Basil Dearden directed the film and the actors included Michael Redgrave, Basil Radford, Ralph Michael, Gordon Jackson, Derek Bond and Guy Middleton as officers, with Jack Warner, Jimmy Hanley and Mervyn Johns as other ranks, and Rachel Kempson, Jane Barrett, Gladys Henson and Rachel Thomas as the women waiting for their men to come home. Redgrave played an imposter, a Czech who had escaped from a concentration camp and adopted the identity of a dead Briton. Taken prisoner, he is forced to keep up the masquerade, even to the extent of corresponding with the dead man's widow who believes that her husband has had a change of heart over their marriage, which was in a shaky state. (The handwriting problem is glossed over with the suggestion that he writes with his left owing to an injury.) Naturally, when repatriation time comes round, the lady gets a shock.

Michael Redgrave leaves a prison camp with a dead man's identity in *The Captive Heart*

The film follows the Ealing method of throwing a disparate group of people together in a situation of adversity, and showing how they cope. When the prisoners are subjected to Nazi loudspeaker indoctrination they respond with a lusty rendering of 'Roll out the barrel'. When, after the commando raid on Sark, the Germans defy the Geneva convention and order the prisoners to be manacled, the spry young cockney (Jimmy Hanley) has everyone's locks picked in a trice. Jack Warner, in his first film for Ealing – not his very first film, which was *The Dummy Talks* in 1943, and who had hitherto been regarded as a popular comedian – is given a characterization, that of a genial corporal, that is in many ways the prototype of those which follow; and even his wife, with whom he has a touching reunion, is played by Gladys Henson, who will later be Mrs Dixon in *The Blue Lamp* when he plays his most famous role of PC Dixon for the first time. By coincidence, although not an extraordinary one since the returned p.o.w. was a popular theme of the period, Michael Redgrave appeared in another film that year on similar lines, called *The Years Between*, a non-Ealing film produced by Sydney Box and directed by Compton Bennett. In it he played a prisoner who returns home after the war to find that he is presumed dead and his wife is on the point of marrying a neighbour, having already taken his seat in Parliament. Of the two films *The Captive Heart* is much the better, giving a well-observed account of life in the p.o.w. compound with all its frustrations, homesickness and tedium. The 'all-pull-together' attitude now seems dated and perhaps artificial but, curiously enough, it is not inaccurate.

The year 1946 saw the fruition of a project begun in the later stages of the war. Jack Beddington, an advertising man under whose control the film-making side of the Ministry of Information had flourished, had asked Balcon to have a look at the Australian war effort, which had been insufficiently depicted in film. With the thought of something like *Nine Men* in mind, its director Harry Watt was sent there with a roving brief to find and film a good war story. It turned out to be a difficult task. The Australians were making *Rats of Tobruk*, a documentary-style reconstruction of the siege of the Libyan port. Watt did not want to go for a similar war subject, and at first found that he was being called upon by Australian government departments to advise them on how to make documentaries. On one such visit to the Australian Ministry of Food, he heard a reference to a great cattle drive in 1942, when 100,000 head were driven halfway across the island continent in order to remove them from the reach of Japanese aerial attack. Watt wanted to make something outdoors – Australian studio facilities were poor – and the idea intrigued him. He flew off immediately to the Northern Territory to reconnoitre the route and find locations, and on his return started hammering out a script in between searching for basic equipment. Even cameras were difficult to obtain, and one of the two Mitchells used had been retrieved from a businessman's safe where it had been held in lieu of an unredeemed debt. Ralph Smart was seconded from the Royal Australian Air Force to act as associate producer and proved to be a great asset as he had considerable experience in British films since his entry as an assistant editor at Elstree in 1927. Osmond Borradaile was sent from England to photograph the film, but Watt recalls

that of the thirty-five people in the unit and the cast, only six had ever worked on a feature film before. Making the film, like the story it told, was an exercise in pragmatism. Dollies, reflectors, mike booms had to be improvised. An abandoned army camp at Alice Springs became home for the first three months of the four-and-a-half month schedule, and after that the unit moved into tents in the outback. Watt had to buy 1,500 head of cattle to make the film, but at the end of shooting was able to sell them at a profit.

The leading role of the drover was given to Chips Rafferty, a tall, cadaverous actor with a lean, leathery face who had previously led an industrious outdoor life. He had already had a leading part in *Rats of Tobruk*, was remarkably at ease in front of the cameras, and was soon established as the best-known Australian screen personality of the day. Another piece of casting caused Watt some problems, when a blonde nursing orderly in a military hospital called Daphne Campbell, chosen to play an energetic young female member of the group who finds time to fall in love with a British sailor, played by Peter Pagan, eloped during the final stages of shooting. The story of the film, *The Overlanders*, was simple, the core of it being the hazardous journey across the vast interior of Australia, hundreds of miles from civilized comforts. There are plenty of mandatory thrills – the cattle swimming across a crocodile-infested river, a full-blown stampede, various accidents. But the most impressive aspect of the film is neither the dialogue, which is basic to the point of banality, nor the incident, which is predictable, but the brilliantly photographed, breathtaking Australian scenery, never shown on a cinema screen before, and a revelation to British audiences.

The Overlanders proved to be a financial success, in spite of all the limitations and difficulties faced by its makers, and as a result Balcon decided that there was a future for Ealing films made in Australia with Australian subjects. Consequently, he asked Watt to return there and establish production. A lease was taken on the Pagewood Studios in Sydney, which were the best-equipped in Australia although they had been closed for a decade. The Australian government was persuaded to lend the army for

Opposite, top: wagon in trouble in *The Overlanders*
Opposite, bottom: Harry Watt directing the film in a
rugged Australian location

Top: Jack Warner, Harry Fowler, a tied-up Valerie
White and Douglas Barr in *Hue and Cry*
Above: Harry Fowler and his gang of *Trump* readers
from the same film, directed by Charles Crichton

crowd scenes in Watt's next film, *Eureka Stockade*,
which was to be an account of an insurrection in the
goldfields of 1854. Meanwhile, the Rank Organisation made *Bush Christmas*, a well-received children's
film which was directed by Ralph Smart. It looked
as though, following Ealing's lead, a British investment would resuscitate the Australian feature film
industry, which had been more or less dormant since
the start of the war. But events were later to prove
otherwise.

Back at Ealing Green an important film emerged –
the first of what were later known as the Ealing
comedies, although at the time it was not realized
that it represented the beginning of a genre. The
writer of *Hue and Cry* was Tibby Clarke, a former
journalist and wartime London policeman, who had
also found time to be a purser on a tramp steamer
and the editor and sole writer of an Australian girls'
weekly paper, among many other improbable jobs.
He had persuaded Balcon to allow him to write
additional dialogue for a comedy section in *Dead of
Night* (the golfing story) and now, with Henry Cornelius as associate producer and Charles Crichton as
director, was given the job of fashioning a story
around the mysterious freemasonry of boys. Its first
title was *The Trump*, which was the name of a boys'
weekly filled with lurid blood-and-thunder yarns.
The leading youth, Joe, played by Harry Fowler,

the young cockney actor who had been a child in *Went the Day Well?*, has more imagination than most and becomes convinced that a hair-raising serial he is reading about a gang of crooks is really happening, and that the pages of *The Trump* are being used by fur thieves as a means of communication. First convincing his pals, he takes his theories to the police, but they dismiss them contemptuously and so the boys decide to go it alone and catch the crooks themselves. The first trap they set in a department store only nets a gaggle of plain-clothes detectives, and the boys make a hasty getaway through the sewers. Then they kidnap *The Trump*'s blonde secretary, who after being tortured by a tame white mouse reveals the plot. The climax of the film involved the coming together of hundreds of boys from all over London to fight it out with the crooks in a spectacular mêlée on a riverside bombsite.

Hue and Cry was billed with the slogan 'The Ealing film that begs to differ' – a line that was later adopted as a sort of unofficial motto for the Studios themselves. Certainly it moved in a new direction, using locations brilliantly as a background to a story of some originality. The character of Ealing comedies could perhaps be described as realistic fantasy, with extravagantly fanciful events taking place in a meticulously believable setting, in this case the shabby streets of early post-war London. The con-

cept of the film took shape from the sequence at the end of the film, with its agglomeration of boys, which illustrated an idea that Cornelius wanted to express. That its patent absurdity is made believable is due to the skill with which the preceding parts of the film are handled. Many of the boys were without acting experience, including one small youth whose special talent was to reproduce the noise of virtually anything that came to mind, and who in the film delivers plenty of sound effects but not a word of dialogue. The presence in the cast of the adult performers required some courage on their parts, but Jack Warner as a Covent Garden wholesaler and master crook, and Alastair Sim as the retiring writer of the stories, who has a lifelong distaste for small boys, are especially effective.

It was another two years before the genre of the Ealing comedy came to full flower, and in 1947 *Hue and Cry* seemed an eccentric element in the studio's output. Nevertheless, it was a great success and was praised by the critics, not least for the strongly indigenous feeling it had – it was, commented the *Monthly Film Bulletin*, 'English to the backbone'.

In the mid-Forties, British films were in an assertive mood. A number of pictures such as *Henry V*, *Brief Encounter* and *Great Expectations* had won admiration and respect abroad, particularly in America. It was perhaps unfortunate that Ealing's

Opposite: *Nicholas Nickleby* on location.
Cavalcanti (centre) directs Sally Ann
Howes at the Cheerybles' cottage

Below: *Nicholas Nickleby* interior set,
Mantalini's fashion house

attempt at Dickens, Cavalcanti's version of *Nicholas Nickleby*, should appear so soon after the accomplished David Lean film, and its comparative failure is in some part due to the choice of book. *Great Expectations* is a much more dramatic story, with a clear narrative line easily disentangled from the usual Dickensian plot-padding; *Nicholas Nickleby*, on the other hand, presents a bewildering parade of minor characters throughout its meandering length, and indeed much of the attraction of the book lies in the detail of the picaresque narrative, so that any process of selection and elimination is bound to alienate its devotees. Although John Dighton's screenplay did its conscientious best, it must have proved an immensely difficult novel to adapt to a screen time of 108 minutes. The eponymous role was taken by Derek Bond who had played an officer

in *The Captive Heart* and who gave a bland but not unlikeable performance that at least provided some continuity through what amounted to a succession of cameos. Some of the casting was distinctly odd – Cyril Fletcher glimpsed as Mantalini, Sir Cedric Hardwicke as a genteel Ralph Nickleby, the villainous usurer into whose hands Nicholas and his mother and sister fall on his father's death. The film is perhaps at its best in the early sequences, showing life at the appalling hellhole of a school, Dotheboys Hall, which is presented with a certain amount of passion; but after Nickleby has left with Smike and joined the ranks of the theatrical Crummles (Stanley Holloway), it becomes anaemic. *Nicholas Nickleby* plainly represented an attempt on the part of Ealing to pursue another kind of cinematic subject, with a nod in the direction of England's greatest novelist,

Opposite, top: Sybil Thorndike as Mrs
Squeers serving gruel at Dotheboys Hall
Bottom: Cedric Hardwicke (right) as the
villainous Ralph Nickleby with Sally Ann
Howes as Kate and Cecil Ramage as the
designing Sir Mulberry Hawk

Googie Withers as a Romney Marsh sheep
farmer in *The Loves of Joanna Godden*,
Chips Rafferty as a shepherd (centre)

whose prolific legacy was interesting other film-
makers at the time, creating something of a Dickens
boom.

The film marked the end of Cavalcanti's association with Ealing, where he had worked happily and
without friction. However, he felt that he was not
making enough money and that he could do better
outside as a freelance. Balcon ascribed his restless
feeling to the change of mood that occurred with the
end of the war, when the Ealing spirit inevitably
changed. Cavalcanti, he felt, did not feel as closely
identified with the Studios as he had before.

Another attempt to transfer a literary work to the
screen was made with *The Loves of Joanna Godden*,
which was adapted by H. E. Bates (with adjust-
ments by Angus MacPhail, Ealing's story supervisor) from a novel of Edwardian rural life by Sheila
Kaye-Smith. Googie Withers played a high-spirited
young woman whose father leaves her a sheep farm
on Romney Marsh and who determines, against the
odds, to run it herself. She refuses assistance from a
neighbouring farmer, one Arthur Alce (John
McCallum) and, encouraged by her new shepherd
to whom she is attracted (Chips Rafferty, temporarily imported from Australia), she embarks on a
disastrous breeding experiment which almost wipes
out a pedigree flock. She becomes engaged to a
pleasantly attractive man who is unlikely to domi-
nate her (Derek Bond) but he is drowned before the
marriage. She then realizes that she would be best
off with Alce, but learns that he has fallen for her
flighty younger sister (Jean Kent) whom he marries.
It is a total failure and, after the sister has run off,
Alce and Joanna finally come together.

Much of the film, which was directed by Charles
Frend (some sequences are by Robert Hamer who
deputized during a period when Frend was ill), was
made on location on Romney Marsh, and a creditable attempt was made to show something of farm
life. A sequence on the handling of an outbreak of
foot-and-mouth disease in Alce's stock was realistic
and uncompromising. Googie Withers was considered by some critics to be too elegantly accoutred
to be a farmer, but she gave the role considerable
strength, and must be regarded as one of Ealing's
best actresses. Lionel Collier in *Picturegoer*
defended her: 'There may be complaints about

expensive dresses and perfect grooming ... but in
my experience I have met a farmer's wife who could
have given points to a Mayfair beauty. And why
not?' One of Ealing's acknowledged weaknesses was
its treatment of women – few are more than ciphers
or supports for the male leads, but Googie Withers
managed on most occasions to take a dominant part.
The choice of a quasi-feminist subject was certainly
unusual, but could be seen as another attempt to
explore a type of film not characteristic of Ealing's
output.

Googie Withers' last Ealing film was *It Always
Rains on Sunday*, directed by Robert Hamer and
adapted by him, Angus MacPhail and Henry Cornelius from a novel by Arthur la Bern about events
one Sunday in the East End. Rose Sandigate is a
former barmaid married to a middle-aged man who
has two teenage daughters from an earlier union.
She is a bossy, strident Bethnal Green housewife,
coping with the difficulties of rationing, near-slum
housing and a dreary environment. A former lover
who was jailed years earlier for robbery with violence escapes from prison and turns to her for help in
making his getaway, hiding in the air raid shelter in
the backyard. It is Sunday morning and the lunch
must be cooked, the girls sorted out for their mis-
demeanours of the previous night and the husband
packed off to the pub out of the way. The strain is

A tense moment for Googie Withers
(right) as her old lover, played by John
McCallum, hides from her stepdaughter,
played by Patricia Plunkett, in *It Always
Rains on Sunday*, set in the East End

John Slater as the flashy Lou Hyams and
Sydney Tafler as his womanizing brother,
Morrie, proprietor of a record shop.
Citizens of Bethnal Green were upset by
the film's bleak view of life there

intolerable and as the day progresses the police net
closes in, a newspaper reporter guessing where the
man might be hiding. By nightfall her secret is out
and she tries to kill herself, while the prisoner once
again flees, only to be cornered in a marshalling yard
and arrested by the patient detective inspector who
has been trailing him.

It is a surprisingly bleak film, in spite of the rich
detailing of East End life. Once again, as in *Pink
String and Sealing Wax*, the woman played by
Googie Withers is a prisoner of her situation, and
even her attempt to escape through suicide is
doomed to fail. It is a difficult part for, in spite of her
bad temper and at one point a violent assault on the
elder, more sluttish of the two stepdaughters (Susan
Shaw), in which she literally tears the girl's dress off
in her rage, we are expected to feel sympathy for her.
The ex-lover, played by John McCallum (by then
Googie's husband), is not a heroic figure, and it
becomes plain that he is only interested in her to save
his own skin. The amiable husband, played by
Edward Chapman, a shuffling, contented, dart-
playing working man of the old school, is perhaps
the only character, apart from the professional-
mannered police inspector (Jack Warner), who is

sound and sympathetic in character, and at the end of the film in a touching hospital scene he quietly forgives his wife for what has happened.

The drab early post-war atmosphere is carefully established – the black street surfaces coated with a film of wet grease, the regulars hanging around a coffee stall scanning the sports pages of *The News of the World*, the Sunday morning street market with its yelling hawkers. The flat-fronted little terrace house at 26 Coronet Grove, where most of the action takes place, is a few yards from a grimy railway bridge which always seems to have a line of goods trucks or a smoke-belching engine crossing it. There is a rich assortment of secondary characters – small-time crooks, a flashy Jewish 'spiv', a womanizing record shop owner, a sanctimonious 'fence', a snide local reporter. When the film was released there were protests from the real inhabitants of Bethnal Green that it painted too black a picture of life there but, as an example of Ealing's pursuit of the slice-of-life technique, *It Always Rains on Sunday* is a skilful work, and one of the best films by the most talented of the directors to emerge from Balcon's stable.

The bold examination of social problems was never one of the particular strengths of British films,

there being a curious distaste for controversy in Wardour Street. Most entertainment film-making followed blandly neutral lines. Those films which took a firm point of view were rare, especially if the chosen stance was potentially unpopular. Consequently, *Frieda*, based on a stage play by Ronald Millar, who co-wrote the screenplay with Angus MacPhail, represented a brave try, in spite of the melodramatic overtones which marred its treatment. Could the Germans be forgiven for the infamy of the Nazis? An RAF officer marries the German girl who helped him to escape from a prison camp, and takes her home to his English county town. 'Would you take Frieda into your home?' asked the posters. They face both the open hostility of the townsfolk and an unhelpful family – his sister in particular is fervently unforgiving. At a cinema, Frieda is publicly humiliated when before the main feature a newsreel showing the concentration camp horrors is screened. But because she appears to be a fundamentally decent and attractive person she overcomes much of the prejudice, and is on the verge of being accepted, when her brother turns up in Polish uniform, reveals that he is still a dedicated Nazi and alleges that she is one also. Surprisingly,

Opposite: returned prisoner-of-war David
Farrar brings home a German bride (Mai
Zetterling) to the consternation of his
family and neighbours in *Frieda*

Below: incompetent agent Gordon
Jackson is arrested by the Gestapo in
Charles Crichton's *Against the Wind*

Simone Signoret 'executes' Jack Warner
when he is revealed as a double agent

although her husband fights and beats her brother,
he believes him and in his disgust rejects Frieda
cruelly. She attempts to commit suicide, but is saved
from drowning at the last moment by her husband
who has finally come to his senses. It is then left to
them both to face the future with all the difficulties it
holds, but with their own guilt purged. Significantly
Frieda's staunchest and, at times, sole supporter is
the widow of her husband's brother who was killed
in action.

Basil Dearden's film tackles its subject with integrity, but there is a nagging feeling throughout that
the issues are not being resolved. The husband,
played by David Farrar, is a stolid, decent British
type, yet he treats his wife with astonishing insensi-
tivity and prefers to believe the worst of her, even
when the source of his information is manifestly
unreliable. Mai Zetterling, the Swedish star of *Hets*
(Frenzy) making her British debut as Frieda, comes
across convincingly and the supporting cast includes
Flora Robson as the hardline sister (who is also a
Labour MP) and Glynis Johns as the young widow,
with Albert Lieven, typecast as ever, as the Nazi
brother.

Mai Zetterling was imported from Sweden for

Frieda; for *Against the Wind* Ealing brought in a
French star, Simone Signoret. Both of them were to
make several British films in their subsequent distinguished careers. *Against the Wind*, directed by
Charles Crichton with a screenplay by Tibby Clarke
and Michael Pertwee, was a return to the wartime
idiom and, as Clarke ruefully observed in his autobiography, 'a classic example of a mistimed film'. It
appeared in early 1948, too soon after the end of the
war to be part of the revival of interest in the subject
which was to occur in the Fifties. As a result its
box-office performance was disappointing. The title
of the film was taken from some lines by Byron: 'Yet
Freedom! yet thy banner, torn but flying, Streams
like the thunderstorm *against* the wind.' It was about
a training school for saboteurs in London, one of
whose number is caught on a mission to Belgium and
has to be rescued by five others who are parachuted
into the enemy-held country. One of them, an
explosives expert played by Gordon Jackson, is disastrously ill-equipped as he is unable to speak
French. Another, played by Jack Warner, turns out
to be a traitor, and is coldly 'executed' by the attractive female member of the team, Simone Signoret,
as if to emphasize the hard, instant decision-making

necessary in wartime. However, in spite of casualties, the mission is a success.

Clarke went to much trouble in his research to gather true incidents from people who had served in the Belgian resistance, and incorporated some of them into the film. One scene, in which Gordon Jackson is obliged to visit a dentist during the mission on account of his raging toothache, was dismissed by contemporary critics as ludicrous and unbelievable, in spite of the fact that something similar had happened to one of Clarke's friends. Exception was also taken to the role of a Catholic priest and a partisan, played by Robert Beatty, on the grounds that it was morally wrong for him to use the confessional for passing on information, and that sabotage involved deception and trickery instead of nice, clean, open fighting – a criticism that once again ignored the facts, for many men of God had been involved in the resistance movement.

The film's failure, in spite of the fact that it was brisk, well-made and exciting, undoubtedly caused the Ealing team to retreat from this particular genre and devote more energies to lighter subjects. *Saraband for Dead Lovers* was not, however, one of them. The first film that Ealing had produced in

Opposite, top: Michael Balcon talks to
director Basil Dearden on the set of
Saraband for Dead Lovers

Bottom: Peter Bull and Joan Greenwood
in a scene from the film, which was
Ealing's first to be made in Technicolor

Moira Lister and Robert Beatty in Charles
Crichton's comedy set in Dublin, *Another
Shore*. A day-dreamer is jerked back to
reality by a girl interested in marriage

Technicolor, it was a period romance with a touch of
swashbuckling based on historical fact, a little-
known incident involving George Louis of Hanover,
the gross prince who was later to become George I of
England. Directed by Basil Dearden, and adapted
by John Dighton and Alexander Mackendrick from
a novel by Helen Simpson, it told the story of how
the prince's young wife, Sophie Dorothea, fell for a
dashing young soldier of fortune, Count Koenigsmark, who was assassinated when the affair became
known. The unfortunate woman spent the remaining thirty years of her life imprisoned in the castle of
Ahlen.

Douglas Slocombe, who had been a cameraman at
Ealing since early in the war when he had been
invited there by Cavalcanti, and who since 1945 had
been director of photography on *Dead of Night*, *The
Captive Heart*, *Hue and Cry*, *The Loves of Joanna
Godden* and *It Always Rains on Sunday*, was responsible for the rich look of the colour, and the film, an
unlikely subject yet again for Ealing to tackle, was an
attempt, at Mr Rank's urging, to go after the 'prestige' market. It is a worthy rather than an outstanding film, with a good central performance by Joan
Greenwood as Sophie. Françoise Rosay reappeared

at Ealing to play the Electress Sophia, and Flora
Robson, slightly miscast, played the fading mistress
of Koenigsmark, who was portrayed by Stewart
Granger in his customary manner – a combination of
athleticism and flared nostrils. Jill Balcon, daughter
of the head of the studio, who had made her debut in
Nicholas Nickleby, was featured in a small role.
While the film was received with reasonable respect
it was not one that fitted happily into the Ealing
style, and this experiment in eighteenth-century
costume drama was not repeated, particularly as in
financial terms it was the Studios' costliest flop.

The three remaining films of the middle period of
Ealing's life were respectively a comedy, a colonial
reconstruction and a heroic epic. The first, the comedy *Another Shore* directed by Charles Crichton, was
set in Dublin and gave a starring role to Robert
Beatty as an Irish day-dreamer who hopes fate will
transport him to a sunny South Seas island. When
he assists a rich man who has been involved in an
accident it begins to look as though his wish will
come true, but he is jerked out of his world of
romantic fantasy by a down-to-earth girl who sets
him on a steadier path which leads to marriage.
There is something sad about a film that curbs the

Dawn attack in *Eureka Stockade*.
Ealing's second Australian film
was set in the goldfields
of the 1850s

imagination of a dreamer and instead pushes him towards a life of banal normality. Moira Lister, a South African actress, made her Ealing debut in this film and Stanley Holloway appeared as the alcoholic reprobate who leads the hero into temptation. Although it preceded the films commonly accepted as Ealing comedies – it was billed as a tragi-comedy – by now the revolution is in sight.

Eureka Stockade was the second film that Harry Watt made in Australia, mostly on location, but with some 20% of its scenes shot in the Ealing-controlled Pagewood Studios in Sydney. Set in the 1850s, it tells the story of the problems following the gold rush in Victoria and New South Wales. After clashes with the police the miners organize themselves under the leadership of Peter Lalor (Chips Rafferty) and engage the authorities in a full-scale battle. But public opinion stands on the side of the miners and their rights, and all the ringleaders are acquitted. Lalor is later elected Member of Parliament for the gold town of Ballarat, and marries a schoolteacher (Jane Barrett) from the goldfields. It was a major production for Australia, with some seventy speaking parts and several hundred extras, most of whom were recruited from the army, with official blessing.

Bad weather and primitive working conditions combined to make it a difficult operation, and many of the unit had not worked on a feature film before. An elaborate set of Ballarat in the 1850s with a main street and miners' tents surrounding it was blown down twice.

There was also a hiatus during shooting when back in Britain the government, worried by the drain on dollars needed to buy American product for British screens, introduced a seventy-five per cent *ad valorem* tax on films from abroad. It was one of the most ineffective treasury imposts ever levied, and its results were wholly negative. Firstly the Americans withdrew entirely all new films from the British market, cutting off the latest offerings from Hollywood in a strictly applied boycott. Secondly there were insufficient British films to fill the newly available screen space, and so a hasty programme of reissues soon flooded the cinemas, with ill effects on audiences. Thirdly the Rank Organisation was persuaded to make a heavy investment in new production to fill screentime, and in consequence overreached itself to the point of bankruptcy, particularly as by the time the new films were completed – it took at least nine months to gestate a film – the government had lifted the tax and allowed a flood of excellent new American films to engulf the exhibition side of the industry. In some respects it was the beginning of the great post-war decline of the British cinema. By the terms of the drafting of the tax law even *Eureka Stockade*, a British film in that it was financed from England, but was made in a Commonwealth country, fell under the 75% duty. Production was held up for nearly three months while an agreement was thrashed out with the Board of Trade which meant that, by bringing in more cast and crew members from England, it could be classified as a British film made on location. The finished film scarcely justified the effort. *Eureka Stockade* is an average feature of its kind, making up in sincerity for what it lacks in polish when compared with the treatment Hollywood might have given the subject. But it did not spell the end of the Australian venture for Ealing, in spite of the considerable difficulties that were placed in the way.

There is something intensely British about *Scott of the Antarctic*, an epic story of great heroism which

Below: John Mills played Robert Falcon
Scott in *Scott of the Antarctic*, here
simulating a famous photograph of the
explorer ensconced in his cabin

ended in failure. Robert Falcon Scott had already
made a name for himself in polar exploration when
he set out in 1910 on an attempt to reach the South
Pole. It took two years for his small party to get to it,
and when they did they found the Norwegian flag
planted by Roald Amundsen flying there. On the
way back everyone perished in the snows, and it was
only after a search party several months later had
found the Scott diaries and pieced together the story
that Edwardian England was able to thrill to the
courage of a small band of gallant men fighting
impossible odds. The film that Ealing made was as
worthy as its subject demanded. The direction was
by Charles Frend who had been responsible for the
wartime story of epic heroism, *San Demetrio London*.
It was made in Technicolor, with Jack Cardiff,
Osmond Borradaile and Geoffrey Unsworth in
charge of photography. The script by Walter Meade
and Ivor Montagu, with sequences by Mary Hayley
Bell, leaned heavily on the diaries and Arne Akermark's art direction gave as authentic a look as pos-

sible to the sets and props. As historical reconstruction it looked impeccable, although it has to be said
that there were difficulties in getting approval from
all the survivors of the expedition, particularly Lord
Mountevans, formerly Lieutenant Evans, who had
objected to his namesake and companion, Petty
Officer Evans, being chosen by Scott for the final
dash to the Pole.

John Mills played Scott, a popular choice as he
had established his reputation portraying level-
headed, stiff upper-lipped men of courage. The
supporting cast included Harold Warrender as Wilson, Derek Bond as Oates, Kenneth More as
Lieutenant Evans, James Robertson Justice as Petty
Officer Evans, Reginald Beckwith as Bowers and
Diana Churchill as Scott's wife. Location photography was shot in Grahamland, Switzerland and
Norway – in the first, which was in Antarctica itself,
without any actors. In addition, there were many
hazardous scenes filmed at Ealing on a sound stage
covered in 'fuff', as the revolting artificial snow was

Below: Studio shooting of *Scott of the Antarctic* in artificial snow

Right: John Mills, Derek Bond and Harold Warrender

Bottom: Mills with James Robertson Justice as Petty Officer Evans

Opposite: the doomed team drags its sled across the snows

called. Because of the difficulties of location shoot-ing it had been decided to use the then new Tech-nicolor monopack system which did away with the cumbersome three-strip camera, and their seventy pounds of film magazines, but it was not so easy to get the new stock from America. The beautiful documentary footage shot on the original expedi-tions on black-and-white nitrate stock by Herbert Ponting was studied closely and some shots were even accurately duplicated. The final touch to enhance the picture's prestige was the vibrant, atmospheric score by Ralph Vaughan Williams, one of the composer's rare and most successful forays into film music, and a triumph for Ealing's musical director, Ernest Irving.

Although there is a tendency nowadays to scoff at hagiographies of national heroes, it would be unfair to deny *Scott of the Antarctic* its excellence. It is a cool, carefully-stated account, which does not flinch from showing the casual, gentlemanly way in which Scott made his plans, leaving far too much to chance and good fortune than was prudent for a determined explorer. He had the ambition, but not the ruthless-ness. In contrast, the unseen Amundsen is the highly-organized professional with luck on his side. Characteristically, the final disaster is seen to begin with a small incident, a cut finger which in the appalling conditions becomes gangrenous and impedes progress. The sacrifice of Oates is simply depicted, and some critics felt that it was not made clear enough that he was giving his life for his fellows, rather than merely absent-mindedly walk-ing out into the snow because he had lost his rational-ity. The film is the perfect evocation of the team spirit, the submergence of individual emotion for the greater good of everyone. Thus the suffering is borne stoically, without complaint. As in so many Ealing films, the women are subordinated to a totally passive role – they wait patiently at home in Britain knowing that they will probably never see their husbands again. At the conclusion we hear John Mills speak Scott's famous last words in his diary: 'Had we lived I should have had a tale to tell of the hardihood, endurance and courage of my com-panions, which would have stirred the heart of every Englishman. It seems a pity, but I don't think I can write more. These rough notes and our bodies must tell the tale.... For God's sake, look after our people.' And on the cross that marked the place in the frozen wilderness where they were found were the words: 'To strive, to seek, to find, and not to yield.' It is the last shot of the film.

Scott of the Antarctic was chosen for the Royal Film Performance of 1948, an annual gala occasion on behalf of film charities, then in its infancy. It had begun in 1946 with the Michael Powell–Emeric Pressburger film, *A Matter of Life and Death*, but in the following year controversy arose with the selec-tion of an American comedy starring Cary Grant, *The Bishop's Wife*. At least here was an offering with all the appropriate ingredients to set before the King.

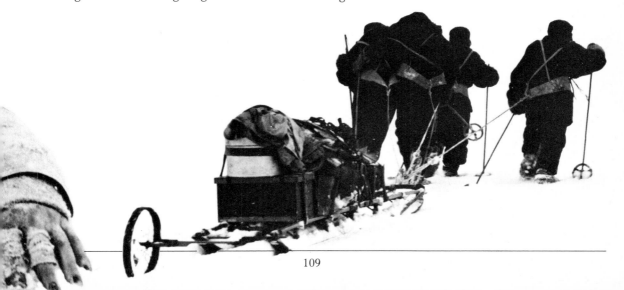

Two of Alec Guinness's many Ealing faces, from (below) *The Man in the White Suit*, 1951, and (right) *The Ladykillers*, 1955

CHAPTER 5

The Ealing comedies

In 1949, Ealing Studios achieved their apotheosis. It was the year in which three outstanding comedies were released, all of them destined to make a permanent contribution to the British film, as well as establishing a genre for which the studio will always be remembered.

The Ealing comedy, so vividly realized in *Passport to Pimlico*, *Whisky Galore!* and *Kind Hearts and Coronets*, had its antecedents years earlier. *Hue and Cry* in 1947 is generally regarded as the harbinger of the Ealing style, but after a study of some of the earliest films it becomes clear that the pattern was developing from the time Balcon took control of production. As far back as *Cheer Boys Cheer*, released in 1939, the conflict of the small, independent, cosy firm and the big, impersonal, ruthless conglomerate can be seen not only as a prototype for many of the Ealing comedies, but as a paradigm of Ealing's own later relationship with the Rank Organisation. Balcon and Baker were obliged to fend off the attempts by Filippo del Guidice to absorb Ealing into the Rank empire, and the favourable contract which gave them autonomy and a guaranteed Rank release was resented. But when Rank was plunged into crisis in 1949, forcing a drastic retrenchment, Ealing's position was relatively strong as most of the films were modestly budgeted and produced satisfactory returns, even in some instances enjoying a reputation for quirky individualism in the United States.

In some ways the comedies also developed from the war films of the early Forties, for many of them – *Whisky Galore!*, *Passport to Pimlico*, *The Titfield Thunderbolt* – adopted the theme of the small group pitted against and eventually triumphing over the superior odds of a more powerful opponent. The quality shown to win is dogged team spirit, the idiosyncrasies of character blended and harnessed for the good of the group. It is a very Ealing-type notion to portray the maverick not as a lone rebel but as someone who finds himself when he becomes part of the team, for example the David Farrar role in *For Those in Peril*, Robert Beatty in *San Demetrio London*, Tommy Trinder in *The Bells Go Down*. There is a constant belief in the saving graces, the innate strengths within the most unlikely people which will enable them to come through when the time is appropriate.

Ealing was basically a middle-class institution of a mildly radical disposition, as well as a determinedly small-scale enterprise. Balcon cast its members, for all their idiosyncrasies, in his own mould. Somehow one feels that the *News Chronicle* rather than the *Daily Telegraph* or even the *Daily Herald* would have been the preferred reading. Balcon was a moderate supporter of the Labour government, but abhorred bureaucracy, state interference in industry and monopolies. He ran his studio on mildly paternalistic lines, encouraging the discussion of ideas and the swapping around of jobs, so that thinkers of original thoughts could have an opportunity to follow them through. He was, as he admitted himself, like a benevolent headmaster of a small, progressive public school, but there were well-defined limits beyond

which he could not be pushed, as most of his staff found out sooner or later.

The reason for Ealing's high-water mark of 1949 has to do with not only the films, but also the period. The euphoria of 1945, when Labour rode to power on the votes of much of the middle class who were looking for a new approach to the national problems, subsided in the face of nationalization, controls, planning and shortages, and by 1949 a mood of jaded despair was becoming general, especially as it became clear that European countries had completed their post-war recoveries considerably in advance of the British, and were now enjoying the advantages of consumerism and prosperity. In Britain the food queues continued, with rigid rationing of many commodities. An attempt to remove children's sweets from the ration was quickly annulled when the authorities realized the scale of the demand. The government instituted the Festival of Britain at around this time, allowing virtually the only non-essential building permits to be issued for the construction of a compact yet grandiose exhibition on the South Bank on both flanks of the Hungerford Bridge, with the intention of extolling to the world the solid virtues of the British. The diversion of energy towards mounting this souped-up folk festival was supposed to diminish the prevailing level of dissatisfaction, by giving the people a

target. Michael Frayn has rightly shown that the 1951 Festival was a turning point, the culmination of the first post-war era, which ended with the passing of the Attlee-led Labour government, austerity, rationing and even the monarch himself. And from that point on Ealing began its decline, for the more affluent Fifties turned to a more robust form of film comedy, the products of Ealing Green representing a whimsical, gentle, folksy humour that was to seem anachronistic.

Not so, however, in 1949. *Passport to Pimlico* fitted the mood of its day. The idea for the plot came from a news item spotted by Tibby Clarke which stated that during the war, in order that a rule be observed whereby members of the Dutch royal succession must be born on Netherlands soil, a room in Ottawa, where the family was in exile from the German occupation, officially became Dutch territory. The film is set in the inner London district of Pimlico, a few narrow streets hemmed in by railway lines and busy main roads, where a delayed bomb explosion reveals a hidden vault containing treasure and an ancient document proving that the land was granted to the Duke of Burgundy in perpetuity. So the inhabitants of this cockney parish suddenly find that officially they are Burgundians. As the realization sinks in that they are no longer subject to the strict laws of austerity England, they are gripped

Opposite: Ealing round-table conference with (from left) Miss Slater, Balcon's secretary, Hal Mason, the production supervisor and general manager, Balcon, Charles Crichton and Margaret Harper Nelson, the casting director

Below: council conference in *Passport to Pimlico*, Arthur Howard chairing Stanley Holloway, Raymond Huntley to his right
Bottom: Huntley and Holloway confront the men from the ministry, Basil Radford and Naunton Wayne

with a wild sense of liberation. The local pub stays open as long as it likes with the constable's blessing, the bank manager sequestrates the reserves in defiance of head office, the dressmaker refuses to acknowledge clothing coupons. Suddenly a grubby set of London backstreets becomes a continental paradise, with sidewalk cafés and unlimited export goods in the shops. Whitehall reacts by closing the 'frontier' and imposing strict currency control and customs inspections on anyone attempting to cross. Soon Pimlico–Burgundy is under siege, blockaded by officialdom, but its defiant stand is supported by other Londoners who hurl food supplies across the barbed wire barricades.

Ultimately Pimlico is readmitted to the United Kingdom, and the relieved inhabitants sit down to a celebratory feast consisting of food rationed according to the law, with a brand new ration book and identity card at every place setting. It is a return to normal after an excursion into the unfamiliar, and perhaps a warning that Britons are not ready for the delights of continental-style emancipation while

Opposite, top: Londoners hurl food to the
beleaguered Burgundians

Bottom: Margaret Rutherford as
Professor Hatton-Jones confuses the
coroner with her analysis

Below: Pimlico is readmitted to the
United Kingdom with a celebratory feast

there is still hard work to do at home. To have ended it otherwise in 1949 would have affronted the sensibilities of the audience, for they, whatever the Burgundians could do, still had to face the rigours of British austerity. Like *Another Shore*, where the young man's fantasy is knocked on the head, it is a coming-down to earth, a moralistic disavowal of the daydream. It is all right to fantasize but ultimately there is a price to be paid. As reinforcement of this message, at the very moment of readmission to the United Kingdom the heavens open, the heatwave is over, and a downpour sends everyone scurrying for shelter, with the exception of a 'Keep Fit' fanatic who had been seen at intervals through the film, and who now delightedly removes his sweater and exults in the rain.

The casting of *Passport to Pimlico*, while using many familiar Ealing faces, is particularly happy. The genial grocer, Pemberton (Stanley Holloway), is admirably contrasted with the timid, precise bank manager, Wix (Raymond Huntley), while outsiders include a delightfully absurd history professor (Margaret Rutherford) and a Burgundian duke (Paul Dupuis) who dashes a girl's romantic dreams of Dijon with chat about the trams in the main square and cement factories. Basil Radford and Naunton Wayne personify Whitehall red tape, and assorted Pimlico residents include Sydney Tafler, Charles Hawtrey, Hermione Baddeley, John Slater, Barbara Murray and Jane Hylton. Perhaps the best line, for its irony sums up the situation with compelling brevity, comes from Betty Warren as the grocer's wife who, when it is suggested that they are now a bunch of foreigners, declares: 'We always were English, and we always will be English, and it's just because we're English we're sticking out for our right to be Burgundians!'

What makes the film delightful is the way a simple idea is elaborated on and taken to ever-increasing heights of fancy, while the setting and details remain disturbingly familiar. Under the direction of Henry Cornelius, the camerawork of Lionel Banes and the art direction of Roy Oxley, the film provides the modern observer with a fascinating impression of how the British capital looked more than three decades ago, with the remains of wartime bombing still apparent as well as the antique collection of trams and buses that made up most of the traffic in the days of heavy petrol rationing. Much of the film was shot on an outdoor set built on a cleared bomb-site off the Lambeth Road, a mile to the east of the real Pimlico, although the original title was kept, largely for its curious foreign-sounding quality and pleasing alliteration.

If *Passport to Pimlico*, a London subject with many studio scenes, needed a contrast, *Whisky Galore!* supplied it. It took the unit to the island of Barra in the Outer Hebrides, as far from Ealing yet still in the British Isles as could be. Monja Danischewsky, who had been Ealing's genial publicity director since 1938, was given the opportunity to produce it, and rather to Balcon's surprise asked for its director to be Alexander Mackendrick, who had not directed before. One novice was enough, Balcon felt, but two could spell disaster, and certainly his foreboding seemed to be justified when the film went heavily over budget (by some £20,000, a fleabite by today's standards, but virtually a hanging matter at Ealing). The main reason was not the inexperience of the production team but the weather, the summer of 1948 being one of the legendarily awful ones.

The story was by Compton Mackenzie, a prolific and imaginative Scottish novelist, and a well-known figure in the islands, where he had a home. It was based on a true incident, when a cargo ship had foundered off the Isle of Eriskay. Some 50,000 cases of Scotch were aboard, as the ship had been destined for the United States. Since it was one of the most difficult commodities to obtain in wartime, and as it held a special place in the lives of the islanders – the word 'whisky' is derived from the Gaelic for 'the water of life' – the decision was taken that it had to be privately salvaged at all costs. So while the ship was breaking up, the small boats were out at night milling around it like sharks nibbling at a piece of meat. The Customs and Excise were powerless to prevent the wholesale scavenging that went on and, while it was never discovered how much of the horde was saved from the depths, there was no shortage of the precious amber fluid in the islands for the rest of the war.

The remote island in Compton Mackenzie's light-hearted, affectionate novel was called Todday, but it was undoubtedly based on Eriskay. The author himself wrote the screenplay in association with Angus MacPhail, and even played a small part in the film. Basil Radford was inspired casting as Captain Waggett, the Englishman in charge of the local Home Guard, who is puzzled by the somnolent demeanour of his troops. Being English, he is unable to comprehend the gloom caused by lack of whisky.

Right: Joan Greenwood as Sibella (top) and Valerie Hobson as Edith (bottom), the two women in Louis Mazzini's life in *Kind Hearts and Coronets*

Opposite, top: Dennis Price as Mazzini daydreams about his ascent to the dukedom of Chalfont

Bottom: Dennis Price watches Ascoyne D'Ascoyne go down with his punt

Then a cargo-laden ship founders on the rocks – but it is the Sabbath, and the islanders are unable to take immediate action. They realize that they will have to thwart Waggett, who is proposing to mount a defence. There was a difference of opinion between the producer and the director on the outcome of the story, for Mackendrick, having been brought up in strict Calvinist surroundings in Glasgow, sided entirely with the unfortunate Waggett, while Danischewsky, a liberal-minded Russian Jew ('So they steal a little!...') could see the islanders' point-of-view. Because of the conflict, and Danny describes in his autobiography how he and Mackendrick fought every inch of the way from script to final cut, it might seem surprising that the film works so well. The humour derives from the fact that Waggett's values are so clearly not those of the natives, and that there is no understanding between them. He is a decent, upright, well-intentioned, slightly pompous Englishman who regards the others as a bunch of half-mad anarchists.

We are told in the film's epilogue that the whisky did not last long and that the islanders of Todday lived unhappily ever after, a concession to the strictly-applied morality code enforced on films shown in America and the director's Calvinism. It does not, of course, have to be believed. Even the title was unacceptable in America, where the name of the familiar beverage (and indeed of all other types of liquor) was not permitted to adorn the marquees of movie houses, and so it became *Tight Little Island*. In France the film was called *Whisky à Go-Go*, and enjoyed such success that a night club was opened bearing the name, and the phrase came into common usage.

The third of the great 1949 comedies, yet another departure in mood, is a classic, the best of all Ealing films. *Kind Hearts and Coronets* is a black comedy, presented in a coolly elegant style with the most articulate and literate of all Ealing screenplays. The title was taken from a Tennysonian couplet quoted by one of the characters: 'Kind hearts are more than coronets, And simple faith than Norman blood'; in France the film was called *Noblesse Oblige*.

It was based on a novel by Roy Horniman published early in the century called *Israel Rank*, but the film credits do not betray the title, merely the

Opposite, top: Alec Guinness plays seven
D'Ascoynes in one shot including the fool
of the family who went into the Church

Bottom: Dennis Price adopts the hobby of
photography to lure one victim, the
husband of the gracious Edith, who will
be his duchess

Below: Miles Malleson as the poetic
hangman and Clive Morton as the
deferential governor on execution day

Bottom: Arthur Lowe as a reporter for
Tit-Bits reminds Louis that he has left his
incriminating memoirs inside the prison

author's name, perhaps as an instance of delicacy,
for another Rank had provided the major part of the
film's finance as well as its British distribution. 'You
are trying to sell that most unsaleable commodity to
the British – irony. Good luck to you,' said Balcon to
its director Robert Hamer, who also wrote the
screenplay with John Dighton. Louis Mazzini, a
young man, the son of a duke's daughter and a
penniless Italian singer who died at his birth, vows
to eliminate the ten people who stand between him
and the dukedom, a desire for vengeance that
becomes intensified when his mother, on her own
death, is refused admission to the family vault. He
works his way through the list, drowning, exploding
and poisoning his rivals and finally shooting the
Duke of Chalfont himself, aided on his way by
departures through natural causes or self-imposed
stupidity. There are two romantic attachments – one
to a headstrong girl called Sibella (Joan Greenwood)
whom he has known since childhood, who marries a
dull man in a fit of pique, and the other to Edith
(Valerie Hobson), the gracious, beautiful widow of
one of his victims, whom he intends to make his
duchess. At the moment of triumph, as he is occupy-
ing the ducal stately home, he is arrested for the
murder, not of any of his genuine victims, but of
Sibella's husband who has really committed suicide.
The story is narrated by the hero, who is spending
the eve of his execution finishing his memoirs. At
dawn he is saved by the 'discovery' of a suicide note,
and as he leaves the prison he is confronted by the
need to make a choice between the two ladies – that is
until a reporter's question reminds him that he has
left his full confession back in the cell.

Alec Guinness played no less than eight of the
D'Ascoynes who stand between Louis and the
dukedom. Yet the film is possessed and dominated
by Dennis Price whose performance as Louis Mazzini is a *tour-de-force*, and his only film part of real
distinction. He too appears in several disguises, such
as that of a colonial bishop, in order to carry out his
lethal work, besides adopting a new demeanour with
each advance up the social scale; yet he never alters
the cool, calm and contained manner that is the
essence of the character, even when he is a lowly
draper's assistant. Price also plays Louis's father in
the brief prologue.

The poster for the film also carried the tag line, 'A hilarious study in the gentle art of murder'. The designer was James Fitton

The ending, like the film as a whole, is ironic, leaving a train of ambiguities. When told by an obsequious prison governor (Clive Morton) that the two women await him outside the gates, Mazzini quotes John Gay's lines, 'How happy could I be with either, Were t'other dear charmer away!', before passing through the gate uncertain what to do because since he has made Edith his wife in a hasty prison ceremony, Sibella has produced her husband's suicide note and is expecting him to honour an agreement to rid himself of his duchess. We never know how he will escape, as he glances first at Edith's carriage and then at Sibella's, for the man from *Tit-Bits* (a walk-on part for Arthur Lowe, who would have to wait twenty years before achieving fame as Captain Mainwaring in *Dad's Army* on television) intervenes to ask about the memoirs. 'My

memoirs?' says Louis, repeating the words three times as he realizes he has forgotten them. In the British version of the film the last shot is a track-in on the manuscript resting where it had been left on the desk in the cell, leaving it open for the audience to suppose that he would turn, ring the prison doorbell, and ask the servile governor to hand over his forgotten property. Such a possibility offended the Johnston Office in America which administered the production code, one of the strictest rules of which was that crime must not be seen to pay. So an additional and aesthetically displeasing scene was appended to the American print in which the auto-biographical manuscript is seen in the hands of the authorities.

Above all, the film is sublimely written. Some of its lines have become immortal nuggets of film dialogue; for instance, that spoken by Guinness playing Canon D'Ascoyne, the doddering, aged fool of the family who was sent into the church, when showing off his parish treasures to a disguised Dennis Price: 'I always say that my west window has all the exuberance of Chaucer, without, happily, any of the concomitant crudities of his period.' Later Price, as a colonial bishop, is called upon to deliver the story of Daniel in the lion's den in Matabele. Robert Hamer, in introducing an extract from the script in *The Cinema 1952*, published by Penguin, wrote: 'What were the possibilities which thus presented themselves? Firstly, that of making a film not noticeably similar to any previously made in the English language. Secondly, that of using this English language, which I love, in a more varied and, to me, more interesting way than I had previously had the chance of doing in a film. Thirdly, that of making a picture which paid no regard whatever to established, although not practised, moral convention. This last was not from my desire to shock, but from an impulse to escape the somewhat inflexible and unshaded characterization which convention tends to enforce in scripts.'

There can be no question of failure on any of these counts, for the film is stylistically far removed from any of the contemporary British works, and remains to this day the most undated of all the Ealing films, many of which are enjoyed as much for their nostalgic value as for their filmic worth. The mood of

Kind Hearts and Coronets is actually ahead of what constituted popular taste in its own day – a sure test of a great film, for example *Citizen Kane*, *The Magnificent Ambersons*, *L'Avventura* or *La Règle du Jeu*. Some critics of 1949 found it cold and even tasteless. It was only two years since *Monsieur Verdoux*, Chaplin's essay in *comédie-noire* with a Landru-like multi-wife murderer, had been virtually hounded off the screen by over-sensitive reviewers. Some found the coldly determined manner in which Mazzini suavely eliminated his victims disturbing; they were unable to appreciate the subtle irony of a remark such as that made when he sends the first D'Ascoyne tumbling over a weir still locked in a carnal embrace with a girl with whom he has been spending an illicit weekend at Maidenhead: 'I was sorry about the girl, but found some relief in the reflection that she had presumably, during the weekend, already undergone a fate worse than death.' Or the highly-charged observation to Sibella's husband Lionel on their wedding day, after Louis, consoling her for her error, has spent the night with her: 'You're a lucky man, Lionel, take my word for it.'

It had not been an easy film to make, and there had been a certain amount of conflict during the production. Ealing's programme during 1948 had become somewhat overloaded and as a result of pressure on studio space - it was suggested that interiors be shot at Pinewood; in an introduction to the script published by Lorrimer in 1974, John Russell Taylor makes much of this fact to explain why the film stands apart from the rest of the Ealing canon. Balcon immediately wrote to *Sight and Sound* categorically denying that any of the film was shot at Pinewood and that, location scenes apart (Leeds Castle in Kent was used as the family seat of the Duke of Chalfont, for instance), it was made at Ealing, commencing production on 1 September 1948. There are plenty of people who can remember being on set at Ealing. However, there were reports in the 1948 trade press that Pinewood was involved. It is possible that some help was given with special effects, such as the fine composite shot featuring six D'Ascoynes, all played by Alec Guinness, seated side by side in church.

With all its problems, Robert Hamer, one of the

Dorothy Alison talks to director Charles Frend during the production of *A Run for Your Money*, the fourth 1949 comedy

most gifted and sadly unfulfilled talents in the British cinema, decided that his career could not progress within Ealing's confines and he left the Studios. None of his subsequent work rose to the heights of *Kind Hearts and Coronets*, and the two further films he made for Balcon, *His Excellency* (1951) and *The Scapegoat* (1958), are particularly disappointing.

There was a fourth Ealing comedy released in 1949, although it tends to be overshadowed by the giants that preceded it. To have had a hat trick was a remarkable feat, and it would have been hoping for too much to expect a fourth winner. *A Run for Your Money* was by no means a failure, but it was somewhat uncertain in manner, and Alec Guinness was wasted in the part of a newspaper gardening correspondent sent, to his disgust, to cover the exploits of two Welsh miners who have come to town to collect the prize money they have won in a productivity competition. It was Charles Frend's first comedy, and several writers were involved in the script, including the Welsh novelist, Richard Hughes, author of *A High Wind in Jamaica*. The theme was that of innocents abroad, the victims of female confidence tricksters and sponging drunks, with

Opposite, top: Hugh Griffith and
Meredith Edwards have problems getting
a harp on a London bus, with Patric
Doonan as an adamant conductor, in *A
Run for Your Money*

Bottom: Meredith Edwards in *The Magnet*
with William Fox (who became James
Fox for his adult career)

Below: Alec Guinness and Stanley
Holloway on location for *The Lavender
Hill Mob*. Cameraman Douglas Slocombe
is on the far right, standing next to
Charles Crichton, the director

occasional bouts of Welsh male voice singing.

Charles Frend directed another comedy in the
following year, which was also less than satisfactory,
although the screenplay came from the firmer comic
hand of Tibby Clarke. The story was based on a
series of misplaced assumptions and concerned a
small boy, played by William Fox (later, as James
Fox, a notable adult actor in *The Servant* and
Performance). The film was called *The Magnet* after
its central prop, a large version of the boyhood toy
which is coveted, won, lost, auctioned and fought
over. But the plot does not have the happy simplicity
of *Hue and Cry*, and the result is an oddly charmless
film in spite of being about children. The inclusion
of jokes about psychiatry and the Labour government give it a middle-class attitude of the kind with
which the British cinema was so frequently associated. The casting was unremarkable with Stephen

Murray as the boy's father, Kay Walsh as his mother
and a tramp played by 'Seamas Mor na Feasag', who
looks suspiciously like James Robertson Justice.

There are still great Ealing comedies to come, as
well as one or two failures. On the positive side are
The Lavender Hill Mob, directed by Charles Crichton, and three by Alexander Mackendrick – *The Man
in the White Suit*, *The Maggie* and *The Ladykillers*.
The Titfield Thunderbolt, directed by Charles
Crichton, and *Barnacle Bill*, by Charles Frend, both
from Tibby Clarke scripts, are sad glimpses of the
Ealing comedy in decline, and at the bottom of the
heap are a few real embarrassments: *Meet Mr
Lucifer*, directed by Anthony Pelissier, *The Love
Lottery* by Charles Crichton, *Touch and Go*, the first
film directed by Michael Truman, and two films at
the tail end of Ealing's existence, *Who Done It?*, a
vehicle for the comedian Benny Hill, directed by

Basil Dearden, and *Davy*, directed by Michael Relph, and starring Harry Secombe.

The idea for *The Lavender Hill Mob* came to Tibby Clarke when he was researching material for a serious Ealing film called *Pool of London*. John Eldridge, who had originated the proposal for the latter film, which was to be a slice-of-life drama centred on dockland, suggested including a villain in the form of a Bank of England employee who uses his privileged position to steal bullion. The more Clarke thought about it, the more humorous the idea seemed; and the chance discovery of a forgotten souvenir from Paris, a gold-painted miniature Eiffel Tower, was all he needed. He immediately scribbled down the outline for a comedy film about a Bank of England employee smuggling bullion abroad in the shape of Birmingham-made tourist knick-knacks. The following morning he took it to Balcon, who wanted to know how *Pool of London* was getting on. The chief erupted in rage when told that the river had been taken out and the story transformed into a comedy about stolen bullion. Clarke retreated, making sure that the outline was left on Balcon's desk. A couple of hours later Balcon sent for him and, as though nothing had happened earlier, told him that the proposed story was very promising, that Clarke should discuss it with Charlie Crichton, and that Jack Whittingham would take over from him on the original *Pool of London*, which was probably more his thing anyway. It is a good illustration of Balcon's manner, and his sharp eye for story possibilities, as well as the Ealing team attitude which could enable switches to be made without causing jealous tantrums.

The Lavender Hill Mob was one of Ealing's most successful pictures. It starred Alec Guinness as the long-serving bank employee, Holland, Stanley Holloway as the souvenir manufacturer, Pendlebury, and Sidney James and Alfie Bass as a pair of crooks recruited to make the caper work. Who could resist Holloway's response as Guinness expounds his dazzling plan for making off with the bullion: 'By Jove, Holland – it's a good job we're both honest men.' The plan was largely concocted by the Bank of England itself, to whom Clarke had turned for advice on how to steal a million pounds' worth of gold, having explained that his eccentric request was on behalf of a film. To his delight an *ad hoc* committee was quickly brought together to work out a way in which the Bank could be robbed. It seems astonishing by today's security-conscious standards, and it was to be hoped that fresh precautions were made after the film's release to prevent real-life imitators.

Inevitably the robbery, which was planned to occur while the bullion was in transit between refinery and vaults, goes wrong, not least because the absent-minded Pendlebury gets arrested in the middle of it for stealing a painting off a market stall. But the chief downfall is caused by a consignment of gold Eiffel Towers getting mixed up with genuine souvenirs on the sales stand of the landmark itself. A batch of English schoolgirls buy them, and Holland and Pendlebury have to chase them back to England to recover them. The last one ends up in a police exhibition, and the now intrepid criminals steal a police car to make their escape, frustrating the hunt by broadcasting false messages from it, eventually causing a threeway collision (the chase sequence is a parody of that in one of Ealing's own films, the police drama *The Blue Lamp*, released early in the preceding year, 1950). Holland escapes, and appears to be narrating the story in a balmy South American paradise to an interested companion. It is only at the end of the film that we realize he is a Scotland Yard detective sent to bring Holland back – the usual sop to the censor, for the audience would certainly have preferred the mild little thief to have got away with it. The luscious dark-haired girl in the Brazilian setting who looks strikingly familiar is Audrey Hepburn, doing a couple of days' bit-part work at Ealing when she was still an unknown. To nobody's credit there, she was not spotted as star material, but then Ealing always had a weak reputation where women were concerned.

One of the curious things about *The Lavender Hill Mob* (the title refers to the seedy South London district between Battersea and Clapham where Holland lives in a dreary boarding-house) was that its running time was a mere seventy-eight minutes, instead of the ninety-plus that was normal for a first feature. Most Ealing films were in fact shorter than the average, which mean that when they went on release they could often be coupled with another

Below: Stanley Holloway is nabbed, but (opposite, bottom) Alec Guinness makes a getaway for South America after a wild chase in a stolen police car in *The Lavender Hill Mob*

Opposite, top: Alec Guinness as the manic inventor Sidney Stratton in *The Man in the White Suit*, the most satirical of all Ealing comedies, with overtones of René Clair's *A Nous la Liberté*

long film, as opposed to the shorter B pictures of the day, which usually had a running time of around seventy minutes. Tibby Clarke explains how the original screenplay for *The Lavender Hill Mob* would have made a 105-minute film, a perfectly normal length today but unacceptable for a comedy in the early Fifties, and how Crichton set about pruning it; certainly the pace is improved by the lack of padding, particularly near the beginning.

The first of the trio of comedies directed by Alexander Mackendrick after *Whisky Galore!* was *The Man in the White Suit*, which appeared in August 1951, two months after *The Lavender Hill Mob* had its premiere. It was scripted by Roger Macdougall, John Dighton and Mackendrick himself, and based on a play by Macdougall. Perhaps its theme was rather more ambitious than those usually tackled in Ealing comedies, for it is an ironic view of both

capital and labour. Alex Guinness, by now the most ubiquitous of Ealing faces, and the most chameleon-like of actors, plays a young would-be research chemist in a textile mill, whose job is confined to washing up the dishes in the laboratory. He constructs his own secret apparatus in an attempt to discover a new fibre, with explosive results, until he eventually makes a miraculous yarn which cannot wear out or even get dirty. When the mill owners realize that their industry could be destroyed as a result, they join forces and wheel in an aged tycoon (Ernest Thesiger) to trick him into signing away his rights. He refuses, and they try to keep him prisoner, but he escapes and runs to the trade union for help. For once they are firmly on the side of management. At the film's climax our hero is pursued through the streets in his dazzling white suit by workers and employers alike. At one point he seizes a

Above: Mandy Miller helps
Alec Guinness to flee from the
enraged mob

Right: Guinness in humble
factory employ

Above: Joan Greenwood as the boss's
daughter takes an interest

Opposite, top: on set with Alexander
Mackendrick (centre), Joan Greenwood and
Michael Gough

Opposite, bottom: Tommy Kearins with
James Copeland in *The Maggie*

dustbin lid and chairleg and confronts his opponents like a medieval warrior. Then, as they move in for the kill, his suit starts to disintegrate – the miracle yarn has an unexpected flaw – and as it falls to pieces he is left standing alone in his underwear. The film ends as, having consulted his notes and exclaimed 'I see!', he strides off more confidently, perhaps to inflict his scientific genius on some other unsuspecting community.

The Guinness figure remains distanced and ambiguous throughout, and even the romantic involvement with Joan Greenwood as the boss's daughter does not bring the audience any closer to what really motivates him. The comedy is partly whimsical, partly satirical, offering a view of Britain conniving with age-old practices and inefficiencies not merely for the sake of the status quo, but for convenience as well. 'Why can't you scientists leave things alone?' cries his old landlady, played by Edie Martin. 'What's to become of my bit of washing when there's no washing to do?' If there seems to be a superficial resemblance to a much earlier Ealing film, the George Formby comedy *Turned Out Nice Again* (1941) which also had a plot set in the textile industry with miracle yarns and bemused industrialists, the common link may possibly be John Dighton, who had a hand in scripting both films, although each had derived from the stage.

Mackendrick's *The Maggie*, released early in 1954, was scripted by William Rose who in the previous year had enjoyed the success of *Genevieve*, the most Ealing-like of non-Ealing films, and made by Rank at Pinewood allegedly because Balcon was unable to find studio space for Henry Cornelius, who was not on the Ealing payroll. From old cars Rose had

Alex Mackenzie as the 'pufferboat' skipper
and Paul Douglas as a frustrated
American millionaire in *The Maggie*

turned to old boats, with a comedy about a small steamer, the *Maggie*, used on the Clyde to transport cargo in modest quantities. Its skipper (Alex Mackenzie) tricks a wealthy American (Paul Douglas) into entrusting the transport of furniture for a new house in the islands to his decrepit vessel; the American then realizes his mistake, and does his best to retrieve his property, but eventually has to concede defeat. It is the come-uppance of a graceless tycoon who, until he is humanized by the quaint old boat, believes that everything can be bought to order, provided that the price is right. But in Ealing

comedies life is not meant to be lived that way; the wily skipper, albeit a deceitful, cunning old rogue, is seen to be lovable, and the *Maggie* lives to sail another day, thanks to the reluctant philanthropy of its victim. But in spite of the healthy atmosphere of Scottish fresh air, *The Maggie* is the least of Mackendrick's comedies, and a long way short of *Whisky Galore!*.

His last, however, could lay claim to being the best. *The Ladykillers* of 1955 came at the end of the Ealing Green period and was premiered in the same month that the sale of the Studios to the BBC was announced. It is the blackest of Ealing comedies, excepting *Kind Hearts and Coronets*. Its central character is a little old lady, played with great taste by Katie Johnson, a familiar performer of little-old-lady roles in British films. She lives in a tumbledown Victorian house near St Pancras Station, and takes in as a lodger a strange 'professor' with prominent dentures (Alec Guinness in one of his most vivid disguises). He has four odd friends who visit regularly for the purpose, she is told, of playing chamber music. In fact they are plotting a large robbery and intend to use the house as their operation base. The group is nicely contrasted: Danny Green is a moronic heavyweight, Cecil Parker an ex-officer confidence trickster type, Peter Sellers a teddy boy crook, Herbert Lom a ruthless Soho-foreign gangster. Inevitably she finds out what they have been up to, and calmly takes them over as though they are little boys who have misbehaved in the nursery. They plot to kill her, but cannot agree who is to perform the deed; the thieves fall out and each in turn is eliminated, the last felled by the arm of a railway signal as he disposes of the penultimate body. The old lady, finding herself the custodian of a gigantic amount of used bank-notes, goes along to the local police station to report it, but the amiable policeman (Jack Warner), who is used to her fantasies, sends her on her way. The film ends as she walks home, wondering what to do with £60,000 and absent-mindedly dropping a pound note to a pavement artist who has drawn Winston Churchill.

The screenplay was again by William Rose, and the film was shot by Otto Heller in Technicolor, colour films becoming more common in the mid-Fifties, although they were still comparatively rare

From *The Ladykillers*: (below, left) Peter Sellers and Alec Guinness with Danny Green, Herbert Lom and Cecil Parker at rear; (below, right and bottom) the gang persuade the landlady Katie Johnson that they are merely chamber musicians

Overleaf: the villains fall out and one by one their bodies are tipped on to freight trains going north. Alec Guinness and Danny Green dispose of Cecil Parker's corpse in *The Ladykillers*

from Ealing. The art direction by Jim Morahan produced a superb house, a lop-sided villa redolent of Victorian faded gentility, with a portrait of the departed husband of some thirty years on the wall, and a parrot answering to the name of General Gordon, which provides some moments of broad farce when it escapes and has to be recaptured by the guests. The main comedy is contained in the contrast between crooks and little old ladies, and one of the best scenes is when the men, their guilty secret already rumbled, are forced to take tea with the circle of friends, who include the diminutive Edie Martin, one of whose previous roles was as the boarding-house landlady in *The Lavender Hill Mob*. It is a case of little old ladies rule, and an explanation for the triumph of Victorian Great Britain and the Empire. Perhaps the fact that William Rose was an American, and Alexander Mackendrick, although raised in Glasgow, was born in Boston, helped to give them a perspective of England that enabled them to fashion a story which unconsciously contained the crystallization of the outsiders' viewpoint. The film is still immensely popular in America, and is given frequent television airings. Its bizarre, almost surreal approach now makes it seem a decade ahead of its time.

The Ladykillers was Mackendrick's last film for Ealing, and when it was completed he left for America to make *Sweet Smell of Success* for Hecht-Hill-Lancaster. From then on his career faltered and his films of the Sixties, *Sammy Going South*, *A High Wind in Jamaica* and *Don't Make Waves*, are un-

Below: duel between road roller and locomotive in *The Titfield Thunderbolt*

Opposite: a wrong turning takes it down the high street without a track

exceptional. He then left the industry for academe in California.

Charles Crichton, of *Hue and Cry* and *The Lavender Hill Mob*, collaborated again with Tibby Clarke for *The Titfield Thunderbolt*, released in 1953. Its theme was the defiance by a group of villagers of the faceless bureaucrats bent on closing down their local railway line. The comedy drew on the English fondness for trains, as well as the commonplace Ealing assumption that small equals beautiful, big equals bad. But there is something that does not quite ring true. The argument for retaining the line seems to be merely for the sake of quaintness and tradition. It was, after all, a few years before the Beeching

revolution would have wiped out all such branch lines anyway. (In fact, the line on which filming took place, near the village of Limpley Stoke, a few miles from Bath, did disappear as a result of one of British Rail's rationalization programmes.) While it is an amusing idea to bring in Godfrey Tearle as a railway-mad bishop, have the entire village appear to steal a locomotive from a museum in order that their sabotaged train can run, and evict the local poacher from his ex-railway carriage home for improvised rolling stock, there is something rather forced about the comedy. Douglas Slocombe's photography was, however, very evocative of West Country England and used Technicolor for the first time for an Ealing comedy. A clue to the film's overall failure to make the same kind of impact as its predecessors is contained in a location report by Hugh Samson in *Picturegoer*: 'Odd point about this railway location: not a single railway enthusiast to be found in the whole crew. T. E. B. 'Tibby' Clarke, writer of the script, loathes trains. Producer Michael Truman can't get out of them quick enough. And director Crichton – well, you won't find him taking engine numbers at Paddington Station.' Perhaps that was it, there was insufficient love of the subject.

Charles Crichton made only one more Ealing comedy, *The Love Lottery*, released in 1954, again photographed by Douglas Slocombe in Technicolor. The object of attack this time was the intemperate fan worship of film stars – not an obvious Ealing target. David Niven played the celebrity, Peggy Cummins the girl who wins him in a lottery, with Anne Vernon and Gordon Jackson in supporting roles. The film is a depressing indication that Ealing usually foundered when it tried to make a film with a feminine viewpoint. The notion of star worship put across in the film must have seemed fairly dated in the Fifties, and viewed today it is ludicrous. A number of feeble dream sequences were inserted to pad out the action, giving the impression that *The Love Lottery* was about to turn into a pastiche of a Hollywood musical, but unfortunately such happy possibilities were ignored and, in spite of Herbert Lom's suavely self-confident head of the world syndicate which makes its money from gambling, the film is an uneasy failure. The only point of interest is the appearance of Humphrey Bogart – in an uncredited walk-on at the end to provide a closing gag.

The Love Lottery was produced by Monja Danis-

Opposite: desperate Titfielders purloin an antique engine from the museum in the dead of night to ensure that they keep their line running

Below: David Niven with Peggy Cummins in *The Love Lottery*
Bottom: Jack Watling and an array of vintage television sets in *Meet Mr Lucifer*

chewsky who, after producing *The Galloping Major*, directed by Henry Cornelius, away from Balcon's orbit, had returned to Ealing in the previous year (1953), to produce and script *Meet Mr Lucifer*. Based on a play called *Beggar My Neighbour* by Arnold Ridley, who in the Twenties had written the melodramatic success, *The Ghost Train* (television fame awaited him in the Seventies, when he played the senile Private Godfrey in *Dad's Army*), it starred Stanley Holloway as the Demon King in an unsuccessful provincial pantomime, who after an accident with the stage trapdoor finds himself in the infernal regions facing Mr Lucifer. The devil believes that people are being made too happy by television when it should be making them miserable, and the film developed into a laboured and limp attempt at satire, showing how television can indeed make a few people unhappy, including Jack Watling and Peggy Cummins as a young married couple and a Scottish bachelor, Gordon Jackson, who falls in love with the Lonely Hearts singer on the screen, Kay Kendall. Perhaps its main interest now is the depiction of the awfulness of television standards in 1953, two years before the first ITV station opened, with appearances by tele-celebrities of the time such as Philip Harben,

Below: Balcon talks to director Michael
Truman and star Jack Hawkins on the set
of *Touch and Go*

Bottom: June Thorburn with Margaret
Johnston and Jack Hawkins in the 1955
kitchen in the film

the bearded cook; Macdonald Hobley, the dinner-
suited announcer; and Gilbert Harding, who based
a career on his talent for irascible boorishness. The
film was directed by Anthony Pelissier, who was not
a member of the Ealing charmed circle, but who had
made a fairly successful film for Two Cities taken
from the D. H. Lawrence story about a boy who
could dream race results, *The Rocking Horse Winner*.

The remaining four comedies made at or by Ealing were all in a minor key. *Touch and Go* starred Jack
Hawkins in an unrewarding part as a furniture
designer who in a fit of pique (brought about largely
by his employer's distrust of 'contemporary' design)
quits his job, sells the house and unilaterally decides
that he and his family must emigrate to Australia.
The edict is wildly unpopular, threatens to destroy
his daughter's romance, fills his wife with mis-
givings and alienates the family cat, who disappears.
At the end of the film the plan is abandoned, the
employer is won round to a new way of thinking and
the cat comes back. The screenplay by William Rose

is perhaps his thinnest; the outcome is totally pre-
dictable and the plot minimal. The Technicolor
photography by Douglas Slocombe succeeds in
making the family's corner of London so charming
and unrealistically quaint that it is hard to see why
anyone should want to leave it, but then that is the
basic premise of the film – better to change with the
times rather than run away altogether.

Who Done It?, inasmuch as it is a vehicle for a
famous comedian, was something of a throwback to
the days of Basil Dean, except that in this case the
reputation had first been made through the new
medium of television rather than on the music-hall
stage that launched Gracie Fields and George
Formby. By 1956 the pudgy-faced Benny Hill had
established himself as the clown on the hearth. In
the film he was cast as an ice-rink attendant and
would-be private detective who uncovers a plot to
assassinate Britain's top scientists and, with the aid
of a blonde, prevents the transmission of secret
plans, getting involved in a chase which ends with
the spies' capture in a stock-car stadium. Such a
plotline would be standard for a Formby or Will Hay
film, and the reappearance of Garry Marsh, a stalwart of the ATP days, reinforces the sense of *déja vu*.

Top: Benny Hill made his film debut in *Who Done It?*
Belinda Lee co-starred
Above: the last Tibby Clarke Ealing
comedy, *Barnacle Bill*, with Alec Guinness

Below: the last Ealing comedy of them all,
and a failure. Harry Secombe with Susan
Shaw in *Davy*, out for Christmas 1957

Surprisingly the screenplay was by Tibby Clarke, a
departure from his usual style, although amidst the
slapstick there were some characteristic touches –
scenes, for instance, of an extravagant ice show
called 'Tropic Nights on Ice'.

Clarke's last and more typical Ealing screenplay
was for *Barnacle Bill*, made after the old place had
been sold to the BBC. Directed by Charles Frend, the
film starred Alec Guinness as the last of a line of
distinguished seafarers (their appearance in a rapid
sequence, all impersonated by Guinness, is a reminder of *Kind Hearts and Coronets*) who, in conquering
his chronic seasickness, takes command of a static
but dilapidated Victorian seaside pier. He finds his
plans to rejuvenate it thwarted by the Mayor who
wants to tear it down for his own profit. So he in turn
thwarts the Mayor by registering it as a ship, a
stationary pleasure cruiser for the seasick. A full-
scale battle, waged on pedalos, ends as the uprooted
pierhead, with Guinness on the bridge, so to speak,
drifts across the Channel to France, after which he is
acclaimed a national hero. Although the central idea
of the film is similar to that of *Passport to Pimlico*, the
passage of nearly a decade has taken a toll, for by the
end of the Fifties the style was clearly seen to be
anachronistic, and a sad reminder of the former
greatness of Ealing. What in the post-war period had
been a sharp, accurate, well-aimed satire now
seemed quaint, feeble and irrelevant – eccentricity
replaced by silliness.

The last Ealing comedy of all, *Davy*, for once
directed by Michael Relph and produced by Basil
Dearden rather than the more usual reversed
arrangement, is even sadder than *Barnacle Bill*.
Harry Secombe, in his first film, plays a member of a
family variety act who wants to be a singer and has to
face the dilemma of pursuing a musical career and
leaving the family act to collapse, or giving up his
ambitions for the sake of the others. It is the latter
course of action which he follows, the old safe values
preventing a clean break into new and exciting territory – further evidence of Ealing's cosiness. Stylistically the film is an awkward combination of broad
farce, Secombe having made his name as one of the
denizens of the celebrated *Goon Show*, and awkward,
turgid scenes of moral conflict.

It was not the most worthy ending for a long and
distinguished story, but it did perhaps reinforce the
message of the preceding film – that the Ealing
comedy belonged to a certain period, and that
attempts to resurrect it were, with the one great
exception of *The Ladykillers*, foredoomed.

CHAPTER 6

The slice of life

Although the abiding memory of Ealing is of the comedies, it is salutary to remember that of the fifty-eight films made there in the post-war years, only eighteen – less than a third – could be so classified. So sparing was the output that except for the *annus mirabilis* of the Ealing comedy, 1949, they were always in the minority of the releases. At the time, the most prominent characteristic of the studio was its desire to show realistically something of British life, and to give the dramatic films backgrounds as authentic as could be achieved in the pre-television age of the British cinema. When Cavalcanti left in 1946 there remained behind him several directors who had been trained in the documentary techniques favoured by Balcon, who firmly believed in verisimilitude and sincerity.

When in 1948 Balcon received his knighthood for services to the British film industry, even then an overdue recognition, he considered it a collective tribute to the Ealing team spirit. 'It isn't me, old boy. It's the studio that has been knighted,' he told Danischewsky. The members of the team were interchangeable – no-one specialized in comedies alone, directors, writers and associate producers being expected to contribute to either genre.

In 1949, there were only two serious films: *Eureka Stockade* (see above, p. 106) and *Train of Events*, an unsuccessful attempt to harness several members of the team in a portmanteau film, a formula that had earlier worked superbly with *Dead of Night*. The plot followed the stories of three sets of people travelling on a night train from Euston to Liverpool, plus the

engine driver (Jack Warner, inevitably saying farewell to Gladys Henson as his wife). The mood of each segment was deliberately contrasted, and the reasons for the presence of the passengers were revealed in flashbacks. An actor has murdered his unfaithful wife, an orphan girl is in love with a fugitive German prisoner-of-war, and a famous conductor cannot choose between his wife and a glamorous pianist. The first two of these three sequences are melodramatic, and directed by Basil Dearden, the third is an unsuccessful attempt at sophisticated comedy by Charles Crichton. The engine driver sequences were directed by Sidney Cole. The problems of some of the characters are solved by the finality of death – the train is doomed to crash, a fact revealed near the beginning, leaving the audience to speculate on who will survive.

Basil Dearden's *The Blue Lamp* showed, however, that it could work if a unified style was imposed. An extended tribute to the Metropolitan Police, stretched in their fight against the post-war crime wave, the film is notable for its introduction of the character Police Constable Dixon (Jack Warner, with Gladys Henson as his long-serving wife). Eliminated halfway through by a gunman's bullet, he was reincarnated and paraded in the BBC television series which ran on and on into the mid-Seventies, and presumably would have gone on running had not Dixon, latterly a station sergeant, become anachronistically aged, since Jack Warner at the close was eighty-two.

The screenplay, based on a story by Ted Willis,

Train of Events was a portmanteau film
telling the stories of four sets of people
involved in a train disaster. The designer
of the poster in this case was Reginald
Mount

was by Tibby Clarke who had himself served in the
Metropolitan Police as a War Reserve Constable,
and thus had some inkling of police routine and
jargon. Unfortunately, the police force he presents
seems to be a highly idealized one, put across in the
best public relations terms, with avuncular, protec-
tive, friendly coppers on the beat, helping old ladies,
giving directions, holding children's hands and
occasionally, cheerfully moving on an obstructive
barrow boy. Against images of police duty on this
banal level a voice-over narration spells out the facts
of the crime wave, blaming it squarely on the new
breed of post-war criminals who 'lack the code,
experience and self-discipline of the professional
thief ... a class apart, all the more dangerous
because of their immaturity'. This thought perhaps
typifies the Ealing view of the world, where even the
criminals have their decencies and acceptable standards of conduct. The new outlaws are giving crime a
bad name.

Below: home life at PC Dixon's. Meredith
Edwards, Jack Warner, Jimmy Hanley
and Gladys Henson in *The Blue Lamp*
Bottom: Dora Bryan and Norman
Shelley, Jimmy Hanley as the new copper

with exciting visual results. The neo-realism of
Italian directors such as Rossellini and De Sica had
inspired some American directors to look to the
streets and producers such as Louis de Rochemont
(Henry Hathaway's *The House on 92nd Street*, Elia
Kazan's *Boomerang*) and Mark Hellinger (Jules Dassin's *The Naked City*) had pioneered techniques of
non-studio shooting that were later to become
commonplace. Dearden made the pavements of
Paddington Green and Ladbroke Grove, Edgware
Road and Leicester Square look refreshingly real,
and the police car chase through the grey streets of
inner West London is dramatic and convincing. It is
the flat and stereotyped characterization which
disappoints, with Hanley and Warner performing
their familiar affectionate notion of working-class
behaviour, and Robert Flemyng representing the
CID and Scotland Yard with a tight-lipped public
school accent redolent of the First XI and the officers' mess, while Peggy Evans, a sort of Rank charm-

On the one hand the story follows the first days of
a rookie policeman settling in at his new post. Andy
(Jimmy Hanley) is fresh-faced, keen, anxious to
shine. PC Dixon shows him the ropes and offers him
lodgings under his roof, a tiny terraced house with
pigeons in the backyard and socks drying on the line
under the mantelpiece. In contrast to this cosy domestic life, which continues in the police station with
shots of choir practice and friendly jossing over
egg-and-chips in the canteen, is set the story of two
young hoodlums, played by Dirk Bogarde and
Patric Doonan, and a raid on a dowdy suburban
cinema in which Dixon is shot down in cold blood. It
seems that shooting a policeman, let alone one as
popular with the community as this one, is simply
not a right and proper way to further a life of crime,
and there is a tacit understanding between the police
and the underworld to help catch the guilty.
Bogarde is eventually tracked to the White City
Stadium during a greyhound meeting, where the
tic-tac signals of the bookies are used to trap him.
The film concludes with young Andy, now an established constable on Dixon's old beat, the embodiment of all the virtues of the old policeman.

Dearden used real London locations in a way that
was relatively novel in British films of the period,

school starlet, plays Bogarde's moll like a girl from Esher pretending to be a cockney. Beyond is the motley parade of tarts, barrow boys and ill-treated wives. Only Bogarde brings anything interesting to a performance – his role has more scope than the others, it is true, but it is clear, even at this stage of his career, that he is a gifted actor, though his talents were later to be execrably wasted in a dreary series of Rank pot-boilers. *The Blue Lamp* is marred because it is phoney, an artificial blend of drama, pathos, action and comic relief – with dialogue suffering from a British film disease so aptly labelled by the perceptive *News Chronicle* critic, Richard Winnington, as 'Huggetry', after a dreadful series of suburban family comedies – starring, as it happens, Jack Warner.

It was followed in June 1950 by *Dance Hall*, one of Ealing's rare attempts to get to grips with a feminine subject. Directed by Charles Crichton, the film contrasted the monotony of factory life with the glamour and excitement of the Palais, following the stories of four girls played by Diana Dors (her only Ealing appearance), Petula Clark, who had only just emerged from children's roles, Jane Hylton, who had been in *It Always Rains on Sunday* and *Passport*

Opposite, top: the murder of PC Dixon.
Dirk Bogarde as a box-office thief

Opposite, below: a stuntman takes a
flying leap during the car chase through
North Kensington streets in *The Blue
Lamp*

Below: Peggy Evans as Bogarde's
hysterical girlfriend

Opposite, top: Charles Tingwell, Chips Rafferty and Gordon Jackson in *Bitter Springs*, third of Ealing's Australian productions

Bottom: David Farrar plays a villain in *Cage of Gold*, a Basil Dearden semi-thriller

Diana Dors jives a little in *Dance Hall*, the only Ealing film in which she appeared

to Pimlico, and Natasha Parry, the future wife of Sir Peter Brook, making her film debut. The storyline is somewhat thin, and the purpose of the film is to get behind the scenes of a big dance hall and show something of the life it represents. Although the background is reasonably authentic, with famous bands such as those of Geraldo and Ted Heath given opportunities to perform on camera, little is revealed about the girls, who are far too actressy to be taken as genuine working-class fugitives from the shop floor having a jolly night out.

The next Ealing release was the third of the films made in Australia, directed this time by Ralph Smart who had been Harry Watt's associate producer on *The Overlanders. Bitter Springs* is the least successful of the trio, and concerns turn-of-the-century pioneers who trek 600 miles to reach land they have bought from the government, only to find it in the possession of an aborigine tribe who have been settled there for centuries and who, as the water supply is only just adequate to support them, are not eager to yield to white settlers. There are nasty incidents, an aborigine is murdered, the whites are rescued from siege by the arrival of mounted troops, and the film ends with promises

between the two factions to behave and co-operate, a somewhat crude and desperate piece of plot construction. The cast included Tommy Trinder as an ex-circus performer who apparently does not even know how to mount a horse; as in the majority of serious Ealing films he made, Trinder's performance is at variance with the prevailing mood. Chips Rafferty, by now the British idea of a professional Australian, leads the settlers, and the party includes the stalwart Gordon Jackson, a favourite Ealing stock player. It was the last Ealing film to be made at Pagewood for, in spite of the efforts Balcon had made to help the establishment of regular Australian production, Canberra decided not to extend the lease any further, arguing that films were non-essential and the leaseholders non-resident. Chips Rafferty, bitter at the 'wowser' attitude in the government, claimed that the Capital Issues Board was cutting the throat of the Australian film industry; the shutdown of Pagewood, which Ealing had turned into a fully-equipped studio at a cost of A$200,000 (including a second stage), blighted Australian film production for seven years. But whatever Balcon personally felt about the Australian government's decision, he was not supported by John Davis, the accountant who had come to the rescue of the Rank empire during its period of crisis at the end of the Forties, and by ruthless pruning had begun to restore its fortunes. Davis made a trip to Australia in 1952 and was plainly unimpressed by what he saw. He told the Australian film producer Norman Rydge, himself a former accountant: 'I could never understand why it was considered necessary to make pictures in Australia. Arthur [Rank] was always keen on it, but I don't know why. After all, we in England have four or five modern, well-equipped studios, and nearly 4,000 people employed. We can make all the pictures you need.'

It was not the last that Ealing saw of Australia, for *The Shiralee* (1957), directed by Leslie Norman, and the last Ealing film of all, *The Siege of Pinchgut* (1959), directed by Harry Watt, were to be based there. But a combination of politics and narrow business interests defeated the brave efforts at Pagewood. And even if *Eureka Stockade* and *Bitter Springs* had enjoyed the same level of success as *The Overlanders*, it is still unlikely that there would have

been a different outcome.

Back at Ealing, 1950 saw the release of *Cage of Gold*, a modestly melodramatic story directed by Basil Dearden, who had a reputation for being the most adept of Ealing film-makers in constructing something showy out of unpromising material. It provided a vehicle for Jean Simmons, playing a young artist infatuated by a caddish ex-RAF officer (David Farrar) who makes her pregnant and then marries her so that he can get her money. When he learns that she has none, he disappears to continue his philandering in Paris. His passport is used by a smuggler whose plane crashes and, thinking he is dead, the girl marries a steadfast doctor (James Donald) who is prepared to bring up the child. Two years later her first husband turns up in London having left his French mistress, and threatens to blackmail the couple. He is shot, and both of them confess to having done it, but the real killer is the French girl, who has followed him to London. The film ends with the doctor and his wife continuing in the socially worthy setting of Battersea where he is a National Health Service practitioner, having scorned the possibilities of a career in Harley Street. *Cage of Gold* is the name of the French night-club

Earl Cameron in Basil Dearden's *Pool of London*, a dockland 'slice of life'

From Australia to East Africa. Harry Watt's *Where No Vultures Fly* starred Anthony Steel as a gamewarden (opposite, on left, with Meredith Edwards). The sequel, *West of Zanzibar*, substituted Sheila Sim (below, with Steel) for Dinah Sheridan

where Farrar's girl friend is a cabaret singer, but it could also be said to symbolize the money trap, and the suggestion that wealth cannot buy happiness. Somehow, the upright, introspective Ealing values assert themselves even in a film of this kind, and not even the slick direction of Dearden can disguise the conventional thinking behind it.

Dearden's next film was *Pool of London*, the subject from which Tibby Clarke was diverted to write *The Lavender Hill Mob*. It has the familiar semi-documentary approach to what is intended to be a slice-of-life story based around the docks, and was jointly written by Jack Whittingham and a documentary director, John Eldridge. The formula is that of *The Blue Lamp*, the use of real locations serving, it was hoped, to authenticate the action. There are three main elements: first, the life of the river, its workings presented in the revelatory style of the documentary, with insights into the routines of customs men and river police; second, a dramatic plot line involving robbery and murder, courage and betrayal; third, social responsibility with an attempt to grapple with the problems of a coloured man and a

white girl, probably for the first time in a British film. The blend is sometimes uneasy, and there is a marked sense of diffidence where the romance with no future is concerned, creating an awkward hiatus in the flow of the narrative. But for all that, *Pool of London* is a workmanlike, well-crafted and sincere picture in Basil Dearden's customary pacey manner, with many excellent set-piece action sequences. The colour theme is an interesting anticipation of his post-Ealing work which was to include a number of 'problem' pictures such as *Sapphire* (colour again) and *Victim* (homosexuality).

Although Australia was no longer an encouraging venue for Ealing's producers, their interest in the Commonwealth had by no means abated. Encouraged by Hal Mason, Balcon's production controller and trouble-shooter who had been at the Studios from almost the start of the post-Dean regime, Harry Watt was sent to East Africa on a story-finding trip. The result was *Where No Vultures Fly*, based on the real-life memoirs of Mervyn Cowie, who had made a reputation as a conservationist. In the film Anthony Steel played a Kenyan game-

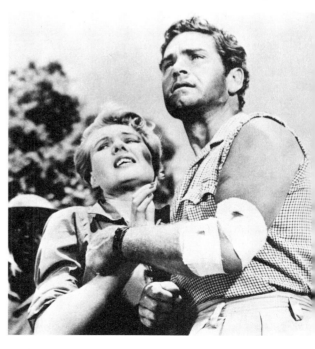

warden, Bob Payton, who, distressed and revolted by the constant attrition of African fauna, decides to set about establishing a national park in Kenya. Having taken over some thousand square miles of territory, he has to do battle with the ivory poachers and hostile tribes who have been enlisted in their support, before he realizes his dream, a land 'where no vultures fly'. Shot in Technicolor by Geoffrey Unsworth, with special wildlife photography by Paul Beeson, the film is a capable travelogue but, at 107 minutes, far longer than any Ealing film since *Scott of the Antarctic*, with flat spots that could have been eliminated by tighter editing. Dinah Sheridan performed gracefully as Mrs Payton, and Harold Warrender played a villain who meets his just desserts. But the film acted as a timely and resounding appeal on behalf of the wildlife preservation cause, and received the accolade of selection as the Royal Film Performance presentation of 1951, which ensured that its box-office receipts were handsome. (Not always a guarantee, however, of either quality or audience appeal – the subsequent choice was an indifferent Mario Lanza musical,

Because You're Mine, followed by a tasteless British costume farrago, *Beau Brummell*, in which the Queen's demented ancestor, the future George IV, was impersonated by Peter Ustinov.)

The success of *Where No Vultures Fly* tempted Ealing into making a sequel which, in the tradition of sequels, was far less enticing than the original. *West of Zanzibar* appeared in the spring of 1954, with Sheila Sim replacing Dinah Sheridan in the role of Mary Payton. The theme this time was the effect of urban Africa on natives forced by drought and soil erosion to leave their tribal lands and resettle near Mombasa. But it quickly turns into an adventure yarn about ivory smugglers off the coast. There is an attempt to get across a message that the Africans are too immature to manage their own affairs and need benevolent white men to protect them from exploitation. Consequently it was banned in Kenya, even though the director argued that his film was firmly on the side of the Africans. Undoubtedly the work's motives were sincere, but Ealing paternalism won out once again. Taken on the level of adventure, with a reprise of the wild life close-ups from the

earlier film, *West of Zanzibar* is acceptable entertainment, but as a message of enlightened counsel for black Africa, it is a non-starter, and may actually have set the British cause back many years.

Colonial affairs were also the theme of Robert Hamer's *His Excellency*, which had Eric Portman cast as the former leader of a dockers' trade union appointed to the post of governor of a British Mediterranean island colony. Adapted from a play by Dorothy and Campbell Christie, *His Excellency* retains a stagebound atmosphere. Its other great fault lies in the way it wastes the theme's potential in a glib and artificial treatment. At times the film is like an Ealing comedy that got away, with familiar stereotypes such as the ladies who form the clientele of the 'Old Tea Shoppe', and the governor's staff. The governor himself tends towards caricature, retaining a shirt-sleeves-and-braces attitude akin to a trade-union rabble rouser long after he should have made a transition to the respectability demanded by his appointment. The key scene has him facing an incipient riot and drawing on his experience of dockyard militancy to win over the mob and the admiration of the sceptical Britons. Not only is it

wildly improbable, but there is something patronizing and offensive in the tone, as though six years of Labour government in which many a working-class minister had sat in Cabinet with no lack of savoir-faire had passed by completely unnoticed. Robert Hamer returned to Ealing specially to make this film, but compared with the promise of his earlier work it is disappointing and marks the beginning of his decline.

Secret People is also concerned with a political theme. The making of Thorold Dickinson's penultimate, and last British, film was followed closely by Lindsay Anderson, who had been a co-founder of the Oxford film magazine *Sequence*, and who later became a film and stage director of considerable eminence. He was granted the privilege of being the fly on the wall throughout the project from conception to completion; and his resulting book, *Making a Film*, is one of the most important Ealing testaments, containing a detailed and accurate description of the Studios' approach. It was unfortunate that the film selected for this treatment should have been directed by someone from outside the mainstream of Ealing directors, worse still that it was

Opposite: Robert Hamer's *His Excellency*
disappointed. Eric Portman (centre) as a
trade unionist elevated to colonial governor

Audrey Hepburn in Thorold Dickinson's
Secret People, in which exiled refugees in
London plan their dictator's assassination

poorly received and is now one of the forgotten
works. Had *The Lavender Hill Mob* or *Kind Hearts
and Coronets* received the benefit of a biographer,
film literature would have been enriched. Nevertheless, the book is one of the best accounts of any film
production, and revealing for its glimpses of life at
Ealing. (Balcon, intervening in a script conference:
'Do you mind if I'm awkward?'; Ernest Irving, the
musical director: 'You can't ask a composer for a
sample'; Dickinson advising an actor: 'Don't act it.
Behave it.')

The story of *Secret People* had been conceived by
Dickinson some years earlier in conjunction with the
novelist Joyce Carey, who had been responsible for
the screenplay of Dickinson's 1946 picture, *Men of
Two Worlds*. For various reasons production of *Secret People* had been put off until finally Balcon,
recognizing it as a change from the usual Ealing
product, invited Dickinson to film it under his aegis.
The plot is reminiscent of Conrad's *The Secret
Agent*, being concerned with a bomb plot in London
planned by nationals of a foreign tyranny who implicate members of the refugee community. Dickinson
and his colleagues viewed Hitchcock's *Sabotage*,
which was based on the Conrad book, before starting their film. There is much of interest in the Ealing
film – the moral dilemma of those who have to resort
to force to overcome force, for instance, though
there is no question of the evil of the dictatorship,
which is maintained by murder, oppression and tor-
ture by secret police. It is also a love story, with a
sensitive performance by the Italian actress, Valentina Cortesa, who had been brought over from
Hollywood where she had been wasted in a number
of unsuitable roles. *Secret People* also gave Audrey
Hepburn a substantial role nearly two years before
Roman Holiday, which most reference books regard
as the start of her film stardom. But the film was
poorly received and was misinterpreted in some
quarters as an attack on the left. It has never been
easy to make a political film in Britain, and few have
ever been attempted. *Secret People* was in some
respects ahead of its time.

For *I Believe in You*, Ealing returned to the slice-
of-life approach, this time looking at the workings of
the probation service, with Basil Dearden directing
a screenplay he wrote with Michael Relph and Jack

Whittingham from a story by Sewell Stokes. Cecil Parker plays Phipps, a middle-aged recruit to the service, a retired colonial civil servant looking for a new and worthwhile occupation. Understanding nothing of his clients' backgrounds, he is at first bewildered, but gradually, with the aid of a dedicated woman officer (Celia Johnson), becomes more humane. The subplot centres on two charges, Hooker (Harry Fowler) and Norma (Joan Collins), who fall in love and wish to marry but are forbidden by their probation officers, with the result that the youth goes back to his old gang to get money and independence from a robbery. The paternalistic Phipps, now thoroughly alive to his responsibilities, intervenes in the theft; expecting to be asked to resign, he is delighted to find that not only does Hooker get out of a jail sentence, but promotion awaits him. The usual quaint characters flit through the drama – the old lady who suspects that the neighbours are poisoning her cat, the deb who periodically gets smashed and ends up in the police cell, the fierce magistrate with an unexpectedly soft heart, the cheerful police sergeant. One performance that really stands out in the picture is that of a seventeen-year-old Joan Collins who projects a powerful aura of confident sexuality far in excess of what would have been intended at Ealing Green. Raymond Durgnat perceptively points to her presence as a symbol of the sub-culture from which the

film is insulated. What is clearly, if unintentionally, shown is the us-and-them attitude of British society, which draws its authority figures from professional and upper middle-class ranks whose members have no inkling of how the other half lives. One is left with the feeling that Phipps, a decent, kindly and compassionate man, will nevertheless remain firmly in his corner, isolated from the gritty realities of working-class life. The film reinforces the patronizing view taken by so many British films, which can only see the world through the eyes of the middle-aged middle class.

Something of the same charge could be laid against *Mandy*, except that she *is* a middle-class child, but one born with a handicap that would be just as devastating no matter what her background – she is stone deaf. It is one of Ealing's most moving films, directed by Alexander Mackendrick (his only non-comedy for the studio) with a script by Jack Whittingham from a novel *The Day is Ours* by Hilda Lewis. Parents as well as the child must suffer, and as the girl reaches school age the family itself is in danger of breaking up. She enters a school for deaf children, run by a dynamic and gifted teacher, brilliantly played by Jack Hawkins, who is beset by the power politics necessary to keep the institution functioning. Some critics in 1952 felt that the documentary view of deaf children – the school scenes were shot at the Royal Residential School for the Deaf in

Below: Mandy Miller, Phyllis Calvert and
Jack Hawkins in *Mandy*, a sympathetic
study of a deaf child

Bottom: Stephen Dalby at the sound
console with director Alexander
Mackendrick and the producer of *Mandy*,
Leslie Norman

Opposite: Lawrence Harvey and Joan
Collins in the dock in *I Believe in You*,
Ealing's view of the probation service

Manchester – was marred by being linked to a story
akin to magazine fiction, but at least the ending was
remarkably honest, as well as touching, clearly stat-
ing that Mandy could never overcome her handicap,
but that she might begin to cope with it. The child
was played by seven-year-old Mandy Miller, whose
acting career, albeit brief, had begun the year before
when she played a little girl in *The Man in the White
Suit*.

The last Ealing film of 1952 was *The Gentle Gunman*, directed by Basil Dearden, an adaptation by
Roger Macdougall from his own play about the
activities of a group of IRA men in London in 1941.
The theme, as in *Secret People*, is the issue of violence as a means of achieving an ideal. Somehow the
events of the more recent past make it difficult to be
truly objective about the film. Its attitudes appear to

John Mills, Dirk Bogarde and, in the background, Gilbert Harding in *The Gentle Gunman*, a film about the IRA

Jack Hawkins in his most famous role, Ericson, in *The Cruel Sea*, with Donald Sinden as his 'Number One', Lockhart

be far too glib and unconvincingly examined to represent any profound statement on the Irish situation. Although the action scenes have a certain excitement, much of the film is stagey and plodding. The naïvety of the overall message, which would have us believe that IRA men can be persuaded to give up their violent calling if something decent enough happens, is but one of the many artificial touches that compound the failure of the film. The cast included John Mills and Dirk Bogarde, neither at their best, and television celebrity Gilbert Harding, playing (to the manor born) the part of a bigoted Englishman who is unable to comprehend anything sensible about the Irish.

In the following year Ealing released an epic. Nicholas Monsarrat's book *The Cruel Sea*, describing corvette life in the Second World War, had been

a monumental best-seller, and it was the author's own wish that the film rights went to a British production company, an altruistic gesture that must have represented a considerable drop in his potential earnings, although wisely he settled for a percentage deal. Balcon arranged a meeting between Monsarrat and Charles Frend, who had directed *San Demetrio London*, and they got on well together. The casting of Jack Hawkins in the central role of Captain Ericson, the professional who leads a bunch of amateur 'wavy navy' sailors, was also popular; at the premiere of *Mandy* the rugged actor, who had been on the stage since the Twenties and in films from 1930, found himself besieged by autograph hunters, and realized that after years of slogging he had become a star. The second major part, that of Lockhart, the second-in-command, went to Donald Sinden, who

had not made a film before; *The Cruel Sea* made his
name, as it did those of Denholm Elliott and Virginia McKenna, whose previous roles had been in-
significant. Bryan Forbes likes to tell the story that
he was turned down for a part because he was not
officer material – it is a good joke against Ealing, and
Balcon somewhat self-consciously denied its truth.

Adapting the novel was a formidable task. Its 416
succinctly-written pages were packed with incident,
some of it horrifying, such as the vivid image of men
from a torpedoed ship, roped together in the water
and supported by their life jackets, grinning and

bowing to each other because they are skeletons.
Eric Ambler manfully prepared the script, discard-
ing many sections and characters, telescoping scenes
and changing emphases. It was estimated that four
million people in Britain alone had read the book,
and so the onus on Ambler was considerable.

Finding a suitable corvette was another problem.
The Admiralty, while anxious to co-operate in the
making of the film, had got rid of all its wartime
corvettes, which were small escort ships that had
been used to protect Atlantic convoys. Eventually
one was located in Malta – the *Coreopsis* of the

Flower Class – which had been loaned to the Greek navy and was now awaiting a tow back to England and the breaker's yard. A naval captain with war service in such vessels, Captain Broome, was dispatched to inspect and report, and he arranged for some repairs before sailing it back to Plymouth under its own steam. Jack Hawkins recalled asking him about the condition of the ship. 'We shall get her going all right,' was the reply, 'but God, what a state she's in. I can only tell you that when those Greek sailors went to the heads they must have turned cartwheels!'

The ship was duly transformed into HMS *Compass Rose* and filming began. It was not without incident. On one occasion, during a run into Plymouth Sound which had been delayed longer than it should have been and was taking place on a fast rising tide, Broome was unable, in spite of his tremendous skill, to prevent the little ship from doing £10,000 worth of damage to HMS *Camperdown*, a destroyer that had just been refitted. An angry sailor, woken from his slumbers, leaned out of a porthole and yelled at Hawkins on the bridge: 'Who's driving your bloody wagon then? Errol Flynn?' Jack Hawkins recalled another occasion when they were sailing past the huge American battleship, USS *Missouri*, then on a goodwill visit, who flashed them the message: 'What ship are you?' Broome delightedly replied, silencing the might of the US Navy: 'We are *Compass Rose* sailing the cruel sea. What ship are you?'

The most traumatic scene in the film occurs after a submarine has caused havoc to the convoy and the ASDIC (sonar detector) reveals that it is beneath a group of British sailors who are struggling in the water, hoping to be rescued. Ericson, faced with an appalling choice, drops the depth charges that will destroy the enemy but will also kill his countrymen. Yet for all his professionalism he is a human being, and he later gets paralytically drunk and bares his feelings to Lockhart. Hawkins, personally moved by the situation, delivered a fitting emotional performance, and at the end of the scene tears were rolling down his face. Two days later, after seeing it cut together, Balcon asked Frend to reshoot it with Hawkins keeping a grip on himself. It was played that way and Balcon pronounced it absolutely perfect. Then two days later, after another viewing, it was decided that a little emotion was needed after all, the scene was reshot with just an odd tear or two, and again the verdict was that it was now dead right.

Opposite: not since *San Demetrio London* had the Ealing tank seen such service. *The Cruel Sea* nobly depicted Nicholas Monsarrat's best-selling novel

Robert Beatty, Alf Hines and Joe Bloom in *The Square Ring*, about an evening's events in a seedy boxing stadium, directed in characteristic style by Basil Dearden

Hawkins was amused to note that the final version of the film used the first take.

Picturegoer was impressed enough by *The Cruel Sea* to award it its Seal of Merit, but one reviewer, the magazine's editor Connery Chappell, found it odd that Ealing should have watered down an outspoken and horrific book that had been read by millions of people into a film that could be granted a 'U' certificate. And as usual, the scenes involving women on shore, the romantic liaisons, were put across in a singularly unexciting way. Chappell wrote of the affair between Lockhart and the Wren operations room girl played by Virginia McKenna: 'I thought it embarrassing and too pukka to be possible, but Ealing women never seem to have any blood in them.'

The Cruel Sea is indisputably worthy, and was well-regarded by the public, but it is not a work on which the reputation of Ealing depends. It fell squarely into the category of stiff-upper-lip British war films which came back into vogue in the Fifties, such as *Angels One Five, Appointment in London, The Dam Busters, The Battle of the River Plate* and the most famous of all, *The Bridge on the River Kwai.* Each of them were decent, capably made and well-acted (often with Jack Hawkins in the cast), with that strange combination of stirring heroism and understatement that was mercilessly ridiculed in 1961 in the satirical revue *Beyond the Fringe.*

One of the last of Ealing's films to look at an institution through the characters involved in its function, as *Dance Hall, Pool of London* and *The Blue Lamp* had done, was Basil Dearden's *The Square Ring*, which dealt with the events of an evening at a provincial boxing stadium, with a cross-section of the people found there. It had originally been a play, but its transition to the screen, with a screenplay by Robert Westerby, worked well, in spite of a plethora of characters and detail, and a rich cast which included Jack Warner as a stalwart trainer, Maxwell Reed, Ronald Lewis, Robert Beatty, Bill Owen and George Rose as a motley assemblage of fighters ranging from the neophyte to the punchdrunk has-been, and even Joan Collins and Kay Kendall as ringside women. *The Square Ring* was regarded as a sort of British version of the American films *The Set-Up* and *Champion*, and the differences in their

approach make for an interesting comparison; even in a story with serious overtones and a tragic outcome, the Ealing film has a folksy jollity with lots of byplay and heavily worked gaglines (two cast members are even billed as First and Second Wiseacres). The bouts themselves were shot with far less blood and gore than the American equivalents and, although Dearden was to make them reasonably dramatic, particularly the climactic encounter between Kid Curtis (Robert Beatty) and Barney Deakon (Alf Hines), there is nothing to equal the bravura camerawork of the American film, *Body and Soul*, in which a handheld Arriflex was used in the ring itself, and which influenced the greatest boxing film of the Eighties, Martin Scorsese's *Raging Bull.* Nevertheless, *The Square Ring* is one of Dearden's better pictures, keeping a straightforward dramatic unity, presenting the professional boxing world convincingly, its seedy, ugly side prominently on view but not overstated. The boxers themselves come across as rounded characters, not stereotypes, and there is a note of genuine suspense in the closing fight sequence.

But now, as the mid-Fifties approached, the Ealing spirit was beginning to turn sour.

Above: the recreation of the evacuation of *Dunkirk*

Left: Charles Crichton working on *Man in the Sky*

CHAPTER 7

The end of Ealing

In 1954 the last vestiges of rationing were finally erased. The Conservative government elected in 1951 was well ensconced, and a new monarch had reigned for two years. The austerity era was clearly over as more and more consumer goods flooded the shops, shiny Ford Consuls and Vauxhall Veloxes filled the streets and for the first time in Britain new television sets came equipped with a channel selector switch, in anticipation of the commercial alternative to the BBC which was due to begin transmissions in the following year. 'Set the people free' had been Churchill's election slogan, and now the promise was coming into effect as the many rigid controls, restrictions, permits, licences and bureaucratic apparatus set up in the war, and carried over as part of the structure of the Welfare State, were set aside. The mood of Britain had changed. The eyesores of the bombsites in the big cities at last began to disappear and were replaced by the eyesores of office blocks. Municipal housing started to flourish and gigantic estates leapt off the architects' drawing boards into the reality of brick and concrete. The recognition of the teenager as an economic force led to a rapid growth in the fashion, cosmetic and confectionery industries. The old wind-up portable gramophones were supplanted by the new compact record players which could handle the newly-established long-play albums, as well as the old 78 rpm singles and their replacements, the 45s.

Ealing did not take happily to the new style of Britain in the Fifties. In general, the British film industry had lost a lot of steam and was entering one of its dreariest periods, faced with spectacularly declining audiences on the one hand, and the growth of television on the other. The American industry had reacted by investing money in new systems in the hope that a touch of showmanship could regenerate the lost audience. Three-dimensional (3D) films were tried but eventually abandoned – the dual projection method was clumsy, and audiences did not relish having to wear special Polaroid glasses – and only one or two worthwhile films were made in the process, which would still have been effective even if they had not been in 3D. Then came CinemaScope, the first of the anamorphic systems in which the image is squeezed on to the standard 35 mm frame and later expanded into a letterbox shape by a corresponding lens in the projector. The anamorphic lens was invented in the Twenties and discarded; it was disinterred by Twentieth Century-Fox with the intention of providing something in the cinema that was impossible on television. Paramount responded with a rival system called VistaVision, subtitled 'Motion Picture High Fidelity', in which the 35 mm film was drawn across the camera aperture horizontally instead of vertically, thus producing a larger image area. When shrunk to a normal release print, it was claimed that greater clarity, sharpness and colour definition ensued. Rank later adopted this system for films made at Pinewood, but unlike CinemaScope, which was supplanted by the much-improved Panavision anamorphic system in use oday, VistaVision did not offer anything different enough to excite the imagi-

Below: young jockey Fella Edmonds and Edward Underdown in *The Rainbow Jacket*

Bottom: *Lease of Life*, Robert Donat's only Ealing film: director Charles Frend rehearses him and Beckett Bould

Women line up for milk in wartime Europe in *The Divided Heart*, a tug-of-love drama Balcon admired

of what could be done, such as trips on rollercoasters or runaway trains. Its prohibitive cost limited it to a handful of theatres in city centres only, while CinemaScope gradually became generally adopted.

The only perceptible technical change at Ealing was the increased use of colour, now applied to films which earlier would not have warranted it. The advent of monopack film made it possible to use conventional cameras instead of the unwieldy three-strip Technicolor camera. At one time only four such cameras existed in Britain, which meant that the number of films shot in the process was severely rationed, with schedules carefully arranged to prevent productions from overlapping.

The paternalistic, cottage-industry style of Ealing Studios seemed at variance with the new thrusting spirit of the day. Even the Ealing comedy no longer reigned unrivalled. In 1953 the most successful film had been *Genevieve*, a comedy about two veteran cars engaged in an unofficial race from Brighton to London after the annual run. Directed by Henry Cornelius, who had made *Passport to Pimlico*, and scripted by William Rose, who was to write *The Maggie* and *The Ladykillers*, it was made by Rank at Pinewood, there being no room on the Ealing lot for the production. Rank had another winner that year with *Trouble in Store*, the first of what became virtually an annual series for many years starring the diminutive, prat-falling, peak-capped comedian, Norman Wisdom. And in 1954 the big comedy success was *Doctor in the House*, a lively recital of the japes and binges of a bunch of medical students (Dirk Bogarde, Donald Sinden and Kenneth More among them) occasionally intimidated by the ill-tempered and sharp-tongued Sir Lancelot Spratt (James Robertson Justice). Based on a popular book by Richard Gordon, the success of the film, with its slapstick routines, mild smut and general air of robust high spirits, led to another series. All Ealing could offer as comic retaliation was the feeble *The Love Lottery* and the outdated *The Maggie*.

The dramatic films were more consistent. *The Rainbow Jacket*, a story about horse racing, reflected a passionate interest of its scriptwriter, Tibby Clark. Pleasing Technicolor photography by Otto Heller evoked the atmosphere of English stables and race courses in a convincing manner, but Basil Dearden's

nation, and after a few years it was quietly dropped. The most spectacular of all the new systems was Cinerama, which used three projectors and a gigantic screen to create a vast scene made up of three adjoining images and the (usually, although not always) barely perceptible seams. It was not a medium that lent itself to ordinary dramatic features, and most of the Cinerama films, starting with *This is Cinerama*, were in the form of demonstrations

direction in his first film collaboration with Clarke since *The Blue Lamp* was dull after his much livelier preceding work, *The Square Ring*. There was something tiresome about the stereotyped characters, particularly Robert Morley as a racing peer and Wilfrid Hyde White and the bushy-moustachioed Michael Trubshawe as his fellow Jockey Club members. A conventional story with heavy-handed plot contrivances, the most disappointing sequences in the film were the races, in which static riders on mechanical mounts were combined with such ragged back projection that the illusion was destroyed. The riders included the celebrated jockey Sir Gordon Richards, who won the 1953 Derby, but even he looked unconvincing.

The Rainbow Jacket had a promising enough opening in the West End but, as sometimes happens with a film that can break house records in Leicester Square, it failed to stir any excitement on general release. Clark recalls that he had deduced that racing films often flopped because of the predictability of the races themselves, as it was always highly probable that the hero would win. For that reason he had two sympathetic characters ride in the main race, to give the audience a selection problem. But it seems that the subterfuge was, in itself, not enough.

Charles Frend's 1954 film took as its basis a more serious domestic subject. *Lease of Life* concerns a Yorkshire vicar given twelve months to live, and the effect this has on his faith and his family. Robert Donat played the central character with his usual care, overcoming the drawbacks of his theatrical technique by sheer strength of personality. Kay Walsh as his wife had to cope with a somewhat implausible part, as Eric Ambler's screenplay failed to supply sufficient motivation for her to misappropriate £100 left in the vicar's care, and Adrienne Corri, a sensitive and beautiful actress who had made an exotic debut in Jean Renoir's *The River*, seemed palpably miscast as the daughter who wants to take up a London piano scholarship. A more central weakness in the film is that a controversial sermon which plays a crucial part in the plot is unremarkable even by the standards of the day, and it is hard to see why, except for plot purposes, it should have caused offence. But in spite of these reservations, *Lease of Life* was a sensitively organized film, admirably sketching in the routine of a North Country vicar's daily round in a rural parish, and the Eastmancolor photography by Douglas Slocombe succeeded in evoking the pastoral English charm of the settings. Although by no means a film to be ashamed of, *Lease of Life* lacked a quality that could have made it, by virtue of its theme, distinguished.

It was soon followed by a serious film that Balcon regarded as one of the best made at Ealing. *The*

Divided Heart was directed by Charles Crichton, representing a notable change of pace for him, and was written by Jack Whittingham with Richard Hughes. The story was based on a heart-rending real-life situation in which a Yugoslav mother, whose baby had been snatched by the Germans during the war along with thousands of others, to be given to childless women in the Fatherland, had managed to trace her child. The baby had grown to be ten years old without knowing anything of his real background, supposing his adoptive parents to be his own. Faced with the judgment of Solomon, the American Control Commission awarded the boy to his real mother without even the bond of a common language between them. In the film, Cornell Borchers and Armin Dahlen play the German couple, with Yvonne Mitchell as the Yugoslav mother and Alexander Knox as the presiding judge. It ends on a highly-charged emotional note, intensified by the closing remark from the court that they are not handing the son into the custody of the mother, but the mother into the custody of the son. After that, there cannot be a dry eye in the house. Nevertheless, *The Divided Heart*, though it was a critics' picture, did not catch fire at the box office. What marred it was a somewhat barren style of construction in which, apart from two flashbacks inserted to show what happened during the war, the story moved at a measured pace towards its climax, losing some of its emotional edge because of an over-deliberate editing pattern. There is a characteristic reticence to become too deeply involved, almost as though, having uncovered an undoubtedly explosively-charged affair of heart-breaking proportions, the film-makers were reluctant to be drawn too close and so risk being forced to make a commitment. Yvonne Mitchell was in general sensitive and moving, conveying an air of sadness and determination, contrasted with the hysterical possessiveness of the other woman. But the ultimate effect is a subdued one, and perhaps the reason for the film's comparative failure with the public lies in its own lack of involvement in the drama which it relates. It is, in essence, far too British about everything.

Out of the Clouds, directed by Basil Dearden, was yet another of Ealing's attempts at a behind-the-scenes approach – this time an anatomy of London Airport, a much smaller community in the mid-Fifties than now. Compared with Arthur Hailey's treatment of the same formula in the Sixties in his novel *Airport*, the result is remarkably tame. As is usual in such Ealing pictures, and in this one more than most, the background and setting are more interesting than the foreground characters, and Paul Beeson's Eastmancolor photography provides a fascinating record of how Heathrow looked in its early days. One of Ealing's largest-ever sets was used for the interior of the terminal. The script, by Michael Relph and John Eldridge, is larded with the customary parade of minor characters – a comic cab driver, a difficult passenger and so on – but so much of the original spirit has by this time deserted Ealing that the peripheral action, far from filling out a rich tapestry of incident, is merely a tiresome diversion from the main thread of the narrative.

Leslie Norman, who worked with Harry Watt as associate producer on his Commonwealth films, made a directorial debut with another air story, *The Night My Number Came Up*. But rather than following the Dearden style of the preceding picture, it returned to an earlier Ealing motif, the occult. A group of people indulge in an after-dinner conversation in which the question of fate and pre-ordained life arises. One of the party, played by Michael Hordern, relates a dream in which another of those present, a senior Royal Air Force officer (Michael Redgrave), together with a girl, an important civilian and five passengers, plus a crew of five, is flying in a DC3 which goes down over Japan and crashes on a rocky shore. Although the Air Marshal is due to fly the following day, he is not disturbed by the story. But on the morrow things begin to take a strange turn: the scheduled Liberator is replaced by a DC3; a girl arrives as a stenographer to a member of the House of Lords who is on the flight; two soldiers hitch a ride, and make the total number flying thirteen, also as in the dream. There is a violent storm, radio failure and the plane seems doomed. The pilot, however, decides to make a forced landing on a rocky beach. Only at the climax does reality differ from the premonition, for everyone aboard is eventually saved.

Some of the dramatic possibilities of the plot were lost in the structure of the film. The story was told in

Top: Michael Howard, Robert Beatty and
Bernard Lee in *Out of the Clouds*: life at
Heathrow Airport

Middle: Michael Redgrave and Nigel
Stock in *The Night My Number Came Up*:
premonitions come true

Bottom: Richard Attenborough and Bill
Owen in *The Ship that Died of Shame*:
servicemen become smugglers

flashback, so it was known right at the start that the plane had crashed, leaving only the question of how it all happened. The remaining content was somewhat thin, particularly as the characterization was of the usual stereotyped kind. It was the only Ealing screenplay by R. C. Sherriff who, besides writing the play *Journey's End*, had been responsible for a number of British and Hollywood hit movies, including *The Four Feathers*, *Lady Hamilton*, *Goodbye Mr Chips* and *Mrs Miniver*, but regrettably his sole work for Balcon turned out to be small beer.

Dearden's *The Ship that Died of Shame*, apart from following what now seemed a tedious fashion for lengthy, gnomic titles, began in a promising Ealing vein as if it was going to be a war film, but developed into a story highlighting the problems of servicemen trying to adjust to the difficulties of civilian life. By 1955 such a theme had become dated and irrelevant – another case of Ealing failing to take into account the shift in attitudes. The script, by John Whiting, Michael Relph and Basil Dearden, was adapted from a novel by Nicholas Monsarrat, the author of *The Cruel Sea*. The film was an uneasy coupling of a routine thriller story with the sentimental notion of the ship with a soul, a concept that might appeal to a few nautical experts but seemed bewildering and absurd to the great mass of landlubbers. The most successful of the performers was Richard Attenborough who attacked the role of a bumptious, smalltime crook with relish. George Baker as the ship's skipper, on the other hand, held himself in check to the point of stiflement.

The Feminine Touch followed the careers of a group of five student nurses in the approved Ealing manner, and was directed by Pat Jackson, a former documentary director (*Western Approaches*) who had made another hospital drama feature five years earlier for Rank called *White Corridors*. The source material this time was a novel, *A Lamp is Heavy* by Sheila Mackay Russell, adapted by Ian McCormick. The contrasted girls were Belinda Lee, Adrienne Corri, Delphi Lawrence, Henryetta Edwards and Barbara Archer, with Diana Wynyard as the upright matron and George Baker as a young house doctor. The hospital routine is presented in the usual straightforward, no-nonsense way, and the various emotional problems of the nurses are gradually

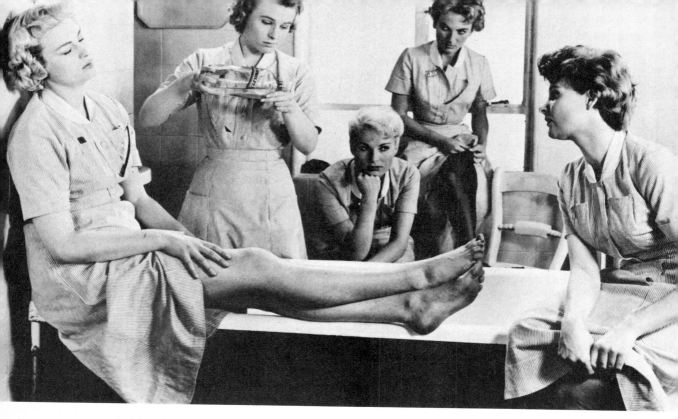

superseded by their sense of vocation, particularly after a patient's life is saved in the course of duty. A worthy if unoriginal film, it provided a view of the probationer nurse's lot in a reasonably entertaining manner, and the Eastmancolor photography by Paul Beeson captured convincingly the atmosphere of the hospital.

The next film made at Ealing, *The Long Arm*, was a police melodrama directed by Charles Frend, with Jack Hawkins as a weary detective on the trail of a murderous safe-cracker, finally captured with his accomplice, who turns out to be his wife, in a trap laid at the Royal Festival Hall. In the seven years since *The Blue Lamp* notable changes have occurred; There is now a markedly cynical view of the attractions of a career in the police. The life of the Scotland Yard man is shown to be tedious and frustrating: no sooner does he reach his far-flung suburban home and his neglected wife than he gets summoned back to the office. Hawkins, as Detective Superintendent Halliday, patiently unravels the case, and copes with the disaffection of his family while encouraging his young assistant, Sergeant Ward (John Stratton) with much banter and chat about 'Chummy' – the Yard name for an unidentified crook. There is something of the flavour of a television police series in the approach, even though at the time that genre was still relatively unexplored. The story originated from Robert Barr, one of the pioneering television documentary writers, and he wrote the script in collaboration with Janet Green,

who was to be responsible for some excellent post-Ealing Relph–Dearden thrillers.

The adjective most frequently used to describe *The Long Arm* is 'efficient' and, while it was not remarkable for its originality, it was by no means a production of which Ealing should be ashamed. This was fortunate as it turned out to be the last film Sir Michael Balcon produced at the Studios. In late 1955 it was announced that the premises were to be sold to the BBC for £350,000. Being in the middle of a residential neighbourhood, there was no opportunity for the site to be converted to any other use except that of a housing estate. The offer from the BBC was therefore an attractive one, since it meant that the buildings would be left intact, and would continue to be used for their intended purpose – the making of films, albeit for television rather than for the cinema. The need to sell the site had arisen because Stephen Courtauld, who had been on the board from the beginning of the Balcon era, and who had been greatly responsible for the financial security of the company, had decided to retire and spend his remaining years abroad. His withdrawal meant that the burden now fell on Balcon and Reg Baker alone. They decided for the first time to secure a loan from the National Film Finance Corporation (NFFC), the body which had been set up during the period in which Harold Wilson had been President of the Board of Trade with the intention of aiding British film production. Balcon had been an honorary advisor to the NFFC, which was one of the

Opposite: student nurses Barbara Archer, Henryetta Edwards, Belinda Lee, Delphi Lawrence and Adrienne Corri in *The Feminine Touch*, directed by Pat Jackson

Below: Jack Hawkins, all-purpose hero, as test pilot in trouble in *Man in the Sky*, and as weary Scotland Yard man (with John Stratton) in *The Long Arm*

reasons why there had been no attempt by Ealing to use its funds, but in any case until this juncture they had been able to finance production from elsewhere. But now a substantial loan was needed, and the Studios, together with the library of films, became the security.

In order for the loan to be repaid in the fullness of time, the sale of the Studios and the switch of production to Pinewood and its more modern facilities seemed to make sense. Balcon had understood from John Davis, the managing director of Rank, that two new stages would be built at Pinewood to be used exclusively for Ealing productions, but it later became apparent that this was not what Davis had in mind. The two new stages were indeed built, but it was made clear that Ealing would have to take its chances with every other contender for the space. Davis had no intention of allowing an autonomous group to operate on its special patch within the gates of Pinewood, although such arrangements are now commonplace in the film industry. Baker felt at the time that a compromise could be reached, but Balcon was adamant that, under the Davis plan, Ealing would lose its independence and simply become another arm of the Rank Organisation. Consequently it was decided that the relationship with Rank should come to an end. Balcon resigned from the board of the Rank Organisation and, after the delivery of *The Long Arm*, the distribution arrangement and joint financing terms were wound up.

Ironically, the company that took over the role of producing and distributing Ealing's films was MGM. It had changed its complexion considerably, however, from the days in the late Thirties when Balcon was for a short time in charge of its British production, until his great falling-out with Louis B. Mayer, who was ousted in 1951 by Dore Schary in one of Hollywood's most famous coups. From now on Ealing production was located in an exclusive wing of the MGM British studios at Borehamwood in Hertfordshire, close to Elstree. The new contract was in many respects less favourable than the one enjoyed with Rank, but it augured well for international sales, as the company had worldwide outlets and was one of the pillars of the film industry in general. Arthur Loew, who had become president of MGM after Schary, had worked with Balcon as far back as

Peter Finch with Dana Wilson in *The Shiralee*, Leslie Norman's view of life in the Australian outback

the Twenties when he was involved in some films with Ivor Novello, and it was he who spearheaded the bringing of Ealing into the MGM fold. However, the new collaboration was shortlived, as shortly after the new contract was signed Loew left the company in a shake-up following an internal dispute, together with Sam Eckman who ran the MGM British operation, and George Muchnic who had been responsible for cementing the agreement with Reg Baker. As a result, the Ealing contingent was faced with having to make a fresh start not only in unfamiliar surroundings, but with a new and unfamiliar management. The contents of the old studios were auctioned off, so that the technicians who transferred to Borehamwood were able to work with new equipment, but that in itself was not adequate compensation for the disruption. 'I don't think any of us welcomed the change,' wrote Tibby Clarke. 'There was little hope of the old team spirit being preserved now that we had ceased to be a self-contained unit, and the intimate atmosphere of our previous home was sadly missing from these new bleak acres of characterless buildings. I was glad I had recently signed a new contract under which I was no longer tied exclusively to Ealing Films.' Even Balcon had to

admit: 'It would be no use pretending that we did not have heavy hearts over leaving Ealing. To comfort myself, I used to say it was people that counted, not buildings. This was not strictly honest, as over the years there had developed at Ealing a spirit which had seeped into the very fabric of the place.'

Life at Borehamwood could never be the same. Only seven more films were to be made bearing the Ealing logo, two of them representing the twilight of the Ealing comedy: *Barnacle Bill* which was Tibby Clarke's last screenplay for the studio that had made his name, and *Davy*, also a valedictory screenplay from William Rose. Rose, together with John Eldridge, had scripted the first of Ealing's Hertfordshire films, *Man in the Sky*, which was the last Balcon production directed by Charles Crichton. A suspenseful drama about a test pilot in trouble with a blazing plane over a built-up area, it was very much a vehicle for Jack Hawkins. The cliff-hanging element was well-handled; less sure however was the psychological battleground and, following *The Long Arm*, it now seemed to be official policy to saddle the harrassed professional with a shaky home life. On his return from his harrowing experience, Hawkins is asked by his wife (Elisabeth Sellars) how his day has been, and tries to pass it off as routine. But she has been watching the drama played out in the air, and bitterly attacks him for putting his job before her and the children. Hawkins then delivers a six-minute speech, a masculine justification for doing a job and staying with it, making the point that if he had not tried to do his best he would never have been able to face her again. In 1957, with Women's Lib then but a whisper, this sort of sentiment was just about acceptable. In the event, the film helped to establish the type of characters that Hawkins was called upon to play – solid, quietly determined, stubborn and ultimately caring, decent men.

Elisabeth Sellars also appeared in *The Shiralee* as the wife of a swagman, that great figure in Australian society, the roamer of the country highways, played in this instance by Peter Finch. Leslie Norman, having worked on Ealing's three previous Australian films, directed this one himself. Made long after Ealing had relinquished its production facilities in Australia, it nevertheless reinforced Balcon's hope that a basis could be found for regular film output in that country; but *The Shiralee*, with its mostly British cast, is much more of a British film made on location than an indigenous product of the country concerned. The restless swagman returns from one of his peripatetic jaunts to find his wife embroiled with a lover (George Rose). Enraged, he takes to the road again, taking his small daughter (Dana Wilson) whom he has snatched from her mother. The child is the 'shiralee', an aboriginal word meaning 'burden'. The film has a great deal of strength in its picture of the rugged Australian individualism of the leading character contrasted with the growing power of the child's unspoken love for her father. The magnificent barren landscapes of the outback, photographed by Paul Beeson with a certain amount of respectful awe, explain the compulsion that makes a man an itinerant, as well as providing the film with stimulating visual interest. There is an episodic quality to the narrative, but Peter Finch's performance, notwithstanding the notorious handicap of sharing the screen with a child, succeeds in welding the structure together. The two women characters are less convincing, and the insertion of broad comedy from Tessie O'Shea and Sidney James as two of the swagman's friends (in other Ealing–Australia days it would have been Tommy Trinder) is an example of the trap that so often ensnares British films generally, and Ealing in particular – that of providing inappropriate comic relief as if the producers had insufficient confidence in their material.

The most ambitious Ealing film during the MGM period was *Dunkirk*, again directed by Leslie Norman, with a script which fused a factual account by Ewan Butler with a novel, *The Big Pick-Up*, by Elleston Trevor. The screenplay was the work of W. P. Lipscomb, with David Divine, a journalist experienced in military affairs and history. It follows the pattern of examining a major event, in this case the rescue of the British army from the French coast in May 1940, by focusing on a small group – a band of soldiers whose officer has been killed and who are now led by a reluctant corporal (John Mills). Because *Dunkirk* is the story of a defeat, though a heroic one, the film has an air of anti-climax, understatement and gritted teeth. There is no flinching from the fact that what is shown is a military disaster, and a journalist who helps in the rescue spends

Filming *Dunkirk*: John Mills and Bernard Lee, who played a war correspondent, in front of the camera for a tracking shot

much time criticizing the brass hats and their conduct of the war which has led to this shambling mess. There is a problem in weaving the individual stories into the larger tapestry of the battle itself; the familiar newsreel and press photograph images of lines of troops snaking through the water from beach to boat, the debris of discarded vehicles, weapons and supplies left behind on the sands, the smoke and tumult of battle are vividly reconstructed, but the insertion of John Mills and his half-dozen men has an awkwardness that diminishes the conviction of the larger set piece.

The subject of *Dunkirk* was perhaps an appropriate one for Ealing, which had made an early name in the area of war films when the Second World War had actually been raging. Few such films had been made in the Fifties, *The Cruel Sea* being the other notable exception. Both films were in a sense concerned not with the glamorous, heroic side of war, but with the wearying, dispiriting absurdity of it, the pointless waste of human resources. *Dunkirk*, the story of a retreat and a defeat, was Ealing's last opportunity to portray a certain idiosyncratic greatness in the British character.

Seth Holt, an editor at Ealing from 1943, made his

John Mills studies his script during a lull
in the location shooting of *Dunkirk*

him to escape from jail, hiding him in a London flat.
There is a tussle for possession of the safety box key,
and Gregory leaves his treacherous partner bound
and gagged, but fails to obtain shelter from other
members of the underworld when it is known that
the man has died of suffocation. A young socialite
(Maggie Smith made her film debut in this role)
decides to protect him and takes him to her parents'
estate in Wales. He is later shot by a farm worker,
and dies believing that the girl has betrayed him.

This essay in criminality is a long way removed
from the simplistic world of *The Blue Lamp*. The
influences are more those of the American and
French crime films of the Fifties. The action moves
along at a crisp rate, helped by the cool jazz sound-
track of Dizzy Reece. The film ends on a resounding
pessimistic chord as the girl reads the thief's farewell
note and then walks off into the landscape away from
camera, a moment of chic despair characteristic of
the period. Holt knew his cinema and could fashion
a modish work with skill and a certain slickness. For
all that, his directorial gifts were considerable, and it
is a matter of tragedy for the British film industry
that they were largely unfulfilled.

One other film was made during the MGM period
which, although serviced by Ealing and produced by
Balcon, was not released as an Ealing film. Directed
by Robert Hamer and starring Alec Guinness, it was
an adaptation by Gore Vidal of Daphne du
Maurier's *The Scapegoat*, in which an Englishman on
holiday exchanges places with a French aristocrat
who is his *doppelgänger*, and is sufficiently convincing to deceive the drug-addicted mother, played by
Bette Davis. The film was not successful and, in
spite of being set in Hamer's beloved France, failed
to be plausible, and it is perhaps as well that it does
not belong within the Ealing canon.

During the three years of the MGM contract there
was an increasing feeling of dissatisfaction with the
impersonal nature of the arrangement, and Balcon
was not happy with the general policy adopted
towards the now rapidly burgeoning medium of
television, which was beginning to show several feature films a week. With considerable foresight, he
looked ahead to the possibility of the cinema and
television aiding each other in joint production, a
view that was anathema to many of his colleagues in

directorial debut in 1958 with *Nowhere to Go*, and
revealed a talent of great promise, though his death
in 1971 meant that he had time to make only half-a-
dozen films, most of them quirkily-conceived thrillers with elements of surprise and shock. His film for
Ealing does not fit the general Balcon tradition,
although it does point the way the cinema will go
long after Ealing is dead and buried. The story was
adapted by Holt and Kenneth Tynan from a thriller
by Donald Mackenzie, in which a crook called
Gregory (played by George Nader in the film) steals
a collection of antique coins from a wealthy American visitor to London, and puts the money he
receives for them into a safety deposit before his
arrest. He is sentenced to ten years rather than the
five which he was expecting, and his partner helps

able to use a true contemporary story as the basis for
a thriller set in modern Sydney. Aldo Ray played a
prisoner on his way to serve a long sentence who
escapes with his younger brother (Neil McCallum)
and two henchmen in a stolen ambulance. They take
refuge on the small island of Pinchgut in Sydney
Harbour and make hostages of the inhabitants – the
caretaker, his wife and daughter. Aldo Ray demands
from the police an assurance that he will be granted a
retrial, so that he can establish his innocence, and
when it is not forthcoming he threatens to detonate
an ammunition ship in the harbour by firing at it
with an ancient naval gun situated on the island. The
police evacuate the city, send in sharpshooters who
eliminate the accomplices, then follow up with a
wave of frogmen. Eventually, after a furious battle,
the ringleader is shot down and his brother is led off
to jail, having formed a romantic liaison with the girl
hostage.

There is an ambivalence in the film which detracts
from its straightforward qualities of entertainment.
The audience is not quite sure who to root for, and
Aldo Ray's heavy playing undermines his protesta-
tions of innocence. But the authorities appear quite
willing to double-cross him, and their attitude forces
him into a violent stand which conciliation would
have made unnecessary. In spite of these problems,
Watt maintained the pace and excitement of the
action and the work has his characteristic stamp of
documentary-like realism. The restitution of law
and order with which *The Siege of Pinchgut* ends
echoes the philosophy of earlier Ealing productions
such as *Passport to Pimlico*, so that at least the last
film made with the famous logo fitted within the
tradition.

Premiered in August 1959, twenty-one years after
Michael Balcon first came to Ealing Green, it was to
be the only film released under the Associated
British arrangement. For the first time Balcon had
no other production in the pipeline, and so an era of
British film-making came to a close, fading away
almost unnoticed, as many had felt that Ealing had
really ended when the old Studios were handed over
to the BBC. Now everyone left was to go their sep-
arate ways, some vanishing from the industry
altogether. Of the great team of Ealing directors,
most were to make further films, although none

the industry at the time. When an offer was made by
the Associated British Picture Corporation for the
Ealing assets, Balcon and Baker decided to accept it.
Associated British was linked to ABC Television
which held the valuable weekend contract for programmes in the Midlands and the North of England,
and was one of the ITV 'big four' which meant that it
had a large share of network programming.

The new deal was agreed on the understanding
that Ealing would continue as an active production
company, and so work was started on *The Siege of
Pinchgut*, made on location in Australia and at the
ABPC Elstree Studios, less than a mile from MGM at
Borehamwood. It gave Harry Watt an opportunity
to return to his favourite Commonwealth country,
and instead of looking to history for a plot he was

achieved the consistent distinction of their Ealing period.

Alexander Mackendrick returned to the United States, the country of his birth, and made the excellent (but in box-office terms, disastrous) *Sweet Smell of Success*, followed by *Sammy Going South*, which was produced by Balcon, *A High Wind in Jamaica* and *Don't Make Waves*. He then dropped out of the industry altogether to teach film at a Californian university. Charles Crichton made a handful of films, including the melodramatic *Floods of Fear* and the comic Peter Sellers vehicle *The Battle of the Sexes*, his last cinema film in 1965, *He Who Rides a Tiger*, and many segments of filmed television series. Charles Frend also worked in television, but made only three post-Ealing feature films – *Cone of Silence*, *Girl on Approval* and *The Sky Bike* – and was second unit director on David Lean's *Ryan's Daughter*. He died in 1977. Henry Cornelius, after *Genevieve*, made *I am a Camera*, *Next to No Time* and with Charles Crichton co-directed *Law and Disorder* before an early death at the age of forty-five in 1958.

Death was also to claim Robert Hamer after only a handful of post-Ealing films, among them *Father Brown* with Alec Guinness as Chesterton's priestly detective, *School for Scoundrels*, based on Stephen Potter's *Lifemanship* books, and his last work, a vehicle for Leo McKern, *A Jolly Bad Fellow*, in 1963. Basil Dearden had the most prolific subsequent career of the Ealing directors, making no less than seventeen films, including *Sapphire*, *The League of Gentlemen*, *Victim*, *Woman of Straw*, *Masquerade*, *Khartoum*, *Only When I Larf*, *The Assassination Bureau* and his last, during the short reign of Bryan Forbes as production chief at Elstree, *The Man Who Haunted Himself*, before being killed in a car crash on a motorway in 1971. Leslie Norman made *Summer of the Seventeenth Doll* in Australia, *The Long and the Short and the Tall* for Balcon, *Spare the Rod* and *Mix Me a Person*, but his other significant contribution to films was as the father of the splendidly knowledgeable television commentator on the cinema, Barry Norman. Harry Watt, on the other hand, did not make any further feature films when Ealing came to an end.

Of directors who had worked at Ealing in the earlier days, Cavalcanti returned to his native Brazil, making films there and later in Italy; Thorold Dickinson, who made *Next of Kin* and *Secret People* at Ealing, left the film industry altogether and became Professor of Film at the Slade School of Art, London; Robert Stevenson of *A Young Man's Fancy* and *Return to Yesterday* became a Hollywood director of high repute, making such films as *Back Street*, *Jane Eyre* and *To the Ends of the Earth* before becoming completely associated with the Disney Organization, for whom he has directed many works including the highly successful *Mary Poppins*, *Bedknobs and Broomsticks* and more recently, at Pinewood, *One of Our Dinosaurs is Missing*. Alone of all the Ealing directors, his career was larger away from the company, but he left at the very beginning of the Balcon era, long before the Studios' character had become properly established.

Screenwriters fared little better than directors in their subsequent working lives, although William Rose, returning to America, achieved some success in association with Stanley Kramer, working on *It's a Mad, Mad, Mad, Mad World* and the Oscar-winning *Guess Who's Coming to Dinner*. Tibby Clarke wrote *Gideon's Day* for John Ford, *Sons and Lovers* which was directed by Jack Cardiff and *A Horse Without a Head* for Disney. Both Roger Macdougall and John Dighton continued their playwriting career after Ealing.

Balcon himself was in his sixties when Ealing finally came to an end. For a while he was chairman of Bryanston Films, a co-operative of independent producers which included Michael Relph and Basil Dearden, George Brown, Monja Danischewsky, Albert Fennell and Ronald Neame, Charles Frend, Michael Truman, Norman Priggen, Kenneth and Gerald Shipman (who controlled Twickenham Studios) and the staunchest of Balcon's Ealing colleagues, Hal Mason. The company worked on a revolving credit principle, whereby projects were financed at one-third of the credit available, the bank recovering its money from the first proceeds and extending the credit or loan accordingly. Bryanston offered producers seventy per cent of a budget, the rest being found from private sources, or from the National Film Finance Corporation. British Lion acted as the distributor. During the period in which Bryanston operated, several major film talents were revealed, including Tony Richardson and John Osborne who brought their Woodfall company into the group and made *The Entertainer* and *Saturday Night and Sunday Morning*, the latter directed by Karel Reisz, followed by *A Taste of Honey* and *The Loneliness of the Long Distance Runner*. What finished Bryanston off was the decline in the overall number of cinemas, which caused a contraction from three releasing circuits to two. It became much harder to get bookings and, since a circuit release was essential for any film to recoup its cost, it meant that it was taking longer and longer for the returns to come in, while at the same time unreleased product was amassing interest charges. It thus became more difficult for the company to make a profit, and when an offer was made for its assets by the London television contractor, Associated Rediffusion, it was accepted.

After Rank and ABPC the third British distributing force was British Lion, but unlike the others it did not own a circuit. For historic reasons the NFFC had a large stake in it and late in 1963 it became known that a plan was in train to sell it to Sydney Box. Balcon, horrified that part of the government's property was being sold off privately in a backdoor manner, started a publicity campaign, leading to a Commons debate. Meanwhile he put in his own bid, along with Richardson and Osborne of Woodfall, Joseph Janni and John Schlesinger, and the American distributor and exhibitor, Walter Reade. It was successful and Balcon foresaw a production programme of between ten and fifteen films a year from Shepperton Studios, with Reade's presence ensuring fair dealing in the United States. Unfortunately, once the company was trading Balcon found that his chairmanship was seen by his fellow directors as a mere figurehead appointment, and there was little desire to engage in the ambitious programme he had put forward. Accordingly, Balcon, believing that in his position he had a public mandate to insist that his proposals were enacted, felt unable to continue, and resigned.

So ended his direct involvement with the British film industry, although he was to serve as a director of Border Television until 1970. He was also a long-serving member of the board of governors of the British Film Institute, a position which enabled him to give substantial encouragement to young filmmakers. He died at the age of eighty-one at his home, Upper Parrock, a fifteenth-century house in Sussex, on 18 October 1977.

If somehow Ealing had survived the Fifties and remained a going concern, its most likely role would have been that of a television production company. Television is the true inheritor of the Ealing legacy, and not merely in the buildings themselves, which remain intact and fully-working, with the BBC dutifully conscious of the historic importance of their fifty-year-old film production premises. The documentary style of so many Ealing films, which aimed to present their fictional stories against realistic, believable backgrounds, is taken for granted in the majority of television drama series, the intimacy of the living room offering a compelling reason to show credible people in appropriate settings, be it hospital, police station, magistrates' court or street corner. One Ealing character, PC Dixon, became a television regular, and although in the Sixties his cosy, avuncular values came in conflict with the raw, coldly cynical, rough northern world of *Z-Cars*, Ealing had made both possible by pointing the way. Britain in the Forties was not ready for *Z-Cars*.

The key to Ealing lies in the context of its time. Much of the pioneering done there later became commonplace, and the innovations are harder to discern today. There is, however, a tremendous legacy of good films, and today they are finding new and wider audiences from frequent showings on television. In the United States, where Ealing is sometimes thought of as the quintessence of the British cinema, they are treated with great respect, and when recently plans were announced for the remake of some of the great comedies, shifted to American settings such as Las Vegas for *The Lavender Hill Mob*, there was understandable concern. The old films remain safe, however, and every week, somewhere or other throughout the world, *The Ladykillers*, *Kind Hearts and Coronets* and the rest will be entertaining someone. The films can now be bought in the form of video tapes, and Ealing fanciers can watch the great performances of Guinness and Holloway, Hawkins and Mills as often as they wish. The flickering ghosts of three decades ago have achieved their immortality.

Filmography

Associated Talking Pictures productions and others made at Ealing before Balcon

The opening date and title are followed by the US title when it differs, the name(s) of the star(s) in italics, and production – distribution details

September 1930 **Escape**
Sir Gerald du Maurier Produced and directed by Basil Dean
ATP (Beaconsfield)–Radio

November 1930 **Birds of Prey**
(US The Perfect Alibi) *Frank Lawton* Produced and directed by Basil Dean
ATP (Beaconsfield)–Radio

July 1931 **Sally in Our Alley**
Gracie Fields Produced by Basil Dean, directed by Maurice Elvey
ATP (Beaconsfield)–Radio

September 1931 **A Honeymoon Adventure**
(US Footsteps in the Night) *Benita Hume* Produced by Basil Dean, directed by Maurice Elvey
ATP (Beaconsfield)–Radio

March 1932 **The Water Gypsies**
Ann Todd, Ian Hunter Produced by Basil Dean, directed by Maurice Elvey
ATP (Beaconsfield)–Radio

March 1932 **Nine Till Six**
Elizabeth Allan Produced and directed by Basil Dean
ATP (first film made at Ealing)–Radio

May 1932 **The Sign of Four**
Arthur Wontner Produced by Basil Dean, directed by Rowland V. Lee and Graham Cutts
ATP–Radio

June 1932 **The Impassive Footman**
(US Woman in Bondage) *Owen Nares* Produced and directed by Basil Dean
ATP–Radio

July 1932 **Love on the Spot**
Richard Dolman Produced by Basil Dean, directed by Graham Cutts
ATP–Radio

September 1932 **Looking on the Bright Side**
Gracie Fields Produced by Basil Dean, directed by Basil Dean and Graham Cutts
ATP–Radio

October 1932 **The Bailiffs**
Bud Flanagan, Chesney Allen Produced by Clayton Hutton, directed by Frank Cadman
ATP–Ideal

January 1933 **Perfect Understanding**
Gloria Swanson, Laurence Olivier Produced by Gloria Swanson, directed by Cyril Gardner
Gloria Swanson British–United Artists

February 1933 **To Brighton With Gladys**
John Stuart Produced by Harry Cohen, directed by George King
George King–Fox

May 1933 **Three Men in a Boat**
Edmund Breon, William Austin, Billy Milton Produced by Basil Dean, directed by Graham Cutts
ATP–ABFD

May 1933 **Loyalties**
Basil Rathbone Produced and directed by Basil Dean
ATP–ABFD

July 1933 **This Week of Grace**
Gracie Fields Produced by Julius Hagen, directed by Maurice Elvey
Real Art–Radio

September 1933 **Tiger Bay**
Anna May Wong Produced by Bray Wyndham, directed by J. Elder Wills
Wyndham–ABFD

October 1933 **The Right to Live**
Davy Burnaby Directed by Albert Parker
Fox British

November 1933 **The Fortunate Fool**
Hugh Wakefield Produced by Jack Eppel, directed by Norman Walker
ABFD

December 1933 **The House of Trent**
John Stuart Produced by W.G.D. Hutchinson, directed by Norman Walker
B & H–Ensign–Butcher

February 1934 **Autumn Crocus**
Ivor Novello, Fay Compton Produced and directed by Basil Dean
ATP–ABFD

March 1934 **Love, Life and Laughter**
Gracie Fields Produced by Basil Dean, directed by Maurice Elvey
ATP–ABFD

March 1934 **Rolling in Money**
Leslie Sarony Produced by John Barrow, directed by Al Parker
Fox British

May 1934 **The Secret of the Loch**
Seymour Hicks Produced by Bray Wyndham, directed by Milton Rosmer
Wyndham–ABFD

June 1934 **The Perfect Flaw**
Ralph Truman, Naomi Waters Directed by Manning Haynes
Fox British

August 1934 **Java Head**
Anna May Wong, John Loder Produced by Basil Dean, directed by J. Walter Ruben
ATP–ABFD

September 1934 **Sing As We Go**
Gracie Fields Produced and directed by Basil Dean
ATP–ABFD

January 1935 **Lorna Doone**
Victoria Hopper, John Loder Produced and directed by Basil Dean
ATP–ABFD

January 1935 **The Public Life of Henry IX**
Leonard Henry Directed by Bernard Mainwaring
Hammer–MGM

February 1935 **The Dictator**
(US The Loves of a Dictator) *Clive Brook, Madeleine Carroll* Produced by Ludovico Toeplitz, directed by Victor Savile and Alfred Santell
Toeplitz–Gau

March 1935 **Death Drives Through**
Dorothy Bouchier Directed by Edward L. Cahn
Clifford Taylor–ABFD

June 1935 **It Happened in Paris**
John Loder, Nancy Burne Produced by Bray Wyndham, directed by Robert Wyler and Carol Reed
Wyndham–ABFD

June 1935 **Look Up and Laugh**
Gracie Fields Produced and directed by Basil Dean
ATP–ABFD

June 1935 **The Silent Passenger**
John Loder, Peter Haddon Produced by Hugh Perceval, directed by Reginald Denham
Phoenix Films–ABFD

September 1935 **Honeymoon for Three**
Stanley Lupino Produced by Stanley Lupino, directed by Leo Mittler
Gaiety Films–ABFD

October 1935 **Midshipman Easy**
(US Men of the Sea) *Margaret Lockwood,
Hughie Green* Produced by Basil Dean and
Thorold Dickinson, directed by Carol Reed
ATP–ABFD

November 1935 **Play Up the Band**
Stanley Holloway Produced by Basil
Humphreys, directed by Harry Hughes
City–ABFD

November 1935 **No Limit**
George Formby Produced by Basil Dean,
directed by Monty Banks
ATP–ABFD

February 1936 **Whom the Gods Love**
(US Mozart) *Victoria Hopper, John Loder*
Produced and directed by Basil Dean
ATP–ABFD

February 1936 **Cheer Up**
Stanley Lupino Directed by Leo Mittler
Stanley Lupino–ABFD

February 1936 **Queen of Hearts**
Gracie Fields Produced by Basil Dean,
directed by Monty Banks
ATP–ABFD

May 1936 **Laburnum Grove**
Edmund Gwenn, Cedric Hardwicke
Produced by Basil Dean, directed by
Carol Reed
ATP–ABFD

July 1936 **Calling the Tune**
Adele Dixon, Sam Livesey Produced by
Hugh Perceval, directed by Reginald
Denham
Phoenix IFP–ABFD

July 1936 **A Woman Alone**
(US Two Who Dared) *Anna Sten, Henry
Wilcoxon* Produced by Robert Garrett and
Otto Klement, directed by Eugene Frenke
Garrett Klement Pictures–United Artists

August 1936 **Guilty Melody**
Nils Asther, Gitta Alpar Produced by F.
Deutschmeister, directed by Richard
Potter
Franco London–ABFD

September 1936 **The Beloved Vagabond**
Maurice Chevalier, Margaret Lockwood
Produced by Ludovico Toeplitz, directed
by Kurt Bernhardt
Toeplitz Productions–ABFD

September 1936 **The Lonely Road**
(US Scotland Yard Commands) *Clive
Brook, Victoria Hopper* Produced by Basil
Dean, directed by James Flood
ATP–ABFD

September 1936 **Keep Your Seats Please**
George Formby, Florence Desmond
Produced by Basil Dean, directed by
Monty Banks
ATP–ABFD

October 1936 **Tropical Trouble**
*Douglass Montgomery, Alfred Drayton,
Betty Ann Davies* Produced by Basil
Humphrys, directed by Harry Hughes
City–General Film Distributors

November 1936 **Dreams Come True**
Frances Day, Nelson Keys, Hugh Wakefield
Produced by Ilya Salkind and John
Gossage, directed by Reginald Denham
London and Continental–Reunion

November 1936 **The House of the
Spaniard**
Peter Haddon, Brigitte Horney Produced
by Hugh Perceval, directed by Reginald
Denham
IFP Phoenix–ABFD

December 1936 **Olympic Honeymoon**
Claude Hulbert, Monty Banks Produced by
Sidney Morgan, directed by Alfred
Goulding
London Screenplays Fanfare–RKO

January 1937 **Take a Chance**
Claude Hulbert, Binnie Hale Produced by
Harcourt Templeman, directed by
Sinclair Hill
Grosvenor–ABFD

March 1937 **Feather Your Nest**
George Formby, Polly Ward Produced by
Basil Dean, directed by William Beaudine
ATP–ABFD

April 1937 **Secret Lives**
(US I Married a Spy) *Neil Hamilton,
Brigitte Horney* Produced by Hugh
Perceval, directed by Edmond T. Greville
IFP Phoenix–ABFD

April 1937 **The Show Goes On**
Gracie Fields, Owen Nares Produced and
directed by Basil Dean
ATP–ABFD

April 1937 **The High Command**
James Mason, Lucie Mannheim Produced
by Gordon Wong Wellesley, directed by
Thorold Dickinson
Fanfare–ABFD

July 1937 **Who's Your Lady Friend?**
Frances Day, Vic Oliver Produced by
Martin Sabine, directed by Carol Reed
Dorian–ABFD

August 1937 **The Girl in the Taxi**
Frances Day, Henri Garat Produced by

Kurt Bernhardt and Eugene Tuscherer,
directed by André Berthomieu
British Unity–ABFD

August 1937 **Brief Ecstasy**
Paul Lukas, Hugh Williams, Linden Travers
Produced by Hugh Perceval, directed by
Edmond T. Greville
IFP Phoenix–ABFD

August 1937 **Keep Fit**
George Formby, Kay Walsh Produced by
Basil Dean, directed by Anthony
Kimmins
ATP–ABFD

February 1938 **I See Ice**
George Formby, Kay Walsh Produced by
Basil Dean, directed by Anthony
Kimmins
ATP–ABFD

October 1938 **Penny Paradise**
Jimmy O'Dea, Betty Driver Produced by
Basil Dean and Jack Kitchin, directed by
Carol Reed
ATP–ABFD

November 1938 **It's in the Air**
(US George Takes the Air) *George
Formby, Polly Ward* Produced by Basil
Dean, directed by Anthony Kimmins
ATP Eltham–ABFD

**Ealing films during the
Balcon era, 1938–1959**

The Gaunt Stranger
US *The Phantom Strikes*
Director: Walter Forde
Associate producer: S. C. Balcon
Cast: Sonnie Hale (Sam Hackett)
Wilfrid Lawson (Maurice Meister)
Louise Henry (Cora Ann Milton)
Alexander Knox (Dr Lomond)
Patricia Roc (Mary Lenley)
Patrick Barr (Insp. Wembury)
John Longden (Insp. Bliss)
Peter Croft (John Lenley)
George Merritt (Sgt. Carter)
Script: Sidney Gilliat, from *The Ringer*
by Edgar Wallace
Photography: Ronald Neame
Art direction: O. F. Werndorff
Editing: Charles Saunders
Opening: November 1938
Running time: 73 mins.
 A suspense thriller in which virtually
the entire cast is under suspicion of
murder. This is the third of four film
versions, one silent. John Longden played
a police inspector in both this and the
preceding talkie of 1931.

The Ware Case
Director: Robert Stevenson

Associate producer: S. C. Balcon
Cast: Clive Brook (Sir Hubert Ware)
Jane Baxter (Lady Margaret Ware)
Barry K. Barnes (Michael Ede)
Francis L. Sullivan (Attorney General)
C. V. France (Judge)
Peter Bull (Eustace Ede)
John Laurie (Hewson)
Ernest Thesiger (Carter)
Dorothy Seacombe (Mrs Slade)
Athene Seyler (Mrs Pinto)
Elliot Mason (Juror)
Frank Cellier (Skinner)
Wally Patch (Taxi Driver)
Script: Robert Stevenson, Roland
Pertwee from the play by G.P. Bancroft,
with additional dialogue by E.V.H.
Emmett
Photography: Ronald Neame
Art direction: O. F. Werndorff
Editing: Charles Saunders
Music: Ernest Irving
Opening: December 1938
Running time: 79 mins.
A play that had been filmed twice as a
silent. Clive Brook plays a part originally
performed by Sir Gerald du Maurier, as a
baronet who is acquitted of murdering his
wife's brother and then commits suicide.
A stagey, melodramatic story, partly set in
a reconstruction of the Old Bailey.

Trouble Brewing
Director: Anthony Kimmins
Producer: Jack Kitchin
Cast: George Formby (George Gullip)
Googie Withers (Mary Brown)
Gus McNaughton (Bill Pike)
Garry Marsh (A. G. Brady)
C. Denier Warren (Major Hopkins)
Beatrix Fielden-Kaye (Housekeeper)
Joss Ambler (Lord Redhill)
Ronald Shiner (Bridgewater)
Martita Hunt (Madame Berdi)
Basil Radford (Guest)
Esma Cannon (Maid)
Script: Anthony Kimmins, Angus
MacPhail, Michael Hogan
Photography: Ronald Neame
Art direction: Wilfred Shingleton
Musical director: Ernest Irving
Editing: Ernest Aldridge
Opening: March 1939
Running time: 87 mins.
Typical George Formby comedy in
which he plays a newspaper compositor
with ambitions to be a detective, who
succeeds in unmasking a gang of
counterfeiters, after adventures on the
racecourse and in the wrestling ring with
Terrible Tiger. The dénouement occurs in
a brewery.

Let's Be Famous
Director: Walter Forde

Cast: Jimmy O'Dea (Jimmy Houlihan)
Betty Driver (Betty Pinbright)
Sonnie Hale (Finch)
Patrick Barr (Johnnie Blake)
Basil Radford (Watson)
Milton Rosmer (Albert Pinbright)
Lena Brown (Polly Pinbright)
Garry Marsh (BBC official)
Hay Plumb (Announcer)
Alf Goddard (Battling Bulger)
Henry Hallett (Grenville)
Script: Roger Macdougall, Allan
Mackinnon
Photography: Ronald Neame, Gordon
Dines
Art direction: O. F. Werndorff
Editing: Ray Pitt
Songs: Noel Gay
Opening: March 1939
Running time: 83 mins.
Comedy with a setting in advertising
and radio, with a performance by Betty
Driver reminiscent of Gracie Fields, the
erstwhile star at Ealing.

The Four Just Men
US *The Secret Four*
Director: Walter Forde
Associate producer: S. C. Balcon
Cast: Hugh Sinclair (Humphrey
Mansfield)
Griffith Jones (James Brodie)
Francis L. Sullivan (Leon Poiccard)
Frank Lawton (Terry)
Anna Lee (Ann Lodge)
Basil Sydney (Frank Snell)
Alan Napier (Sir Hamar Ryman)
Lydia Sherwood (Myra Hastings)
Roland Pertwee (Mr Hastings)
Edward Chapman (B. J. Burrell)
George Merritt (Insp. Falmouth)
Garry Marsh (Bill Grant)
Eliot Makeham (Simmons)
Frederick Piper (Pickpocket)
Ellaline Terriss (Lady Willoughby)
Athole Stewart (Commissioner)
Script: Roland Pertwee, Angus MacPhail,
Sergei Nolbandov
Photography: Ronald Neame
Art direction: Wilfred Shingleton
Music: Ernest Irving
Editing: Stephen Dalby
Opening: June 1939
Running time: 85 mins.
Another Edgar Wallace story, first
filmed in 1921 as a silent, but in this 1939
version fulfilling a topical patriotic need.
The four are an assorted band of
successful men who secretly join together
to protect the British Empire from foreign
megalomaniacs. It is an entertaining if
implausible thriller. The 1944 reissue had
an updated and amended ending to bring
in the fact of the Second World War.

There Ain't No Justice
Director: Penrose Tennyson
Associate producer: Sergei Nolbandov
Cast: James Hanley (Tommy Mutch)
Edward Rigby (Pa Mutch)
Mary Clare (Ma Mutch)
Phyllis Stanley (Elsie Mutch)
Edward Chapman (Sammy Sanders)
Jill Furse (Connie Fletcher)
Nan Hopkins (Dot Ducrow)
Richard Ainley (Billy Frost)
Michael Wilding (Len Charteris)
Gus McNaughton (Alfie Norton)
Richard Norris (Stan)
Al Millen (Perce)
Script: Penrose Tennyson, Sergei
Nolbandov, James Curtis, from a novel
by James Curtis
Photography: Mutz Greenbaum
Art direction: Wilfred Shingleton
Editing: Ray Pitt
Music: Ernest Irving
Opening: June 1939
Running time: 83 mins.
Pen Tennyson's first film was a
'programmer' about a young boxer in a
working-class London milieu who, on
turning professional, learns that his fights
are being fixed, with subsequent damage
to his conscience.

Young Man's Fancy
Director: Robert Stevenson
Associate producer: S. C. Balcon
Cast: Griffith Jones (Lord Alban)
Anna Lee (Ada)
Seymour Hicks (Duke of Beaumont)
Martita Hunt (Duchess of Beaumont)
Felix Aylmer (Sir Caleb Crowther)
Meriel Forbes (Miss Crowther)
Billy Bennett (Capt. Boumphrey)
Edward Rigby (Gray)
Phyllis Monkman (Esme)
Francis L. Sullivan (Blackbeard)
Athene Seyler (Milliner)
George Benson (Booking Clerk)
George Carney (Chairman)
Aimos (Tramp)
Script: Roland Pertwee, from a story by
Robert Stevenson, with additional
dialogue by E.V.H. Emmett, Rodney
Ackland
Photography: Ronald Neame
Art direction: Wilfred Shingleton
Editing: Charles Saunders, Ralph
Kemplen
Music: Ernest Irving
Opening: August 1939
Running time: 77 mins.
A romantic comedy set in 1870 in
which a young nobleman resists his
domineering mother's attempt to force
him into an unsuitable marriage, and falls
in love instead with a human cannonball.
They elope to Paris, facing both the siege

and parental wrath. Naturally, all ends well.

Cheer Boys Cheer
Director: Walter Forde
Associate producer: S. C. Balcon
Cast: Edmund Gwenn (Edward Ironside)
Peter Coke (John Ironside)
C. V. France (Tom Greenleaf)
Nova Pilbeam (Margaret Greenleaf)
Jimmy O'Dea (Matt Boyle)
Alexander Knox (Saunders)
Graham Moffatt (Albert)
Moore Marriott (Geordie)
Ivor Barnard (Naseby)
Jean Webster Brough (Belle)
Script: Roger Macdougall, Allan Mackinnon, from a story by Ian Dalrymple, Donald Bull
Photography: Ronald Neame
Art direction: Wilfred Shingleton
Editing: Ray Pitt
Music: Ernest Irving
Opening: August 1939
Running time: 85 mins.

Early Ealing comedy set in the world of brewing, with a traditional family firm fighting a takeover by the slickly-organized modern giant. Familiar farce elements such as mistaken identity, messy fights, slapstick, drunkenness, are mixed in the brew.

Come On George
Director: Anthony Kimmins
Producer: Jack Kitchin
Cast: George Formby (George)
Pat Kirkwood (Ann Johnson)
Joss Ambler (Sir Charles Bailey)
Meriel Forbes (Monica Bailey)
Cyril Raymond (Jimmy Taylor)
George Hayes (Bannerman)
George Carney (Sgt. Johnson)
Ronald Shiner (Nat)
Gibb McLaughlin (Dr MacGregor)
James Hayter (Banker)
Hal Gordon (Stableboy)
Davy Burnaby (Col. Bollinger)
C. Denier Warren (Barker)
Syd Cronley (Policeman)
Script: Anthony Kimmins, Leslie Arliss, Val Valentine
Photography: Ronald Neame
Art direction: Wilfred Shingleton
Editing: Ray Pitt
Music: Ernest Irving
Opening: November 1939
Running time: 88 mins.

George Formby befriends a horse, only to discover just before a big race that it destroys any jockey who comes near it. There are inevitably bands of crooks, car chases, a comic brain specialist, and a girl whose true love enables our hero to overcome his fear.

Return to Yesterday
Director: Robert Stevenson
Associate producer: S. C. Balcon
Cast: Clive Brook (Robert Maine)
Anna Lee (Carol Sands)
David Tree (Peter Thropp)
O. B. Clarence (Truscott)
Dame May Whitty (Mrs Truscott)
Hartley Power (Regan)
Milton Rosmer (Sambourne)
Olga Lindo (Grace Sambourne)
Garry Marsh (Charlie Miller)
Elliot Mason (Mrs Priskin)
Arthur Margetson (Osbert)
Frank Pettingell (Prendergast)
David Horne (Morrison)
H. F. Maltby (Inspector)
Wally Patch (Watchman)
Script: Robert Stevenson, Roland Pertwee, Angus MacPhail, from the play *Goodness How Sad* by Robert Morley
Photography: Ronald Neame
Art direction: Wilfred Shingleton
Editing: Charles Saunders
Music: Ernest Irving
Opening: January 1940
Running time: 69 mins.

A successful actor returns to his home town and falls in love with an aspiring young actress for whom he is much too old. He parts wiser and sadder. It is a stagey film about a stagey subject.

The Proud Valley
Director: Penrose Tennyson
Associate producer: Sergei Nolbandov
Cast: Paul Robeson (David Goliath)
Edward Rigby (Bert)
Edward Chapman (Dick Parry)
Rachel Thomas (Mrs Parry)
Simon Lack (Emlyn Parry)
Janet Johnson (Gwen Owen)
Dilys Davies (Mrs Owen)
Clifford Evans (Seth Jones)
Jack Jones (Thomas)
Allan Jeayes (Mr Trevor)
Edward Lexy (Commissionaire)
Noel Howlett (Clerk)
Script: Penrose Tennyson, Jack Jones, Louis Goulding, from a story by Herbert Marshall, Alfredda Brilliant
Photography: Glen MacWilliams, Roy Kellino
Art direction: Wilfred Shingleton
Editing: Ray Pitt
Music: Mendelssohn and others, arranged by Ernest Irving
Opening: March 1940
Running time: 76 mins.

Drama set in the Welsh coalfields in the slump years. A black American gets a job in the pit only to lose it when the colliery is closed following an accident. The miners march on London to petition the owners, but the war starts and there is a

national need for coal. The film ends with the newcomer's death as he tries to rescue his friends in another pit collapse.

Let George Do It
Director: Marcel Varnel
Associate producer: Basil Dearden
Cast: George Formby (George)
Phyllis Calvert (Mary)
Garry Marsh (Mendez)
Romney Brent (Slim)
Bernard Lee (Nelson)
Coral Browne (Ivy)
Diana Beaumont (Greta)
Torin Thatcher (U-boat Commander)
Donald Calthrop (Strickland)
Ronald Shiner (Musician)
Bill Shine (Steward)
Albert Lieven (Radio Operator)
Hal Gordon (Arbuckle)
Script: John Dighton, Austin Melford, Angus MacPhail, Basil Dearden
Photography: Ronald Neame
Art direction: Wilfred Shingleton
Editing: Ray Pitt
Musical director: Ernest Irving
Opening: July 1940
Running time: 82 mins.

George, a member of a pier concert party, inadvertently finds himself on a boat to Bergen instead of Blackpool, and at once up to his neck in fifth-column intrigue in Norway before the Nazi invasion. He thwarts a U-boat attack and returns covered in glory, with a beautiful British spy on his arm.

Convoy
Director: Penrose Tennyson
Associate producer: Sergei Nolbandov
Cast: Clive Brook (Capt. Armitage)
John Clements (Lieut. Cranford)
Judy Campbell (Lucy Armitage)
Penelope Dudley Ward (Mabel)
Allan Jeayes (Cdr. Blount)
Harold Warrender (Lieut-Cdr. Martin)
Michael Wilding (Dot)
Stewart Granger (Sutton)
David Hutcheson (Capt. Sandeman)
Edward Chapman (Capt. Eckersley)
Charles Farrell (Walker)
Edward Rigby (Matthews)
Charles Williams (Shorty Howard)
George Carney (Bates)
Al Millen (Knowles)
John Laurie (Gates)
Albert Lieven (U-boat Commander)
Hay Petrie (Skipper)
Mervyn Johns (Mate)
Edward Lexy (Skipper)
John Glyn Jones (Mate)
Script: Penrose Tennyson, Patrick Kirwan
Photography: Wilkie Cooper, Gordon Dines

Art direction: Wilfred Shingleton
Editing: Ray Pitt
Music: Ernest Irving
Opening: July 1940
Running time: 90 mins.

Ealing's first serious war film and Pen Tennyson's last. It shows the way the Royal Navy guarded merchant convoys, and how an escort ship takes on a German pocket battleship. The consensus was that propaganda had combined well with entertainment. A boyish Stewart Granger appears briefly on Clive Brook's bridge.

Saloon Bar
Director: Walter Forde
Associate producer: Culley Forde
Cast: Gordon Harker (Joe Harris)
Elizabeth Allan (Queenie)
Mervyn Johns (Wickers)
Anna Konstam (Ivy)
Joyce Barbour (Sally)
Judy Campbell (Doris)
Cyril Raymond (Harry Small)
Helena Pickard (Mrs Small)
Laurence Kitchin (Peter)
Mavis Villiers (Joan)
Alec Clunes (Eddie Graves)
Norman Pierce (Bill Hoskins)
Felix Aylmer (Mayor)
O. B. Clarence (Sir Archibald)
Manning Whiley (Evangelist)
Al Millen (Fred)
Roddy Hughes (Doctor)
Script: Angus MacPhail, John Dighton, from the play by Frank Harvey Jr
Photography: Ronald Neame
Art direction: Wilfred Shingleton
Editing: Ray Pitt
Music: Ernest Irving
Opening: October 1940
Running time: 76 mins.

A talkative, stagey thriller featuring Gordon Harker, the professional cockney, as a bookie who becomes an amateur detective, solving the identity of the murderer before closing time, even though it is the night of the execution. An authentic pub atmosphere does not disguise the pedestrian pace.

Sailors Three
US *Three Cockeyed Sailors*
Director: Walter Forde
Associate producer: Culley Forde
Cast: Tommy Trinder (Tommy Taylor)
Claude Hulbert ('Admiral')
Michael Wilding (Johnny)
Carla Lehmann (Jane)
Henry Hewitt (Professor Pilkington)
Jeanne de Casalis (Mrs Pilkington)
James Hayter (Hans)
John Laurie (MacNab)
Harold Warrender (Mate)
Manning Whiley (German Commander)

Allan Jeayes (British Commander)
Alec Clunes (British Pilot)
Derek Elphinstone (Observer)
John Glyn Jones (Best Man)
Julian Vedey (Resident)
Danny Green (Bouncer)
E.V.H. Emmett (Newsreel Commentator)
Robert Rendel (Captain)
Script: Angus MacPhail, John Dighton, Austin Melford
Photography: Gunther Krampf
Art direction: Wilfred Shingleton
Editing: Ray Pitt
Musical director: Ernest Irving
Opening: December 1940
Running time: 86 mins.

A comedy with songs, in which a trio of British matelots find themselves, after a binge in a South American port, on a German battleship. It was Forde's farewell to Ealing, and the end of the *ancien régime* as Balcon got into his stride.

Spare a Copper
Director: John Paddy Carstairs
Associate producer: Basil Dearden
Cast: George Formby (George)
Dorothy Hyson (Jane)
Bernard Lee (Jake)
John Warwick (Shaw)
Eliot Makeham (Fuller)
George Merritt (Brewster)
Warburton Gamble (Sir Robert Dyer)
John Turnbull (Insp. Richards)
Edward Lexy (Night Watchman)
Ellen Pollock (Lady Hardstaff)
Charles Carson (Admiral)
Grace Arnold (Customer)
Jack Melford (Dame)
Hal Gordon (Sergeant)
Jimmy Godden (Manager)
Script: Roger Macdougall, Basil Dearden, Austin Melford
Photography: Bryan Langley
Art direction: Wilfred Shingleton
Editing: Ray Pitt
Music: Louis Levy
Opening: December 1940
Running time: 77 mins.

The fifth-column menace is flourishing on Merseyside, with well-placed traitors sabotaging the shipyards. George is a wartime special constable who overcomes his ineptitude to foil a dastardly Nazi plot.

The Ghost of St Michael's
Director: Marcel Varnel
Associate producer: Basil Dearden
Cast: Will Hay (William Lamb)
Claude Hulbert (Hilary Teasdale)
Charles Hawtrey (Percy)
Derek Blomfield (Sunshine)
Felix Aylmer (Dr Winter)
Raymond Huntley (Mr Humphries)

Elliot Mason (Mrs Wigmore)
John Laurie (Jamie)
Roddy Hughes (Amberley)
Hay Petrie (Procurator Fiscal)
Brefni O'Rourke (Sgt. Macfarlane)
Manning Whiley (Stock)
Script: Angus MacPhail, John Dighton
Photography: Derek Williams
Art direction: Wilfred Shingleton in consultation with Alberto Cavalcanti
Editing: E.B. Jarvis
Opening: April 1941
Running time: 82 mins.

Will Hay's first Ealing film. He plays a teacher (the job, as usual, acquired through bogus references) in a school that has been evacuated to a remote Scottish castle, where the matron turns out to be a Nazi spy.

Turned Out Nice Again
Director: Marcel Varnel
Associate producer: Basil Dearden
Cast: George Formby (George Pearson)
Peggy Bryan (Lydia)
Elliot Mason (Mrs Pearson)
Edward Chapman (Uncle Arnold)
O. B. Clarence (Mr Dawson)
Mackenzie Ward (Gerald Dawson)
Ronald Ward (Nelson)
John Salew (Largos)
Wilfrid Hyde White (Removal Man)
Michael Rennie (Diner)
Hay Petrie (Drunk)
Script: Austin Melford, John Dighton, Basil Dearden, from the play *As You Are* by Hugh Mills, Wells Root
Photography: Gordon Dines
Art direction: Wilfred Shingleton, in consultation with Alberto Cavalcanti
Editing: Robert Hamer
Music: Ernest Irving
Opening: August 1941
Running time: 81 mins.

George Formby's last Ealing film had a more serious plot than usual, with no slapstick chases. He is in the textile industry, in a firm that is declining because it will not move with the times. He comes across a revolutionary new yarn but his employer is unimpressed and fires him. His wife saves the day. A sort of precursor to *The Man in the White Suit*.

Ships with Wings
Director: Sergei Nolbandov
Associate producer: S. C. Balcon
Cast: John Clements (Lieut. Dick Stacey)
Michael Wilding (Lieut. Grant)
Michael Rennie (Lieut. Peter Maxwell)
Hugh Burden (Lieut. Wetherby)
Jane Baxter (Celia Wetherby)
Leslie Banks (Admiral Wetherby)
Basil Sydney (Capt. Fairfax)
Ann Todd (Kay Gordon)

Betty Marsden (Jean)
Edward Chapman (Papadopoulos)
Hugh Williams (Wagner)
Frank Pettingell (Fields)
Frank Cellier (Gen. Scarapa)
Cecil Parker (German Air Marshal)
John Stuart (Commander Hood)
Charles Victor (MacDermott)
John Laurie (Reid)
Morland Graham (CPO Marsden)
Script: Patrick Kirwan, Austin Melford,
Diana Morgan, Sergei Nolbandov
Photography: Mutz Greenbaum, Wilkie
Cooper (interiors), Roy Kellino, Eric
Cross (exteriors)
Art direction: Wilfred Shingleton
Editing: Robert Hamer
Music: Geoffrey Wright
Opening: November 1941
Running time: 103 mins.
This dramatic story involving life in
the Fleet Air Arm was marred by
unconvincing modelwork, as well as a
convoluted plot. The film was attacked by
Churchill, though not, it would seem, for
aesthetic reasons.

The Black Sheep of Whitehall
Directors: Will Hay, Basil Dearden
Associate producer: S. C. Balcon
Cast: Will Hay (William Davis)
Henry Hewitt (Professor Davys)
John Mills (Bobby)
Basil Sydney (Costello)
Felix Aylmer (Crabtree)
Frank Cellier (Dr Innsbach)
Joss Ambler (Sir John)
Thora Hird (Joyce)
Leslie Mitchell (Interviewer)
George Woodbridge (Hospital Nurse)
Roddy Hughes (Official)
Katie Johnson (Train Passenger)
Margaret Halstan (Matron)
Script: Angus MacPhail, John Dighton
Photography: Gunther Krampf
Art direction: Tom Morahan
Editing: Ray Pitt
Opening: January 1942
Running time: 80 mins.
Will Hay farce in which an indigent
faker is mistaken for an economics
professor who is meanwhile kidnapped by
Nazi spies. Will Hay spends much of the
film disguised as a nursing sister, but
there is a lively chase sequence near the
close. John Mills is an unhappy stooge.

The Big Blockade
Director: Charles Frend
Associate producer: Alberto Cavalcanti
Cast: Leslie Banks (Taylor)
Michael Redgrave (Russian)
John Mills (Tom)
Michael Rennie (George)
Will Hay (Skipper)

Bernard Miles (Mate)
Frank Cellier (Schneider)
Robert Morley (Von Geiselbrecht)
Alfred Drayton (Direktor)
Marius Goring (Propaganda Officer)
Austin Trevor (U-boat Captain)
Albert Lieven (Gunter)
Joss Ambler (Stoltenhoff)
George Woodbridge (Quisling)
Michael Wilding (Captain)
John Stuart (Naval Officer)
Ronald Adam (German Businessman)
Frederick Piper (Malta Official)
Morland Graham (Dock Official)
David Evans (David)
Quentin Reynolds (Himself)
David Bowes-Lyon (Himself)
Frank Owen (Himself)
Hugh Dalton (Himself)
Script: Angus MacPhail
Commentary: Frank Owen
Photography: Wilkie Cooper
Art direction: Tom Morahan
Editing: Charles Crichton, Compton
Bennett
Music: Richard Addinsell
Opening: January 1942
Running time: 73 mins.
Overt propaganda in the form of
entertainment, the purpose of this film
was to explain the meaning of economic
warfare, by means of dramatized
documentary. The effect was spotty and
often unintentionally comical.

The Foreman Went to France
US *Somewhere in France*
Director: Charles Frend
Associate producer: Alberto Cavalcanti
Cast: Tommy Trinder (Tommy)
Clifford Evans (Ted Carrick)
Constance Cummings (Girl)
Gordon Jackson (Jock)
Robert Morley (Mayor)
Paul Bonifas (Prefect)
Ernest Milton (Stationmaster)
François Sully [Francis L. Sullivan]
(Skipper)
John Williams ('Captain')
Ronald Adam (Sir Charles Fawcett)
Charles Victor (Spotter)
Bill Blewitt (Spotter)
Mervyn Johns (Official)
John Boxer (Official)
Anita Palacine (Barmaid)
Thora Hird (Barmaid)
Script: John Dighton, Angus MacPhail,
Leslie Arliss from a story by J. B.
Priestley, based on the experiences of
Melbourne Johns to whom the film is
dedicated
Photography: Wilkie Cooper
Art direction: Tom Morahan
Editing: Robert Hamer
Music: William Walton

Opening: April 1942
Running time: 87 mins.
A vital piece of machinery is recovered
from under the noses of the advancing
Germans during the fall of France. The
story is based on fact, but the adventures
of the hero, who en route meets two
stranded tommies and a pretty American
girl, are piled on thickly. An Ealing
preoccupation with spies and traitors is
exercised when the team is nearly trapped
by a bogus British officer, spotted because
his badges are not quite right.

Next of Kin
Director: Thorold Dickinson
Associate producer: S. C. Balcon
Cast: Mervyn Johns (Davis)
John Chandos (Contact)
Nova Pilbeam (Beppie Leemans)
Stephen Murray (Mr Barratt)
David Hutcheson (Intelligence Officer)
Reginald Tate (Major Richards)
Geoffrey Hibbert (Private John)
Philip Friend (Lieut. Cummins)
Basil Sydney (Naval Captain)
Jack Hawkins (Major)
Brefni O'Rourke (Brigadier)
Frederick Leister (Colonel)
Charles Victor (Seaman)
Torin Thatcher (German General)
Mary Clare (Miss Webster)
Phyllis Stanley (Miss Clare)
Thora Hird (ATS Girl)
Joss Ambler (Mr Vernon)
Basil Radford (Careless Talker)
Naunton Wayne (Careless Talker)
Alexander Field (Private Durnford)
Script: Thorold Dickinson, Angus
MacPhail, John Dighton, with Captain
Sir Basil Bartlett (Military Supervisor)
Photography: Ernest Palmer
Art direction: Tom Morahan
Editing: Ray Pitt
Music: William Walton
Opening: May 1942
Running time: 102 mins.
The so-called 'Hush-Hush Film' was
made at the invitation but minimal
funding of the War Office, with Ealing
putting up the rest of the finance. It told
of the infiltration of a German spy into a
coastal area, and the ease with which he
thwarted a surprise raid on France, with
the resulting deaths of many British
commandos. Churchill thought it bad for
public morale.

The Goose Steps Out
Directors: Will Hay, Basil Dearden
Associate producer: S. C. Balcon
Cast: Will Hay (William Potts/Muller)
Frank Pettingell (Professor Hoffman)
Julien Mitchell (Gen. von Glotz)
Raymond Lovell (Schmidt)

Anne Firth (Lena)
Charles Hawtrey (Max)
Leslie Harcourt (Vagel)
Barry Morse (Kurt)
Peter Ustinov (Krauss)
Jeremy Hawk (ADC)
Aubrey Mallalieu (Rector)
Lawrence O'Madden (Colonel Truscott)
Script: John Dighton, Angus MacPhail,
from a story by Bernard Miles, Reg
Groves
Photography: Ernest Palmer
Art direction: Tom Morahan
Editing: Ray Pitt
Music: Bretton Byrd
Opening: August 1942
Running time: 79 mins.

Will Hay is parachuted into Germany,
charged with getting a sample secret
weapon from a research laboratory, and
finds himself teaching Hitler Youth how
to be spies. Abetted by disaffected class
members he escapes to England at the
controls of a stolen aircraft. Without
exception, the German ruling classes are
shown as idiots.

Nine Men
Director: Harry Watt
Associate producer: Charles Crichton
Cast: Jack Lambert (Sgt. Watson)
Gordon Jackson (Young 'Un)
Frederick Piper ('Banger' Hill)
Grant Sutherland (Jock Scott)
Bill Blewitt (Bill Parker)
Eric Micklewood ('Booky' Lee)
John Varley ('Dusty' Johnstone)
Jack Horsman (Joe Harvey)
Richard Wilkinson (Officer)
Giulio Finzi (Italian Mechanic)
Script: Harry Watt, from a story by
Gerald Kersh
Photography: Roy Kellino
Art direction: Duncan Sutherland
Editing: Charles Crichton
Supervising editor: Sidney Cole
Music: John Greenwood
Opening: January 1943
Running time: 68 mins.

A bunch of recruits are told the story of
a group of soldiers cut off in the North
African desert who hold out against the
enemy until they are relieved. Harry
Watt, triumphant from his documentary
of an RAF Wellington crew, *Target for
Tonight*, directed on a shoestring.

The Bells Go Down
Director: Basil Dearden
Associate producer: S. C. Balcon
Cast: Tommy Trinder (Tommy Turk)
Beatrice Varley (Ma Turk)
James Mason (Ted Robbins)
Norman Pierce (Pa Robbins)

Muriel George (Ma Robbins)
Mervyn Johns (Sam)
Finlay Currie (Station Officer McFarlane)
Billy Hartnell (Brooks)
Philip Friend (Bob)
Meriel Forbes (Susie)
Philippa Hiatt (Nan)
Ralph Michael (Dunkirk Survivor)
Charles Victor (Dunkirk Survivor)
Johnny Schofield (Milkman)
Grace Arnold (Canteen Lady)
Julian Vedey (Lou Freeman)
Lesley Brook (June)
Script: Roger Macdougall, Stephen Black
Photography: Ernest Palmer
Art direction: Michael Relph
Editing: Mary Habberfield
Supervising editor: Sidney Cole
Music: Roy Douglas
Opening: April 1943
Running time: 90 mins.

Documentary-style drama set in the
London Blitz with an assortment of
auxiliary firemen coping with incendiary
destruction. Tommy Trinder, in spite of
his cheery persona, dies saving his
peppery station officer. Basil Dearden
however managed to avoid too many
heroic clichés, and the film is a creditable
portrayal of the hard civilian war.

Undercover
US *Underground Guerrillas*
Director: Sergei Nolbandov
Associate producer: S. C. Balcon
Cast: John Clements (Milosh Petrovitch)
Tom Walls (Kossan Petrovitch)
Rachel Thomas (Maria Petrovitch)
Stephen Murray (Dr Stevan Petrovitch)
Mary Morris (Anna Petrovitch)
Godfrey Tearle (Gen. von Staengel)
Robert Harris (Col. von Brock)
Michael Wilding (Constantine)
Charles Victor (Sergeant)
Niall McGinnis (Dr Jordan)
Ivor Barnard (Stationmaster)
Stanley Baker (Peter)
Norman Pierce (Lieut. Frank)
Script: John Dighton, Monja
Danischewsky, Sergei Nolbandov, Milosh
Sokulich, from a story by George
Slocombe
Photography: Wilkie Cooper
Art direction: Duncan Sutherland
Editing: Eileen Boland
Supervising editor: Sidney Cole
Music: Fredric Austin
Opening: July 1943
Running time: 80 mins.

War story set in Yugoslavia, although
shot in Wales. Partisanship appears to be
a family affair, with the son of a guerrilla
leader remaining in the city, posing as a
quisling, in order to aid the cause. It is
one of the less convincing Ealing war

films; somehow the Petrovitch family
seems much too British.

My Learned Friend
Directors: Will Hay, Basil Dearden
Associate producer: S. C. Balcon
Cast: Will Hay (William Fitch)
Claude Hulbert (Claude Babbington)
Mervyn Johns (Grimshaw)
Laurence Hanray (Sir Norman)
Aubrey Mallalieu (Magistrate)
Charles Victor ('Safety' Wilson)
Derna [later Hy] Hazell (Gloria)
Leslie Harcourt (Barman)
Eddie Phillips ('Basher' Blake)
G. H. Mulcaster (Dr Scudamore)
Ernest Thesiger (Ferris)
Lloyd Pearson (Col. Chudleigh)
Gibb McLaughlin (Butler)
Maudie Edwards (Aladdin)
Script: John Dighton, Angus MacPhail
Photography: Wilkie Cooper
Art direction: Michael Relph
Editing: Charles Hasse
Music: Ernest Irving
Opening: June 1943
Running time: 74 mins.

Will Hay's last film is something of a
black comedy in which he and Claude
Hulbert realize that a madman is killing
everyone on a private hit list which
includes them. The film is basically a
chase, with sequences in a tacky
provincial pantomime, an East End
drinking den, and a climax with the duo
disguised as Yeomen of the Guard
dangling from the clockface of Big Ben.

Went the Day Well?
US *48 Hours*
Director: Alberto Cavalcanti
Associate producer: S. C. Balcon
Cast: Leslie Banks (Oliver Wilsford)
Basil Sydney (Major Ortler)
Marie Lohr (Mrs Frazer)
Valerie Taylor (Nora)
C. V. France (Vicar)
Frank Lawton (Tom Sturry)
Elizabeth Allan (Peggy)
Thora Hird (Land Girl)
Mervyn Johns (Sims)
John Slater (German Sergeant)
David Farrar (German Officer)
Muriel George (Mrs Collins)
Patricia Hayes (Daisy)
Edward Rigby (Poacher)
Harry Fowler (George Truscott)
Norman Pierce (Jim Sturry)
Grace Arnold (Mrs Owen)
Script: John Dighton, Diana Morgan,
Angus MacPhail, from a story by Graham
Greene
Photography: Wilkie Cooper
Art direction: Tom Morahan
Editing: Sidney Cole

Music: William Walton
Opening: October 1943
Running time: 92 mins.

An English village is taken over by German paratroops disguised as British soldiers on an exercise. When the villagers learn of the duplicity they react fiercely, mustering an uncharacteristic fervour to fight the enemy on the home turf. A rare Graham Greene contribution to Ealing.

San Demetrio London
Director: Charles Frend
Associate producer: Robert Hamer
Cast: Walter Fitzgerald (Chief Engineer Pollard)
Ralph Michael (Hawkins)
Frederick Piper (Bosun Fletcher)
Gordon Jackson (John Jamieson)
Mervyn Johns (John Boyle)
Robert Beatty ('Yank' Preston)
Charles Victor (Deckhand)
James McKechnie (Colum McNeil)
Arthur Young (Capt. Waite)
Nigel Clarke (Dodds)
David Horne (Mr Justice Langton)
Barry Letts (John Jones)
Lawrence O'Madden (Capt. Fogarty Fegan)
Script: Robert Hamer, Charles Frend, from the factual narrative by F. Tennyson Jesse
Photography: Ernest Palmer
Art direction: Duncan Sutherland
Editing: Eily Boland
Supervising editor: Sidney Cole
Music: John Greenwood
Opening: December 1943
Running time: 104 mins.

Heroic war picture in which the crew of an abandoned blazing tanker reboard her after drifting for three days on the Atlantic, and manage to sail her the rest of the way into the Clyde. In spite of unconvincing scenes shot in the studio tank, the film has a powerful sense of integrity.

Halfway House
Director: Basil Dearden
Associate producer: Alberto Cavalcanti
Cast: Mervyn Johns (Rhys)
Glynis Johns (Gwyneth)
Tom Walls (Capt. Meadows)
Françoise Rosay (Alice Meadows)
Esmond Knight (David Davies)
Guy Middleton (Fortescue)
Alfred Drayton (Oakley)
Valerie White (Jill French)
Richard Bird (Squadron Leader French)
Sally Ann Howes (Joanna)
Philippa Hiatt (Margaret)
Pat McGrath (Terence)
John Boxer (Doctor)
C. V. France (Solicitor)

Joss Ambler (Pinsent)
Rachel Thomas (Landlady)
Roland Pertwee (Prison Governor)
Script: Angus MacPhail, Diana Morgan, T. E. B. Clarke, from the play *The Peaceful Inn* by Denis Ogden
Photography: Wilkie Cooper
Art direction: Michael Relph
Editing: Charles Hasse
Supervising editor: Sidney Cole
Music: Lord Berners
Opening: April 1944
Running time: 95 mins.

Ealing's first foray into the occult, with a curious story about a bunch of travellers staying at an inn that was bombed out of existence a year earlier. Through contact with the strange landlord and his daughter, each makes some personal readjustment and goes away a changed person. There was a short-lived vogue for this kind of thing, probably started by J. B. Priestley.

For Those in Peril
Director: Charles Crichton
Associate producer: S. C. Balcon
Cast: David Farrar (Murray)
Ralph Michael (Rawlings)
Robert Wyndham (Leverett)
John Slater (Wilkie)
John Batten (Wireless Operator)
Robert Griffith (Griffiths)
Peter Arne (Junior Officer)
James Roberston Justice (Ops Room Officer)
Script: Harry Watt, J. O. C. Orton, T. E. B. Clarke, from a story by Richard Hillary
Photography: Douglas Slocombe (exteriors), Ernest Palmer (interiors)
Art direction: Duncan Sutherland
Editing: Erik Cripps
Supervising editor: Sidney Cole
Music: Gordon Jacob
Opening: June 1944
Running time: 67 mins

War film about the Air-Sea Rescue Service, with a chip-on-the-shoulder officer, who would rather be flying, having to take command and prove his heroism. The picture has a documentary feel to it, with much factual description of life in a little-known department of the war, and David Farrar and Ralph Michael perform their roles realistically.

They Came to a City
Director: Basil Dearden
Associate producer: Sidney Cole
Cast: John Clements (Joe Dinmore)
Googie Withers (Alice)
Raymond Huntley (Malcolm Stritton)
Renée Gadd (Mrs Stritton)
A. E. Matthews (Sir George Gedney)

Mabel Terry Lewis (Lady Loxfield)
Frances Rowe (Philippa)
Ada Reeve (Mrs Batley)
Norman Shelley (Mr Cudworth)
Ralph Michael, Brenda Bruce (Couple on Hillside)
J. B. Priestley (Himself)
Script: Basil Dearden, Sidney Cole, from the play by J. B. Priestley
Photography: Stan Pavey
Art direction: Michael Relph
Editing: Michael Truman
Music: Scriabin
Opening: August 1944
Running time: 78 mins.

The cast of Priestley's sociological fantasy repeated their roles in this strange film, one of the few attempts in British cinema history to put across a socialist message. A group of people arrive at a city. Within is Utopia. The question is, which of them will be admitted? It is tempting to ascribe the mood of Britain to this film, a few months before the 1945 landslide election of a Labour government, but in fact it was a box-office failure.

Champagne Charlie
Director: Alberto Cavalcanti
Associate producer: John Croydon
Cast: Tommy Trinder (George Leybourne)
Stanley Holloway (The Great Vance)
Betty Warren (Bessie Bellwood)
Jean Kent (Dolly Bellwood)
Robert Wyndham (Duckworth)
Austin Trevor (Duke)
Peter de Greeff (Lord Petersfield)
Leslie Clarke (Fred Sanders)
Eddie Phillips (Tom Sayers)
Eric Boon (Clinker)
Norman Pierce (Landlord)
Vida Hope (Barmaid)
Harry Fowler ('Orace)
Billy Shine (Stage Manager)
Guy Middleton (Patron)
James Robertson Justice (Patron)
Frederick Piper (Learoyd)
Drusilla Wills (Dresser)
Andrea Malandrinos (Gatti)
Paul Bonifas (Targetino)
Script: Austin Melford, Angus MacPhail, John Dighton
Photography: Wilkie Cooper
Art direction: Michael Relph
Editing: Charles Hasse
Musical director: Ernest Irving
Opening: August 1944
Running time: 105 mins.

Victorian comedy set in the music halls of the day, recalling the rivalries of the singers George Leybourne and the Great Vance, and their united front against the theatre owners who are trying to close them down. Although it is an antiseptic view of London in the 1860s, the film is zestful and agreeable, and the closest Balcon's Ealing ever got to a musical.

Fiddlers Three
Director: Harry Watt
Associate producer: Robert Hamer
Cast: Tommy Trinder (Tommy)
Frances Day (Poppaea)
Sonnie Hale (Professor)
Francis L. Sullivan (Nero)
Elizabeth Welch (Thora)
Mary Clare (Volumnia)
Diana Decker (Lydia)
Frederick Piper (Auctioneer)
Russell Thorndike (High Priest)
Danny Green (Lictor)
James Robertson Justice (Centurion)
Ernest Milton (Titus)
Robert Wyndham (Lionkeeper)
Script: Harry Watt, Diana Morgan
Photography: Wilkie Cooper
Art direction: Duncan Sutherland
Editing: Eily Boland
Music: Spike Hughes
Opening: October 1944
Running time: 88 mins.

Comedy, with modern servicemen falling asleep at Stonehenge and waking up in Ancient Rome in Nero's day. Opportunities are taken to invest the script with topical jokes, many now incomprehensible.

Johnny Frenchman
Director: Charles Frend
Associate producer: S. C. Balcon
Cast: Françoise Rosay (Lanec Florrie)
Tom Walls (Nat Pomeroy)
Patricia Roc (Sue Pomeroy)
Ralph Michael (Bob Tremayne)
Paul Dupuis (Yan Kerverac)
Frederick Piper (Zacky Penrose)
Arthur Hambling (Steven Matthews)
Grace Arnold (Mrs Matthews)
Judith Furse (June Matthews)
Bill Blewitt (Dick Trewhiddie)
Carol O'Connor (Mr Harper)
Alfie Bass (Corporal)
Beatrice Varley (Mrs Tremayne)
Drusilla Wills (Miss Bennett)
Paul Bonifas (Jerome)
Richard George (Charlie West)
James Harcourt (Joe Pender)
Stan Paskin (Tim Bassett)
Script: T. E. B. Clarke
Photography: Roy Kellino
Art direction: Duncan Sutherland
Editing: Michael Truman
Music: Clifton Parker
Opening: August 1945
Running time: 112 mins.

Hands-across-the-Channel war drama, in which Cornish and Breton fisherfolk forget their ancient rivalries in the face of

Hitler. Although it was filmed entirely in England, Françoise Rosay contributed a powerful French presence. The war ended before the film was released.

Painted Boats
US *The Girl on the Canal*
Director: Charles Crichton
Associate producer: Henry Cornelius
Cast: Jenny Laird (Mary Smith)
Bill Blewitt (Pa Smith)
May Hallatt (Ma Smith)
Robert Griffith (Ted Stoner)
Madoline Thomas (Mrs Stoner)
Harry Fowler (Alf Stoner)
Grace Arnold (Miss Stoner)
Megs Jenkins (Barmaid)
James McKechnie (Narrator)
Script: Stephen Black with Micky McCarthy
Commentary: Louis MacNeice
Photography: Douglas Slocombe
Art direction: Jim Morahan
Editing: Leslie Allen
Music: John Greenwood
Opening: September 1945
Running time: 63 mins.

Canal life in England is the subject of this modest film which nevertheless incorporates the familiar Ealing theme of the two factions, one favouring the traditional methods, in this case horse-drawn motive power, and the other the modern, a motor-driven boat. Marriage unites the opposed families, as does the effect of war. The pace is as measured as the flow of the canals.

Dead of Night
Directors: Alberto Cavalcanti, Charles Crichton, Basil Dearden, Robert Hamer
Associate producers: Sidney Cole, John Croydon
Cast: Mervyn Johns (Walter Craig)
Renée Gadd (Mrs Craig)
Roland Culver (Eliot Foley)
Mary Merrall (Mrs Foley)
Frederick Valk (Dr Van Straaten)
Barbara Leake (Mrs O'Hara)
Christmas Party:
Sally Ann Howes (Sally O'Hara)
Michael Allan (Jimmy Watson)
Robert Wyndham (Dr Albury)
The Haunted Mirror:
Googie Withers (Joan)
Ralph Michael (Peter)
Esme Percy (Antique Dealer)
Hearse Driver:
Anthony Baird (Hugh Grainger)
Judy Kelly (Joyce Grainger)
Hearse Driver (Miles Malleson)
Golfing Story:
Basil Radford (George)
Naunton Wayne (Larry)
Peggy Bryan (Mary)

The Ventriloquist's Dummy:
Michael Redgrave (Maxwell Frere)
Hartley Power (Sylvester Kee)
Elizabeth Welch (Beulah)
Magda Kun (Mitzi)
Garry Marsh (Harry Parker)
Script: John V. Baines, Angus MacPhail, with additional dialogue by T.E.B. Clarke from stories by Angus MacPhail, E.F. Benson, John V. Baines, H.G. Wells
Photography: Douglas Slocombe, Stan Pavey
Art direction: Michael Relph
Editing: Charles Hasse
Music: Georges Auric
Opening: September 1945
Running time: 102 mins.

Ealing's great portmanteau ghost story in which the guests at a country weekend tell of their occult experiences.

Pink String and Sealing Wax
Director: Robert Hamer
Associate producer: S. C. Balcon
Cast: Mervyn Johns (Edward Sutton)
Googie Withers (Pearl Bond)
Gordon Jackson (David Sutton)
Sally Ann Howes (Peggy Sutton)
Mary Merrall (Mrs Sutton)
Jean Ireland (Victoria Sutton)
Colin Simpson (James Sutton)
David Wallbridge (Nicholas Sutton)
John Carol (Dan Powell)
Catherine Lacey (Miss Porter)
Garry Marsh (Joe Bond)
Frederick Piper (Doctor)
Valentine Dyall (Policeman)
Maudie Edwards (Mrs Webster)
Margaret Ritchie (Madame Patti)
Don Stannard (John Bevan)
Charles Carson (Editor)
Pauline Letts (Louise)
Script: Diana Morgan, Robert Hamer, from the play by Roland Pertwee
Photography: Richard Pavey
Art direction: Duncan Sutherland
Editing: Michael Truman
Music: Norman Demuth
Opening: November 1945
Running time: 89 mins.

Robert Hamer's first full-length film was a late-Victorian melodrama, with a puritanical father, a rebellious son, a highly-sexed publican's wife and a poisoned husband. Googie Withers made the most of her part as the villainess, and the film exhibited the occasional baroque touch. Googie's death was shot first.

The Captive Heart
Director: Basil Dearden
Associate producer: Michael Relph
Cast: Michael Redgrave (Capt. Hasek)
Mervyn Johns (Private Evans)
Basil Radford (Major Dalrymple)

Jack Warner (Cpl. Horsfall)
James Hanley (Private Matthews)
Gordon Jackson (Lieut. Lennox)
Ralph Michael (Capt. Thurston)
Derek Bond (Lieut. Hartley)
Guy Middleton (Capt. Grayson)
Karel Stepanek (Forster)
Jack Lambert (Padre)
Rachel Kempson (Celia Mitchell)
Meriel Forbes (Beryl Curtess)
Gladys Henson (Mrs Horsfall)
Rachel Thomas (Mrs Evans)
Jane Barrett (Caroline Hartley)
Frederick Leister (Mr Mowbray)
Robert Wyndham (Lieut-Cdr. Marsden)
Margot Fitzsimmons (Elspeth Macdougall)
Script: Angus MacPhail, Guy Morgan, from a story by Patrick Kirwan
Photography: Douglas Slocombe
Art direction: Michael Relph
Editing: Charles Hasse
Music: Alan Rawsthorne
Opening: March 1946
Running time: 104 mins.

The dreary life of a prisoner-of-war camp in Germany, with flashes of life beyond the barbed wire, culminating in a homecoming in which a man who has assumed the identity of a dead officer confronts the astonished wife.

The Overlanders
Director: Harry Watt
Associate producer: Ralph Smart
Cast: Chips Rafferty (Dan McAlpine)
John Nugent Hayward (Bill Parsons)
Daphne Campbell (Mary Parsons)
Jean Blue (Mrs Parsons)
Helen Grieve (Helen Parsons)
John Fernside (Corky)
Peter Pagan (Sinbad)
Frank Ransome (Charlie)
Clyde Combo (Jackie)
Script: Harry Watt
Research: Dora Birtles
Photography: Osmond Borradaile
Editing: E. M. Inman Hunter
Supervising editor: Leslie Norman
Music: John Ireland
Opening: October 1946
Running time: 91 mins.

Ealing's first venture in the Antipodes was a wartime drama showing the evacuation of a vast herd of cattle from an area threatened by Japanese attack, involving a drive of 2,000 miles across rough terrain. The documentary aspects of the film are better than its fictionalized human interest.

Hue and Cry
Director: Charles Crichton
Associate producer: Henry Cornelius
Cast: Alastair Sim (Felix H. Wilkinson)

Jack Warner (Nightingale)
Valerie White (Miss Davis)
Jack Lambert (Inspector Ford)
Harry Fowler (Joe Kirby)
Frederick Piper (Mr Kirby)
Vida Hope (Mrs Kirby)
Gerald Fox (Dicky)
Grace Arnold (Dicky's Mother)
Joan Dowling (Clarry)
Douglas Barr (Alec)
Stanley Escane (Roy)
Ian Dawson (Norman)
Paul Demel (Jago)
Bruce Belfrage (BBC Announcer)
Script: T. E. B. Clarke
Photography: Douglas Slocombe
Art direction: Norman G. Arnold
Editing: Charles Hasse
Music: Georges Auric
Opening: February 1947
Running time: 82 mins.

A boy's comic comes to life as an intelligent lad suddenly realizes that the pages are being used by a gang of crooks to communicate with each other. The fierce battle involving seemingly half the youth of London is a satisfying climax to an original and well-conceived Ealing comedy in an *Emil and the Detectives* vein.

Nicholas Nickleby
Director: Alberto Cavalcanti
Associate producer: John Croydon
Cast: Derek Bond (Nicholas Nickleby)
Cedric Hardwicke (Ralph Nickleby)
Mary Merrall (Mrs Nickleby)
Sally Ann Howes (Kate Nickleby)
Bernard Miles (Newman Noggs)
Athene Seyler (Miss la Creevy)
Alfred Drayton (Wackford Squeers)
Sybil Thorndike (Mrs Squeers)
Vida Hope (Fanny Squeers)
Roy Hermitage (Wackford Junior)
Aubrey Woods (Smike)
Patricia Hayes (Phoebe)
Cyril Fletcher (Mr Mantalini)
Fay Compton (Mme Mantalini)
Catherine Nesbitt (Miss Knag)
Stanley Holloway (Vincent Crummles)
Vera Pearce (Mrs Crummles)
Una Bart (The Infant Phenomenon)
June Elvin (Mrs Snevellici)
Drusilla Wills (Mrs Crudden)
James Hayter (Ned Cheeryble/Charles Cheeryble)
Emrys Jones (Frank Cheeryble)
Roddy Hughes (Tim Linkinwater)
George Relph (Mr Bray)
Jill Balcon (Madeleine Bray)
Michael Shepley (Mr Gregory MP)
Cecil Ramage (Sir Mulberry Hawk)
Tim Bateson (Lord Verisopht)
John Salew (Mr Lillyvick)
Dandy Nichols (Mantalini Employee)
John Chandos (Employment Agent)

Frederick Burtwell (Mercury)
Script: John Dighton, from the novel by Charles Dickens
Photography: Gordon Dines
Art direction: Michael Relph
Editing: Leslie Norman
Music: Lord Berners
Opening: March 1947
Running time: 108 mins.

Cavalcanti's attempt to film Dickens' novel was overshadowed on its release by David Lean's version of *Great Expectations*, and unfairly compared. In retrospect it can be seen that the narrative flow sustains itself, and that incidents and characters are wisely selected.

The Loves of Joanna Godden
Director: Charles Frend
Associate producer: Sidney Cole
Cast: Googie Withers (Joanna Godden)
Jean Kent (Ellen Godden)
John McCallum (Arthur Alce)
Derek Bond (Martin Trevor)
Henry Mollison (Harry Trevor)
Chips Rafferty (Collard)
Sonia Holm (Louise)
Josephine Stuart (Grace Wickens)
Alec Faversham (Peter Relf)
Edward Rigby (Stuppeny)
Frederick Piper (Isaac Turk)
Fred Bateman (Young Turk)
Grace Arnold (Martha)
Barbara Leake (Mrs Luckhurst)
Ethel Coleridge (Lighthouse Woman)
William Mervyn (Huxtable)
Script: H. E. Bates, from the novel *Joanna Godden* by Sheila Kaye-Smith
Photography: Douglas Slocombe
Art direction: Duncan Sutherland
Editing: Michael Truman
Music: Ralph Vaughan Williams
Opening: June 1947
Running time: 89 mins.

An Edwardian pastoral drama with much location footage shot on Romney Marsh. Googie Withers is an ardent young woman, determined to be a farmer in her own right, but eventually succumbing to the love of a good neighbour and his masculine skills. This pre-Women's Lib story was by a notable woman novelist.

Frieda
Director: Basil Dearden
Associate producer: Michael Relph
Cast: David Farrar (Robert Dawson)
Glynis Johns (Judy Dawson)
Mai Zetterling (Frieda)
Flora Robson (Nell Dawson)
Barbara Everest (Mrs Dawson)
Ray Jackson (Tony Dawson)
Patrick Holt (Alan Dawson)
Gladys Henson (Edith)

Albert Lieven (Richard)
Barry Jones (Headmaster)
Norman Pierce (Crawley)
D. A. Clarke-Smith (Herriot)
Renée Gadd (Mrs Freeman)
Garry Marsh (Beckwith)
Milton Rosmer (Tom Merrick)
Barry Letts (Jim Merrick)
Arthur Howard (Official)
Script: Angus MacPhail, Ronald Millar
from latter's play
Photography: Gordon Dines
Art direction: Jim Morahan
Editing: Leslie Norman
Music: John Greenwood
Opening: July 1947
Running time: 98 mins.

Anti-German prejudice nearly scuppers the new marriage of a returned POW who brings home the girl who helped him to escape. A fervent Nazi brother-in-law does not help, and the husband is too ready to believe the worst in his wife. For all that, it faces squarely the problem of post-war relations.

It Always Rains on Sunday
Director: Robert Hamer
Associate producer: Henry Cornelius
Cast: Googie Withers (Rose Sandigate)
Edward Chapman (George Sandigate)
Susan Shaw (Vi Sandigate)
Patricia Plunkett (Doris Sandigate)
David Lines (Alfie Sandigate)
John McCallum (Tommy Swann)
Sydney Tafler (Morrie Hyams)
Betty Ann Davies (Sadie Hyams)
John Slater (Lou Hyams)
Jane Hylton (Bessie Hyams)
Meier Tzelnicker (Solly Hyams)
Jack Warner (Det-Sgt. Fothergill)
Frederick Piper (Det-Sgt. Leech)
Michael Howard (Slopey Collins)
Nigel Stock (Ted Edwards)
Hermione Baddeley (Mrs Spry)
Grace Arnold (Landlady)
Betty Baskomb (Barmaid)
Edie Martin (Mrs Watson)
Al Millen (Bill Hawkins)
Vida Hope (Mrs Wallis)
John Salew (Caleb Neesley)
Gladys Henson (Mrs Neesley)
James Hanley (Whitey)
John Carol (Freddie)
Alfie Bass (Dicey)
Script: Angus MacPhail, Robert Hamer,
Henry Cornelius, from the novel by
Arthur la Bern
Photography: Douglas Slocombe
Art direction: Duncan Sutherland
Editing: Michael Truman
Music: Georges Auric
Opening: November 1947
Running time: 92 mins.

East End slice-of-life with Googie

Withers sheltering her ex-lover, an escaped convict who suddenly turns up while the Sunday lunch is in the oven. By nightfall he is recaptured and she has tried to kill herself, but her faithful middle-aged husband stands by her. Hamer's direction is assured.

Against the Wind
Director: Charles Crichton
Associate producer: Sidney Cole
Cast: Robert Beatty (Father Phillip)
Jack Warner (Max Cronk)
Simone Signoret (Michele)
Gordon Jackson (Johnny Duncan)
Paul Dupuis (Jacques)
Gisele Preville (Julie)
John Slater (Emile)
Peter Illing (Andrew)
James Robertson Justice (Ackerman)
Eugene Deckers (Marcel)
André Morell (Abbot)
Sybilla Binder (Malou)
Helen Hanson (Marcel)
Olaf Olsen (German Officer)
Script: T. E. B. Clarke, Michael Pertwee,
from a story by J. Elder Wills
Additional dialogue: P. Vincent Carroll
Photography: Lionel Banes
Art direction: J. Elder Wills
Editing: Alan Osbiston
Music: Leslie Bridgewater
Opening: February 1948
Running time: 96 mins.

Saboteurs at work against the Nazis in wartime Belgium, with Jack Warner as a double agent. The film was not too well received at the box office, largely because the public was no longer in a mood for war films.

Saraband for Dead Lovers
US *Saraband*
Director: Basil Dearden
Associate producer: Michael Relph
Cast: Stewart Granger (Koenigsmark)
Joan Greenwood (Sophie Dorothea)
Flora Robson (Countess Platen)
Françoise Rosay (Electress Sophia)
Frederick Valk (Elector Ernest Augustus)
Peter Bull (Prince George Louis)
Anthony Quayle (Durer)
Michael Gough (Prince Charles)
Megs Jenkins (Frau Busche)
Jill Balcon (Knesbeck)
David Horne (Duke George William)
Cecil Trouncer (Major Eck)
Noel Howlett (Count Platen)
Barbara Leake (Maria)
Miles Malleson (Lord of Misrule)
Allan Jeayes (Governor)
Guy Rolfe (Envoy)
Mercia Swinburne (Countess Eleanore)
Script: John Dighton, Alexander
Mackendrick, from the novel by Helen

Simpson
Photography: Douglas Slocombe, in
Technicolor
Art direction: Michael Relph, Jim
Morahan, William Kellner
Editing: Michael Truman
Music: Alan Rawsthorne
Opening: September 1948
Running time: 96 mins.

Ealing's expensive 'prestige' film, a historical drama about the unhappy Hanoverian, Sophie Dorothea, incarcerated for life following her illicit affair with the dashing Count Koenigsmark. While sumptuous to look at (it was Ealing's first Technicolor film), the storyline is depressing and sparkless.

Another Shore
Director: Charles Crichton
Associate producer: Ivor Montagu
Cast: Robert Beatty (Gulliver)
Moira Lister (Jennifer)
Stanley Holloway (Alastair McNeil)
Michael Medwin (Yellow)
Maureen Delaney (Mrs Gleeson)
Dermot Kelly (Boxer)
Michael Golden (Broderick)
Wilfred Brambell (Moore)
Irene Worth (Socialite)
Bill Shine (Socialite)
Edie Martin (Woman in Park)
Fred O'Donovan (Coghlan)
Sheila Manahan (Nora)
Desmond Veane (Parkes)
W. A. Kelly (Roger)
Script: Walter Meade, from the novel by
Kenneth Reddin
Photography: Douglas Slocombe
Art direction: Malcolm Baker-Smith
Editing: Bernard Gribble
Music: Georges Auric
Opening: November 1948
Running time: 91 mins.

A comedy set in Dublin, with Robert Beatty as a day-dreaming Irishman, yearning for a sybaritic life in the South Seas, who appears to get his chance, but is stopped by a no-nonsense young woman who wakes him up to realities. Stanley Holloway is excellent.

Scott of the Antarctic
Director: Charles Frend
Associate producer: Sidney Cole
Cast: John Mills (Capt. Scott)
Derek Bond (Capt. Oates)
Harold Warrender (Dr Wilson)
James Robertson Justice (PO Taff Evans)
Reginald Beckwith (Lieut. Bowers)
Kenneth More (Lieut. Teddy Evans)
James McKechnie (Lieut. Atkinson)
John Gregson (PO Green)
Barry Letts (Apsley Cherry-Gerrard)
Clive Morton (Herbert Ponting)

Christopher Lee (Bernard Day)
Bruce Seton (Lieut. Pennell)
Anne Firth (Oriana Wilson)
Diana Churchill (Kathleen Scott)
Norman Williams (Stoker Lashley)
Dennis Vance (Charles Wright)
Script: Walter Meade, Ivor Montagu,
Mary Hayley Bell
Photography: Jack Cardiff, Osmond
Borradaile, Geoffrey Unsworth, in
Technicolor
Art direction: Arne Akermark, Jim
Morahan
Editing: Peter Tanner
Music: Ralph Vaughan Williams
Opening: December 1948
Running time: 111 mins.
   Ealing's other great 'prestige'
production of 1948, which was selected
for the Royal Film Performance. The epic
failure of Robert Falcon Scott was told
with as much honesty and accuracy as
could be mustered while some of the
associates were still alive, and John Mills
gave an exceptional performance.

Eureka Stockade
Director: Harry Watt
Associate producer: Leslie Norman
Cast: Chips Rafferty (Peter Lalor)
Jane Barrett (Alicia Dunne)
Jack Lambert (Commissioner Rede)
Peter Illing (Raffaelo)
Gordon Jackson (Tom Kennedy)
Ralph Truman (Governor Hotham)
Sydney Loder (Vern)
Dorothy Alison (Mrs Bentley)
John Fernside (Sly Grog Seller)
Grant Tyler (Sgt. Milne)
Script: Harry Watt, Walter Greenwood
Photography: George Heath
Art direction: Charles Woolveridge
Editing: Leslie Norman
Music: John Greenwood
Opening: January 1949
Running time: 103 mins.
   Insurrection in the Australian
goldfields was the subject of Ealing's
second production there but, in spite of
this promising theme, the film lacks
excitement.

Passport to Pimlico
Director: Henry Cornelius
Associate producer: E. V. H. Emmett
Cast: Stanley Holloway (Arthur
Pemberton)
Betty Warren (Connie Pemberton)
Barbara Murray (Shirley Pemberton)
Paul Dupuis (Duke of Burgundy)
Margaret Rutherford (Professor
Hatton-Jones)
John Slater (Frank Huggins)
Jane Hylton (Molly)

Raymond Huntley (Mr Wix)
Philip Stainton (PC Spiller)
Sydney Tafler (Fred Cowan)
Hermione Baddeley (Edie Randall)
Frederick Piper (Garland)
Charles Hawtrey (Bert Fitch)
Stuart Lindsell (Coroner)
Naunton Wayne (Straker)
Basil Radford (Gregg)
Michael Hordern (Insp. Bashford)
Arthur Howard (Bassett)
Bill Shine (Captain)
Harry Locke (Sergeant)
Sam Kydd (Sapper)
Fred Griffiths (Spiv)
James Hayter (Commissionaire)
Grace Arnold (Woman on Tube)
E.V.H. Emmett (Newsreel
Commentator)
Script: T.E.B. Clarke
Photography: Lionel Banes
Art direction: Roy Oxley
Editing: Michael Truman
Music: Georges Auric
Opening: April 1949
Running time: 84 mins.
   First of 1949's classic trio of comedies,
in which the inhabitants of a London
district find that they are legally
Burgundians, and therefore immune to
the rationing and restrictions of post-war
Britain. Their freedom is hard to handle.

Whisky Galore!
US *Tight Little Island*
Director: Alexander Mackendrick
Associate producer: Monja Danischewsky
Cast: Basil Radford (Capt. Waggett)
Catherine Lacey (Mrs Waggett)
Bruce Seton (Sgt. Odd)
Joan Greenwood (Peggy Macroon)
Gabrielle Blunt (Catriona Macroon)
Wylie Watson (Joseph Macroon)
Gordon Jackson (George Campbell)
Jean Cadell (Mrs Campbell)
James Robertson Justice (Dr Maclaren)
Morland Graham (The Biffer)
John Gregson (Sammy)
James Anderson (Hector)
Jameson Clark (Constable Macrae)
Duncan Macrae (Angus McCormac)
Mary MacNeil (Mrs McCormac)
Henry Mollison (Farquharson)
Compton Mackenzie (Capt. Buncher)
A. E. Matthews (Col. Linsey-Wolsey)
James Woodburn (Roderick MacBurie)
Finlay Currie (Narrator)
Script: Compton Mackenzie, Angus
MacPhail, from Compton Mackenzie's
novel
Photography: Gerald Gibbs
Art direction: Jim Morahan
Editing: Joseph Sterling
Music: Ernest Irving
Opening: June 1949

Running time: 82 mins.
   The second great comedy, in which the
islanders of Todday purloin the cargo of
whisky carried by a war-wrecked
freighter. Celtic cunning is pitted against
the forces of authority and Sassenach rule,
and it is not surprising which side wins.
Even interiors were shot on location.

Kind Hearts and Coronets
Director: Robert Hamer
Associate producer: Michael Relph
Cast: Alec Guinness (Lord D'Ascoyne,
Henry D'Ascoyne, Canon D'Ascoyne,
General D'Ascoyne, Admiral D'Ascoyne,
Ascoyne D'Ascoyne, Lady Agatha
D'Ascoyne, and Duke of Chalfont)
Dennis Price (Louis Mazzini)
Joan Greenwood (Sibella)
Valerie Hobson (Edith)
Audrey Fildes (Mrs Mazzini)
John Penrose (Lionel)
John Salew (Mr Perkins)
Anne Valery (Girl in Punt)
Barbara Leake (Schoolmistress)
Peggy Ann Clifford (Maud)
Cecil Ramage (Counsel)
Hugh Griffith (Lord High Steward)
Clive Morton (Prison Governor)
Miles Malleson (Hangman)
Arthur Lowe (Reporter)
Script: Robert Hamer, John Dighton,
from the novel *Israel Rank* by Roy
Horniman
Photography: Douglas Slocombe
Art direction: William Kellner
Editing: Peter Tanner
Music: Mozart
Opening: June 1949
Running time: 106 mins.
   Third and finest of the 1949 classic
comedies and in some respects the
apotheosis of Ealing's output. Dennis
Price never bettered his part of a fringe
member of a titled family murdering his
way to a dukedom, while Alec Guinness
sailed through eight parts with ease.

Train of Events
Directors: Sidney Cole, Charles Crichton,
Basil Dearden
Associate producer: Michael Relph
Cast: *Engine Driver:*
Jack Warner (Jim Hardcastle)
Gladys Henson (Mrs Hardcastle)
Susan Shaw (Doris Hardcastle)
Patric Doonan (Ron Stacey)
Miles Malleson (Time Keeper)
Philip Dale (Fireman)
Leslie Phillips (Fireman)
Prisoner-of-war:
Joan Dowling (Ella)
Laurence Payne (Richard)
Olga Lindo (Mrs Bailey)

Conductor:
Valerie Hobson (Stella)
John Clements (Raymond Hillary)
Irina Baranova (Irina)
John Gregson (Malcolm)
Gwen Cherrell (Charmian)
Jacqueline Byrne (TV Announcer)
Actor:
Peter Finch (Philip)
Mary Morris (Louise)
Laurence Naismith (Joe Hunt)
Doris Yorke (Mrs Hunt)
Michael Hordern (Plain-clothes Man)
Charles Morgan (Plain-clothes Man)
Guy Verney (Producer)
Mark Dignam (Bolingbroke)
Philip Ashley (Actor)
Bryan Coleman (Actor)
Henry Hewitt (Actor)
Lyndon Brook (Actor)
Script: Basil Dearden, T. E. B. Clarke,
Ronald Millar, Angus MacPhail
Photography: Lionel Banes, Gordon
Dines
Art direction: Malcolm Baker-Smith, Jim
Morahan
Editing: Bernard Gribble
Music: Leslie Bridgewater
Opening: August 1949
Running time: 88 mins.
    Ealing's second attempt at the port-
manteau approach with three directors
recounting the stories of people on a
night express which is doomed to crash.
Compared with *Dead of Night*, the result
is disappointing and lifeless.

A Run for Your Money
Director: Charles Frend
Associate producer: Leslie Norman
Cast: Donald Houston (Dai)
Meredith Edwards (Twm)
Moira Lister (Jo)
Alec Guinness (Whimple)
Hugh Griffith (Huw)
Julie Milton (Bronwen)
Clive Morton (Editor)
Joyce Grenfell (Mrs Pargeter)
Dorothy Bramhall (Jane)
Edward Rigby (Beefeater)
Gabrielle Brune (Crooner)
Patric Doonan (Conductor)
Leslie Perrins (Barney)
Peter Edwards (Davies)
Desmond Walter-Ellis (Announcer)
Mackenzie Ward (Photographer)
Script: Charles Frend, Leslie Norman,
Richard Hughes from a story by Clifford
Evans
Additional dialogue: Diana Morgan
Photography: Douglas Slocombe
Art direction: William Kellner
Editing: Michael Truman
Music: Ernest Irving
Opening: November 1949

Running time: 85 mins.
    Wales' turn in the comedy series did not
produce anything as sparkling as *Whisky
Galore!*. Two Welsh miners arrive in
London to collect prize money and go on
a minor spree. Alec Guinness was
singularly miscast as an inept reporter.

The Blue Lamp
Director: Basil Dearden
Producer: Michael Relph
Cast: Jack Warner (PC Dixon)
James Hanley (PC Mitchell)
Robert Flemyng (Sgt. Roberts)
Bernard Lee (Insp. Cherry)
Dirk Bogarde (Tom Riley)
Patric Doonan (Spud)
Peggy Evans (Diana Lewis)
Frederick Piper (Mr Lewis)
Betty Ann Davies (Mrs Lewis)
Dora Bryan (Maisie)
Norman Shelley (Jordan)
Gladys Henson (Mrs Dixon)
Bruce Seton (PC Campbell)
Meredith Edwards (PC Hughes)
Clive Morton (Sgt. Brooks)
William Mervyn (Chief Insp. Hammond)
Campbell Singer (Station Sergeant)
Michael Golden (Mike Randall)
Muriel Aked (Mrs Waterbourne)
Glyn Houston (Barrow Boy)
Renée Gadd (Woman Driver)
Tessie O'Shea (Herself)
Script: T. E. B. Clarke, from a story by
Ted Willis, Jan Read
Additional dialogue: Alexander
Mackendrick
Photography: Gordon Dines
Art direction: Tom Morahan
Editing: Peter Tanner
Music: Ernest Irving
Opening: January 1950
Running time: 82 mins.
    Ealing's tribute to the Metropolitan
Police, with the daily round and perils
recorded in a documentary-like manner,
using the experiences of Tibby Clarke
who was a wartime special. Exciting, full
of action, and too good to be true. The
police helped enthusiastically.

Dance Hall
Director: Charles Crichton
Associate producer: E. V. H. Emmett
Cast: Natasha Parry (Eve)
Jane Hylton (Mary)
Diana Dors (Carole)
Petula Clark (Georgie)
Donald Houston (Phil)
Bonar Colleano (Alec)
Douglas Barr (Peter)
Fred Johnson (Mr Wilson)
Gladys Henson (Mrs Wilson)
Dandy Nichols (Mrs Crabtree)

Sydney Tafler (Manager)
James Carney (Mike)
Kay Kendall (Doreen)
Eunice Gayson (Mona)
Grace Arnold (Mrs Bennett)
Harold Goodwin (Jack)
Michael Trubshawe (Colonel)
Harry Fowler (Amorous Youth)
Script: E. V. H. Emmett, Diana Morgan,
Alexander Mackendrick
Photography: Douglas Slocombe
Art direction: Norman Arnold
Editing: Seth Holt
Music: orchestras of Geraldo and Ted
Heath plus Hy Hazell, Wally Fryer and
Margaret Barnes
Opening: June 1950
Running time : 80 mins.
    This film examines the emotional lives
of four girls at a London dance hall,
Ealing for once showing an interest in the
female half of the population. All, except
Diana Dors, are a bit too classy to be
believable factory girls, but the
contemporary setting seems authentic.

Bitter Springs
Director: Ralph Smart
Associate producer: Leslie Norman
Cast: Tommy Trinder (Tommy)
Chips Rafferty (Wally King)
Gordon Jackson (Mac)
Jean Blue (Ma King)
Charles Tingwell (John King)
Nonnie Piper (Emma King)
Nicky Yardley (Charlie)
Michael Pate (Trooper)
Henry Murdoch (Black Jack)
Script: W. P. Lipscomb, Monja
Danischewsky, from a story by Ralph
Smart
Photography: George Heath
Art direction: Charles Woolveridge
Editing: Bernard Gribble
Music: Ralph Vaughan Williams
Opening: July 1950
Running time: 89 mins.
    The promise of Ealing's Australian
venture evaporated with the third of the
films made there, which examined the
problems of white settlers in the 1900s
contending with the aboriginal population
for land rights. The casting of Tommy
Trinder militated against the serious
theme; it was not the first time that his
presence upset the mood of a film.

Cage of Gold
Director: Basil Dearden
Associate producer: Michael Relph
Cast: Jean Simmons (Judith)
David Farrar (Bill Brennan)
James Donald (Dr Alan Kearn)
Harcourt Williams (Dr Kearn Senior)

Gladys Henson (Nanny)
Herbert Lom (Rahman)
Gregoire Aslan (Dupont)
Madeleine Lebeau (Madeleine)
Maria Mauban (Antoinette)
Bernard Lee (Insp. Gray)
Martin Boddey (Adams)
Campbell Singer (Constable)
George Benson (Registrar)
Arthur Howard (Bridegroom)
Script: Jack Whittingham, from a story
by Jack Whittingham, Paul Stein
Photography: Douglas Slocombe
Art direction: Jim Morahan
Editing: Peter Tanner
Music: Georges Auric
Opening: September 1950
Running time: 83 mins.
   Slightly uneasy melodrama, with Jean
Simmons menaced by a former lover who
turns up just as she is about to marry a
decent doctor. The action flits between
London and Paris and David Farrar
enjoys himself in a caddish role, while
Basil Dearden disguises many of the sags
in the story with brisk direction.

The Magnet
Director: Charles Frend
Associate producer: Sidney Cole
Cast: Stephen Murray (Dr Brent)
Kay Walsh (Mrs Brent)
William [later James] Fox (Johnny Brent)
Meredith Edwards (Harper)
Julien Mitchell (Mayor)
Wylie Watson (Pickering)
Joss Ambler (Businessman)
Gladys Henson (Nanny)
Thora Hird (Nanny)
Joan Hickson (Mrs Ward)
Grace Arnold (Mrs Archer)
Harold Goodwin (Man at Pin Table)
Michael Brooke Jr. (Kit)
Keith Robinson (Spike)
Thomas Johnson (Perce)
Sam Kydd (Postman)
Seamas Mor na Feasag [James Robertson
Justice] (Tramp)
Bryan Michie (Announcer)
Script: T. E. B. Clarke
Photography: Lionel Banes
Art direction: Jim Morahan
Editing: Bernard Gribble
Music: William Alwyn
Opening: October 1950
Running time: 79 mins.
   Comedy about a young psychiatrist's
son who acquires a magnet from another
child and then becomes involved in some
curious adventures, mostly based on
misplaced assumptions. It is not one-tenth
as impressive as *Hue and Cry*, although
Tibby Clarke wrote both. James
Robertson Justice appears under a Celtic
name in a bit part as a tramp.

Pool of London
Director: Basil Dearden
Associate producer: Michael Relph
Cast: Bonar Colleano (Dan MacDonald)
Earl Cameron (Johnny)
Leslie Phillips (Harry)
Susan Shaw (Pat)
Renée Asherson (Sally)
Moira Lister (Maisie)
Joan Dowling (Pamela)
James Robertson Justice (Trotter)
Max Adrian (Vernon)
Alfie Bass (Alf)
Laurence Naismith (Commissionaire)
Beckett Bould (Watchman)
Victor Maddern (Tram Conductor)
Michael Golden (Andrews)
John Longden (Insp. Williamson)
Script: Jack Whittingham, John Eldridge
Photography: Gordon Dines
Art direction: Jim Morahan
Editing: Peter Tanner
Music: John Addison
Opening: February 1951
Running time: 85 mins.
   A ship docks near London Bridge; the
film shows how the crew takes to a
weekend ashore, with action that includes
a smuggling attempt, a rapid romance
between a black seaman and a white
theatre cashier, and a glimpse of the
operations of the river police. Filmed in
Dearden's *Blue Lamp* style.

The Lavender Hill Mob
Director: Charles Crichton
Associate producer: Michael Truman
Cast: Alec Guinness (Holland)
Stanley Holloway (Pendlebury)
Sidney James (Lackery)
Alfie Bass (Shorty)
Marjorie Fielding (Mrs Chalk)
Edie Martin (Miss Evesham)
Ronald Adam (Bank Official)
Clive Morton (Police Sergeant)
John Gregson (Farrow)
Sydney Tafler (Clayton)
Patrick Barr (Inspector)
Meredith Edwards (PC Edwards)
Robert Shaw (Police Scientist)
Michael Trubshawe (British Ambassador)
Audrey Hepburn (Chiquita)
Jacques Brunius (French Official)
Gibb McLaughlin (Godwin)
Marie Burke (Señora Gallardo)
Script: T.E.B. Clarke
Photography: Douglas Slocombe
Art direction: William Kellner
Editing: Seth Holt
Music: Georges Auric
Opening: June 1951
Running time: 78 mins.
   Tibby Clarke won an Oscar for his
screenplay and it was the 1951 British
Film Academy's Best Film. This classic

comedy about a meek bank clerk who
masterminds a bullion heist is one of the
best in Ealing's output, and even gently
pokes fun at *The Blue Lamp*.

The Man in the White Suit
Director: Alexander Mackendrick
Associate producer: Sidney Cole
Cast: Alec Guinness (Sidney Stratton)
Joan Greenwood (Daphne Birnley)
Cecil Parker (Alan Birnley)
Michael Gough (Michael Corland)
Ernest Thesiger (Sir John Kierlaw)
Howard Marion Crawford (Cranford)
Henry Mollison (Hoskins)
Russell Waters (Davidson)
Joan Harben (Miss Johnson)
Vida Hope (Bertha)
Patric Doonan (Frank)
Duncan Lamont (Harry)
Roddy Hughes (Accountant)
Colin Gordon (Accountant)
Harold Goodwin (Wilkins)
Judith Furse (Nurse Gamage)
Miles Malleson (Tailor)
Edie Martin (Mrs Watson)
Mandy Miller (Little Girl)
Olaf Olsen (Knudsen)
Frank Atkinson (Baker)
Billy Russell (Night Watchman)
John Rudling (Wilson)
Brian Worth (King)
Script: Roger Macdougall, Alexander
Mackendrick, John Dighton, from Roger
Macdougall's play
Photography: Douglas Slocombe
Art direction: Jim Morahan
Editing: Bernard Gribble
Music: Benjamin Frankel
Opening: August 1951
Running time: 85 mins.
   Comedy with a sharp edge, in which a
young inventor of a miracle cloth makes
the painful discovery that nobody wants
it. Guinness invests him with a sense of
remoteness; he is an alien being who
unites unions and bosses in joint hostility
towards him.

Where No Vultures Fly
US *Ivory Hunter*
Director: Harry Watt
Associate producer: Leslie Norman
Cast: Anthony Steel (Bob Payton)
Dinah Sheridan (Mary Payton)
William Simons (Tim Payton)
Harold Warrender (Mannering)
Meredith Edwards (Gwyl)
Orlando Martins (M'Kwongwi)
Andrew Cruickshank (Governor)
Philip Birkinshaw (District
Commissioner)
Script: W. P. Lipscomb, Ralph Smart,
Leslie Norman, from a story by Harry
Watt

Photography: Geoffrey Unsworth, in Technicolor
Wildlife photography: Paul Beeson
Editing: Gordon Stone
Music: Alan Rawsthorne
Opening: December 1951
Running time: 107 mins.

Harry Watt switches his sights from Australia to Africa, and takes as his subject the battle between a young idealistic gamewarden and the ivory poachers. He achieves his dream of a great national park 'where no vultures fly'. There is some excellent animal photography, but the screenplay has moments of unintentional naïvety.

His Excellency
Director: Robert Hamer
Producer: Michael Truman
Cast: Eric Portman (George Harrison)
Cecil Parker (Sir James Kirkman)
Helen Cherry (Lady Kirkman)
Susan Stephen (Peggy Harrison)
Edward Chapman (Admiral)
Clive Morton (GOC)
Robin Bailey (Charles)
Alec Mango (Jackie)
Geoffrey Keen (Morellos)
John Salew (Fernando)
Elspeth March (Mrs Fernando)
Eric Pohlman (Dobrieda)
Paul Demel (Chef)
Henry Longhurst (Lord Kynaston)
Howard Marion Crawford (Teashop Owner)
Barbara Leake (Woman in Teashop)
Barbara Cavan (Woman in Teashop)
Basil Dignam (Security Officer)
Laurence Naismith (Soldier)
Victor Maddern (Soldier)
Script: Robert Hamer, W. P. Lipscomb, from the play by Dorothy and Campbell Christie
Photography: Douglas Slocombe
Art direction: Jim Morahan
Editing: Seth Holt
Music: Handel
Opening: January 1952
Running time: 82 mins.

A curious choice of subject for Robert Hamer, being an uninspired adaptation of a stage play about a trade unionist who becomes governor of a British island colony. The subject is more promising than the treatment. Location footage was shot in Sicily.

Secret People
Director: Thorold Dickinson
Producer: Sidney Cole
Cast: Valentina Cortesa (Maria Brentano)
Serge Reggiani (Louis)
Audrey Hepburn (Nora)
Angela Fouldes (Nora as a child)

Charles Goldner (Anselmo)
Megs Jenkins (Penny)
Irene Worth (Miss Jackson)
Reginald Tate (Insp. Eliot)
Athene Seyler (Mrs Kellick)
Geoffrey Hibbert (Steenie)
Sydney Tafler (Syd Burnett)
John Ruddock (Daly)
Michael Shepley (Manager)
Michael Allan (Rodd)
John Field (Fedor Luki)
Norman Williams (Sgt. Newcombe)
Bob Monkhouse (Barber)
Charlie Cairoli and Paul (Themselves)
Script: Thorold Dickinson, Wolfgang Wilhelm, Christiana Brand, from a story by Thorold Dickinson, Joyce Carey
Photography: Gordon Dines
Art direction: William Kellner
Editing: Peter Tanner
Music: Roberto Gerhard
Opening: February 1952
Running time: 96 mins.

Two sisters in pre-war London, refugees from a foreign tyranny, become involved in terrorist activities against its head of state who is visiting England; the elder feels a sense of revulsion at being used by fanatics and tries to save her sister from the same fate. An unusual subject for Ealing, and a neglected film, although its history has been told in detail by Lindsay Anderson.

I Believe in You
Director: Basil Dearden
Producer: Michael Relph
Cast: Cecil Parker (Henry Phipps)
Celia Johnson (Matty)
Harry Fowler (Hooker)
Joan Collins (Norma)
George Relph (Mr Dove)
Godfrey Tearle (Mr Pyke)
Ernest Jay (Mr Quayle)
Laurence Harvey (Jordie)
Ursula Howells (Hon. Ursula)
Sidney James (Sgt. Brodie)
Katie Johnson (Miss Macklin)
Ada Reeve (Mrs Crockett)
Brenda de Banzie (Mrs Hooker)
Alex McCrindle (Mr Haines)
Fred Griffiths (Crump)
Richard Hart (Eric Stevens)
Gladys Henson (Mrs Stevens)
Judith Furse (Athletics Secretary)
Laurence Naismith (Sgt. Braxton)
Script: Michael Relph, Basil Dearden, Jack Whittingham, from the memoir *Court Circular* by Sewell Stokes
Additional scenes: Nicholas Phipps
Photography: Gordon Dines
Art direction: Maurice Carter
Editing: Peter Tanner
Music: Ernest Irving
Opening: March 1952

Running time: 95 mins.

Life in the probation service, with Cecil Parker as a retired colonial civil servant making a career switch, and coming up against realities of which he never dreamt. A seventeen-year-old Joan Collins makes a formidable debut as a teenage sexpot, otherwise the film is the usual avuncular Ealing view of life.

Mandy
US *Crash of Silence*
Director: Alexander Mackendrick
Producer: Leslie Norman
Cast: Jack Hawkins (Richard Searle)
Terence Morgan (Henry Garland)
Phyllis Calvert (Christine Garland)
Mandy Miller (Mandy Garland)
Godfrey Tearle (Mr Garland Senior)
Marjorie Fielding (Mrs Garland)
Nancy Price (Miss Ellis)
Dorothy Alison (Miss Stockton)
Patricia Plunkett (Miss Cricker)
Eleanor Summerfield (Lily)
Edward Chapman (Ackland)
Colin Gordon (Woollard)
Gabrielle Brune (Secretary)
Julian Aymes (Jimmy Tabor)
Jane Asher (Nina)
Script: Jack Whittingham, Nigel Balchin, from the novel *The Day is Ours* by Hilda Lewis
Photography: Douglas Slocombe
Art direction: Jim Morahan
Editing: Seth Holt
Music: William Alwyn
Opening: July 1952
Running time: 93 mins.

Jack Hawkins, an actor who had been around for more than twenty years, became a star as a result of this film, playing the headmaster of a school for deaf children who becomes closely involved with the mother of an afflicted little girl. The film is moving without becoming mawkish, and excellently written.

The Gentle Gunman
Director: Basil Dearden
Producer: Michael Relph
Cast: John Mills (Terence Sullivan)
Dirk Bogarde (Matt Sullivan)
Elisabeth Sellars (Maureen Fagan)
Barbara Mullen (Molly Fagan)
Robert Beatty (Shinto)
Eddie Byrne (Flynn)
Joseph Tomelty (Dr Brannigan)
Gilbert Harding (Henry Truethorne)
Liam Redmond (Tom Connolly)
Michael Golden (Murphy)
Jack McGowran (McGuire)
James Kenney (Johnny Fagan)
Patric Doonan (Sentry)

Script: Roger Macdougall, from his play
Photography: Gordon Dines
Art direction: Jim Morahan
Editing: Peter Tanner
Music: John Greenwood
Opening: October 1952
Running time: 86 mins.

This rare attempt to examine the Anglo-Irish conflict is unfortunately far too loaded with dialogue to excite as a film, and betrays its stage origins. The celebrated television boor of the day, Gilbert Harding, played the part of a bigoted Englishman.

The Titfield Thunderbolt
Director: Charles Crichton
Producer: Michael Truman
Cast: Stanley Holloway (Valentine)
George Relph (Rev. Mr Weech)
Naunton Wayne (Blakeworth)
John Gregson (Gordon)
Godfrey Tearle (Bishop)
Edie Martin (Emily)
Hugh Griffith (Dan)
Sidney James (Hawkins)
Gabrielle Brune (Joan)
Jack McGowran (Crump)
Ewan Roberts (Pearce)
Reginald Beckwith (Coggett)
Michael Trubshawe (Ruddock)
John Rudling (Inspector)
Frank Atkinson (Police Sergeant)
Nancy O'Neil (Mrs Blakeworth)
Script: T. E. B. Clarke
Photography: Douglas Slocombe, in Technicolor
Art direction: C. P. Norman
Editing: Seth Holt
Music: Georges Auric
Opening: March 1953
Running time: 84 mins.

The first Ealing comedy in Technicolor is a postcard-pretty view of bucolic West Country England, with united villagers fighting a branch line closure by taking over the railway operation themselves. In spite of the 'playing with trains' theme, there is less verve than in earlier Tibby Clarke screenplays.

The Cruel Sea
Director: Charles Frend
Producer: Leslie Norman
Cast: Jack Hawkins (Lieut-Cdr. Ericson)
Donald Sinden (Lieut. Lockhart)
Denholm Elliott (Lieut. Morell)
John Stratton (Ferraby)
Stanley Baker (Bennett)
Virginia McKenna (Julie Hallam)
Moira Lister (Elaine Morell)
June Thorburn (Doris Ferraby)
Liam Redmond (Jim Watts)
Bruce Seton (Bob Tallow)

Megs Jenkins (Glad Tallow)
Meredith Edwards (Yeoman Wells)
John Warner (Baker)
Glyn Houston (Phillips)
Alec McCowen (Tonbridge)
Andrew Cruickshank (Doctor)
Walter Fitzgerald (Warden)
Script: Eric Ambler, from the novel by Nicholas Monsarrat
Photography: Gordon Dines
Art direction: Jim Morahan
Editing: Peter Tanner
Music: Alan Rawsthorne
Opening: March 1953
Running time: 126 mins.

Ealing's respectful version of a celebrated best-seller about the ravages on corvette crews of a long war, with Jack Hawkins as a professional leading a ship of volunteers. It was one of Ealing's most successful pictures in box-office terms, and consolidated Jack Hawkins' reputation.

The Square Ring
Director: Basil Dearden
Producer: Michael Relph
Cast: Jack Warner (Danny Felton)
Robert Beatty (Kid Curtis)
Bill Owen (Happy Burns)
Maxwell Reed (Rick Martell)
George Rose (Whitey Johnson)
Bill Travers (Rowdie Rawlings)
Alfie Bass (Frank Forbes)
Ronald Lewis (Eddie Lloyd)
Sidney James (Adams)
Joan Collins (Frankie)
Bernadette O'Farrell (Peg Curtis)
Kay Kendall (Eve Lewis)
Eddie Byrne (Lou Lewis)
Joan Sims (Bunty)
Sydney Tafler (Wiseacre)
Alexander Gauge (Wiseacre)
Ben Williams (Mr Lloyd)
Madoline Thomas (Mrs Lloyd)
Harry Herbert (De Grazos)
C. M. Nichols (Timekeeper)
Kid Berg (Referee)
Joe Bloom (Referee)
Alf Hines (Barney Deakon)
Script: Robert Westerby, from the play by Ralph W. Peterson
Additional dialogue: Peter Myers, Alec Grahame
Photography: Otto Heller
Art direction: Jim Morahan
Editing: Peter Bezencenet
Opening: July 1953
Running time: 83 mins.

Although originally a play, the concept is typically Ealing – we are shown what goes on behind the scenes at a provincial boxing stadium, and follow the stories of several contenders, who form the customary cross-section of types.

Meet Mr Lucifer
Director: Anthony Pelissier
Producer: Monja Danischewsky
Cast: Stanley Holloway (Sam Hollingsworth)
Peggy Cummins (Kitty Norton)
Jack Watling (Jim Norton)
Barbara Murray (Patricia Pedelty)
Joseph Tomelty (Mr Pedelty)
Gordon Jackson (Hector McPhee)
Jean Cadell (Mrs Macdonald)
Kay Kendall (Lonely Hearts Singer)
Charles Victor (Mr Elder)
Humphrey Lestocq (Arthur Simmonds)
Raymond Huntley (Mr Patterson)
Ernest Thesiger (Mr Macdonald)
Frank Pettingell (Mr Roberts)
Olive Sloane (Mrs Stannard)
Joan Sims (Fairy Queen)
Ian Carmichael (Man Friday)
Geoffrey Keen (Mr Lucifer's Voice)
Gladys Henson (Woman on Bus)
Edie Martin (Deaf Woman)
Dandy Nichols (Mrs Clarke)
Roddy Hughes (Billings)
Gilbert Harding (Himself)
Philip Harben (Himself)
Macdonald Hobley (Himself)
David Miller (Himself)
Script: Monja Danischewsky, from the play *Beggar My Neighbour* by Arnold Ridley
Additional dialogue: Peter Myers, Alec Grahame
Photography: Desmond Dickinson
Art direction: Wilfred Shingleton
Editing: Bernard Gribble
Music: Eric Rogers
Opening: November 1953
Running time: 83 mins.

A restrained attempt to debunk the increasingly popular medium of television marks this comedy in which a pantomime demon king dreams of placing a curse on viewing so that it makes people miserable. There is not enough wit to make the satire effective, but it is of interest to see how dire television was in 1953.

The Love Lottery
Director: Charles Crichton
Producer: Monja Danischewsky
Cast: David Niven (Rex Allerton)
Peggy Cummins (Sally)
Anne Vernon (Jane)
Herbert Lom (Amico)
Gordon Jackson (Ralph)
Charles Victor (Jennings)
Felix Aylmer (Winant)
Theodore Bikel (Parsimonious)
Hattie Jacques (Chambermaid)
John Chandos (Gulliver Kee)
Hugh McDermott (Rodney Wheeler)
Stanley Maxted (Stanton)
June Clyde (Viola)

Sebastian Cabot (Suarez)
Eugene Deckers (Vernet)
Humphrey Bogart (Himself)
Script: Henry Kurnitz, from a story by
Charles Neilson-Terry, Zelma Bramley
Moore
Photography: Douglas Slocombe, in
Technicolor
Art direction: Jim Morahan
Editing: Seth Holt
Music: Benjamin Frankel
Opening: January 1954
Running time: 89 mins.

The only Ealing film to star David
Niven is a comedy in which he plays a
movie star who is first prize in a lottery.
The subject of girlish fan worship is not
one easily handled by the studio and the
Technicolored result is more like the
typical Rank product of the Fifties – a
glass of flat champagne. Someone
persuaded Humphrey Bogart to do a
walk-on at the end of the picture.

The Maggie
US *High and Dry*
Director: Alexander Mackendrick
Producer: Michael Truman
Cast: Paul Douglas (Calvin B. Marshall)
Alex Mackenzie (Captain Mactaggart)
Tommy Kearins (Dougie)
James Copeland (Mate)
Abe Barker (Engineer)
Hubert Gregg (Pusey)
Dorothy Alison (Miss Peterson)
Andrew Keir (Reporter)
Geoffrey Keen (Campbell)
Mark Dignam (Laird)
Jameson Clark (Dirty Dan)
Moultrie Kelsall (Captain)
Meg Buchanan (Sarah)
Fiona Clyne (Sheena)
Script: William Rose
Photography: Gordon Dines
Art direction: Jim Morahan
Editing: Peter Tanner
Music: John Addison
Opening: February 1954
Running time: 92 mins.

Comedy set in Scotland about a roguish
old pufferboat skipper who tricks a
wealthy American into allowing him to
transport his furniture and then defies all
demands to yield. It is a case of wealth
and power versus indigent wiliness, with
the millionaire eventually capitulating.

West of Zanzibar
Director: Harry Watt
Producer: Leslie Norman
Cast: Anthony Steel (Bob Payton)
Sheila Sim (Mary Payton)
William Simons (Tim Payton)
Orlando Martins (M'Kwongwi)
Edric Connor (ushingo)

Martin Benson (Dhofar)
Peter Illing (Khingoni)
Juma (Juma)
Howard Marion Crawford (Wood)
Alan Webb (Official)
R. Stuart Lindsell (Colonel Ryan)
Script: Jack Whittingham, Max Catto,
from a story by Harry Watt
Photography: Paul Beeson, in
Technicolor
Art direction: Jim Morahan
Editing: Peter Bezencenet
Music: Alan Rawsthorne
Opening: March 1954
Running time: 94 mins.

Sequel to *Where No Vultures Fly* with
Sheila Sim taking over the Dinah
Sheridan role. Following drought, the
tribe is resettled on the coast near
Mombasa, but bright city lights subvert
some of the younger members who get
caught up with the ivory smuggling trade.
But Bob Payton saves them.

The Rainbow Jacket
Director: Basil Dearden
Producer: Michael Relph
Cast: Bill Owen (Sam Lilley)
Kay Walsh (Barbara Crain)
Fella Edmonds (Georgie Crain)
Edward Underdown (Geoffrey Tyler)
Honor Blackman (Mrs Tyler)
Robert Morley (Lord Logan)
Wilfrid Hyde White (Lord Stoneleigh)
Charles Victor (Ross)
Frederick Piper (Lukey)
Howard Marion Crawford (Travers)
Sidney James (Harry)
Michael Trubshawe (Gresham)
Ronald Ward (Bornie Rudd)
Brian Roper (Ron Saunders)
Gordon Richards (Himself)
Raymond Glendenning (Himself)
Script: T. E. B. Clarke
Photography: Otto Heller, in Technicolor
Art direction: Tom Morahan
Editing: Jack Harris
Music: William Alwyn
Opening: May 1954
Running time: 99 mins.

Tibby Clarke always wanted to write a
racing screenplay, but the result was less
original than would have been expected,
with the usual plot of crooks trying to
persuade a young lad to throw a race.
Behind-the-scenes glimpses of stable life
and Jockey Club deliberations enliven it,
and the colour photography is pleasant,
apart from obvious studio race shots.

Lease of Life
Director: Charles Frend
Associate producer: Jack Rix
Cast: Robert Donat (Rev. William
Thorne)
Kay Walsh (Mrs Thorne)

Adrienne Corri (Susan Thorne)
Denholm Elliott (Martin Blake)
Walter Fitzgerald (Dean)
Cyril Raymond (Headmaster)
Reginald Beckwith (Journalist)
Richard Wattis (Solicitor)
Frank Atkinson (Verger)
Frederick Piper (Jeweller)
Alan Webb (Dr Pembury)
Beckett Bould (Mr Sproatley)
Vida Hope (Mrs Sproatley)
John Salew (Doctor)
Richard Leech (Carter)
Jean Anderson (Miss Calthorp)
Edie Martin (Her Friend)
Russell Walters (Russell)
Robert Sandford (Boy)
Mark Daley (Spooner)
Script: Eric Ambler, from a story by
Frank Baker, Patrick Jenkins
Photography: Douglas Slocombe, in
Eastmancolor
Art direction: Jim Morahan
Editing: Peter Tanner
Music: Alan Rawsthorne
Opening: October 1954
Running time: 94 mins.

Robert Donat's only Ealing film has
him playing a Yorkshire clergyman,
stricken with a fatal illness, who eschews a
comfortable incumbency because the
terms offend his conscience. A sincere,
well-wrought film with an impressive
central performance.

The Divided Heart
Director: Charles Crichton
Producer: Michael Truman
Cast: Cornell Borchers (Inga Hartl)
Yvonne Mitchell (Sonja Slavko)
Armin Dahlen (Franz Hartl)
Michael Ray (Toni)
Alexander Knox (Chief Justice)
Liam Redmond (Justice)
Eddie Byrne (Justice)
Geoffrey Keen (Marks)
Theodore Bikel (Josip)
Ferdy Mayne (Dr Muller)
Martin Stephens (Hans)
John Schlesinger (Ticket Collector)
Alec McCowen (Reporter)
André Mikhelson (Professor Miran)
Pamela Stirling (Mlle Poncet)
Script: Jack Whittingham, Richard
Hughes
Photography: Otto Heller
Art direction: Edward Carrick
Editing: Peter Bezencenet
Music: Georges Auric
Opening: November 1954
Running time: 89 mins.

An attempt at a tug-of-love emotional
drama, with two mothers facing up to
each other in a post-war court. The true
mother has returned from Auschwitz; the

adoptive mother, her husband a prisoner of the Russians, has raised the child as her own. Having acquired a powerful situation, Ealing does not know what to do with it.

Out of the Clouds
Director: Basil Dearden
Producer: Michael Relph
Cast: Anthony Steel (Gus Randall)
Robert Beatty (Nick Melbourne)
David Knight (Bill Steiner)
Margo Lorenz (Leah Roche)
James Robertson Justice (Capt. Brent)
Eunice Gayson (Penny Henson)
Isabel Dean (Mrs Malcolm)
Marie Lohr (Rich Woman)
Esma Cannon (Her Companion)
Bernard Lee (Customs Officer)
Gordon Harker (Taxi Driver)
Abraham Sofaer (Indian)
Megs Jenkins (Landlady)
Melissa Stribling (Jean Osmond)
Sidney James (Gambler)
Nicholas Phipps (Hilton Davidson)
Jill Melford (Eleanor)
Arthur Howard (Booking Clerk)
Cyril Luckham (Doctor)
Michael Howard (Purvis)
Jack Lambert (Designer)
Katie Johnson (Passenger)
Script: Michael Relph, John Eldridge, Rex Reinits
Photography: Paul Beeson, in Eastmancolor
Art direction: Jim Morahan
Editing: Jack Harris
Music: Richard Addinsell
Opening: February 1955
Running time: 88 mins.
   London Airport is fogbound, leaving a number of passengers stranded. The film follows some of the stories in the standard manner, but the result is jaded in comparison with earlier Dearden–Relph exercises. A massive Heathrow terminal interior was built on Ealing's biggest stage.

The Night My Number Came Up
Director: Leslie Norman
Associate producer: Tom Morahan
Cast: Michael Redgrave (Air Marshal John Hardie)
Sheila Sim (Mary Campbell)
Alexander Knox (Owen Robertson)
Ursula Jeans (Mrs Robertson)
Denholm Elliott (Flt-Lieut. Mackenzie)
Ralph Truman (Lord Wainwright)
Michael Hordern (Cdr. Lindsay)
Nigel Stock (Sqdn-Ldr. Walker)
George Rose (Walter Bennett)
Bill Kerr (Soldier)
Alfie Bass (Soldier)
Victor Maddern (Engineer)

Stratford Johns (Sergeant)
Script: R. C. Sherriff, from a story by Air Vice-Marshal Sir Victor Goddard
Photography: Lionel Banes
Art direction: Jim Morahan
Editing: Peter Tanner
Music: Malcolm Arnold
Opening: March 1955
Running time: 94 mins.
   A late Ealing foray into the occult, with a story about a dream that foretells a plane crash. Some of the suspense is diminished due to the flashback construction of the film, but it is still a good yarn.

The Ship that Died of Shame
US *PT Raiders*
Director: Basil Dearden
Producer: Michael Relph
Cast: Richard Attenborough (George Hoskins)
George Baker (Bill Randall)
Bill Owen (Birdie Dick)
Virginia McKenna (Helen Randall)
Roland Culver (Fordyce)
Ralph Truman (Sir Richard)
Bernard Lee (Sam Brewster)
Harold Goodwin (Customs Officer)
John Chandos (Raines)
John Longden (Detective)
David Langton (Man in Bar)
Stratford Johns (Garage Man)
Script: John Whiting, Michael Relph, Basil Dearden, from the novel by Nicholas Monsarrat
Photography: Gordon Dines
Art direction: Bernard Robinson
Editing: Peter Bezencenet
Music: William Alwyn
Opening: April 1955
Running time: 95 mins.
   Wartime colleagues join up afterwards to indulge in smuggling activities, having bought their old boat for the purpose of running contraband across the English Channel. They become involved with a murderer on the run, and it all develops into a routine thriller.

Touch and Go
US *The Light Touch*
Director: Michael Truman
Associate producer: Seth Holt
Cast: Jack Hawkins (Jim Fletcher)
Margaret Johnston (Helen Fletcher)
June Thorburn (Peggy Fletcher)
John Fraser (Richard Kenyon)
Roland Culver (Reg Fairbright)
Alison Leggatt (Alice Fairbright)
Henry Longhurst (Mr Pritchett)
Margaret Halstan (Mrs Pritchett)
James Hayter (Kimball)
Basil Dignam (Stevens)
Bessie Love (Mrs Baxter)
Gabrielle Brune (Waitress)

Heather Sears (Student)
Margaret Courtenay (Kimball's Secretary)
Script: William Rose, from a story by William and Tania Rose
Photography: Douglas Slocombe, in Technicolor
Art direction: Edward Carrick
Editing: Peter Tanner
Music: John Addison
Opening: September 1955
Running time: 85 mins.
   A trendy furniture designer, tired of his employer's lack of appreciation, decides to emigrate to Australia, to the chagrin of his family. After much *angst* all round he changes his mind. A thin, over-worked situation yields a few good moments, but it is a disappointment from the writer of *Genevieve*.

The Ladykillers
Director: Alexander Mackendrick
Associate producer: Seth Holt
Cast: Katie Johnson (Mrs Wilberforce)
Alec Guinness (Professor Marcus)
Cecil Parker (Major Courtney)
Herbert Lom (Louis)
Peter Sellers (Harry)
Danny Green (One-Round)
Jack Warner (Superintendent)
Philip Stainton (Sergeant)
Ewan Roberts (Constable)
Frankie Howerd (Barrow Boy)
Kenneth Connor (Taxi Driver)
Fred Griffiths (Junk Man)
Harold Goodwin (Parcels Clerk)
Stratford Johns (Security Guard)
Edie Martin (Lettice)
Helen Burls (Hypatia)
Evelyn Kerry (Amelia)
Phoebe Hodgson (Old Lady)
Leonard Sharp (Pavement Artist)
Jack Melford (Detective)
Script: William Rose
Photography: Otto Heller, in Technicolor
Art direction: Jim Morahan
Editing: Jack Harris
Music: Tristram Cary
Opening: December 1955
Running time: 97 mins.
   Ealing's last comic masterpiece, in which a gang of ill-matched bankroll thieves lodge in a genteel house near King's Cross, to be thwarted by their aged innocent landlady, and meet sudden ends. Alec Guinness with astonishing false teeth is outstanding as their leader, as is Katie Johnson, an Ealing bit-player achieving stardom at the age of seventy-seven.

Who Done It?
Director: Basil Dearden
Producer: Michael Relph
Cast: Benny Hill (Hugo Dill)

Belinda Lee (Frankie Mayne)
David Kossoff (Zacco)
Garry Marsh (Insp. Hancock)
George Margo (Barakov)
Ernest Thesiger (Sir Walter)
Thorley Walters (Raymond Courtney)
Nicholas Phipps (Scientist)
Gibb McLaughlin (Scientist)
Charles Hawtrey (Disc Jockey)
Stratford Johns (Policeman)
Denis Shaw (Otto Stumpf)
Frederick Schiller (Gruber)
Irene Handl (Customer)
Jeremy Hawk (Himself)
Robert McDermott (Himself)
Dagenham Girl Pipers (Themselves)
Script: T. E. B. Clarke
Photography: Otto Heller
Art direction: Jim Morahan
Editing: Peter Tanner
Music: Philip Green
Opening: March 1956
Running time: 85 mins.

Almost a throwback to the days of
George Formby and Will Hay, in that this
film is unashamedly a vehicle for a
comedian who had made his reputation
elsewhere. Benny Hill plays an ice-rink
sweeper who aspires to be a detective and
uncovers a spy plot.

The Feminine Touch
US *The Gentle Touch*
Director: Pat Jackson
Associate producer: Jack Rix
Cast: George Baker (Jim Alcott)
Belinda Lee (Susan Richards)
Delphi Lawrence (Pat Martin)
Adrienne Corri (Maureen O'Brien)
Henryetta Edwards (Ann Bowland)
Barbara Archer (Liz Jenkins)
Diana Wynyard (Matron)
Christopher Rhodes (Ted Russell)
Joan Haythorne (Home Sister)
Beatrice Varley (Sister Snow)
Richard Leech (Casualty Doctor)
Dandy Nichols (Skivvy)
Newton Blick (Porter)
Mandy Miller (Jessie)
Dorothy Alison (The Suicide)
Joss Ambler (Bateman)
Script: Ian McCormick, from the novel *A
Lamp is Heavy* by Sheila Mackay Russell
Photography: Paul Beeson, in
Eastmancolor
Art direction: Edward Carrick
Editing: Peter Bezencenet
Music: Clifton Parker
Opening: March 1956
Running time: 91 mins.

A group of young nurses are followed
through their training, facing the familiar
trials of arduous duties, romantic
complications, nightmare patients, jolly
doctors, stern matrons. *Doctor in the*

House had trod the same ground a year or
two earlier, but humorously.

The Long Arm
US *The Third Key*
Director: Charles Frend
Associate producer: Tom Morahan
Cast: Jack Hawkins (Supt. Tom
Halliday)
Dorothy Alison (Mary Halliday)
Michael Brooke Jr. (Tony Halliday)
John Stratton (Sgt. Ward)
Geoffrey Keen (Supt. Jim Malcolm)
Newton Blick (Cdr. Harris)
Ralph Truman (Col. Blenkinsop)
Joss Ambler (Cashier)
Sydney Tafler (Stone)
Richard Leech (Night Watchman)
Meredith Edwards (Thomas)
Ian Bannen (Workman)
Maureen Davis (His Wife)
George Rose (Slob)
Glyn Houston (Sergeant)
Nicholas Parsons (PC Bates)
Alec McCowen (Surgeon)
Ursula Howells (Mrs Elliott)
John Welsh (Estate Agent)
Gillian Webb (Housewife)
Maureen Delaney (Daily)
Harry Locke (Dealer)
William Mervyn (Manager)
Harold Goodwin (Official)
Sam Kydd (Policeman)
Stratford Johns (Policeman)
Script: Janet Green, Robert Barr, from a
story by Robert Barr
Additional dialogue: Dorothy and
Campbell Christie
Photography: Gordon Dines
Art direction: Edward Carrick
Editing: Gordon Stone
Music: Gerbrand Schurmann
Opening: June 1956
Running time: 96 mins.

The last film made at Ealing was this
Scotland Yard thriller, with Jack Hawkins
as a weary, overworked detective
superintendent pursuing an ingenious safe
breaker. There is a televisual style to the
filming, anticipating the shape of
programmes to come.

Man in the Sky
US *Decision Against Time*
Director: Charles Crichton
Associate producer: Seth Holt
Cast: Jack Hawkins (John Mitchell)
Elisabeth Sellars (Mary Mitchell)
Catherine Lacey (Her Mother)
Jeremy Bodkin (Nicholas Mitchell)
Gerald Lohan (Philip Mitchell)
John Stratton (Peter Hook)
Walter Fitzgerald (Conway)
Eddie Byrne (Ashmore)
Donald Pleasance (Crabtree)

Victor Maddern (Joe Biggs)
Lionel Jeffries (Keith)
Ernest Clark (Maine)
Russell Waters (Sim)
Howard Marion Crawford (Ingram)
Megs Jenkins (Mrs Ingram)
Script: William Rose, John Eldridge,
from a story by William Rose
Photography: Douglas Slocombe
Art direction: Jim Morahan
Editing: Peter Tanner
Music: Gerbrand Schurmann
Opening: January 1957
Running time: 87 mins.

A test pilot struggles against the odds to
prevent a crash which could put a
company out of business, and is attacked
by his wife for taking unnecessary risks. A
combination of psychological drama and
cliff-hanger, which does not entirely
satisfy. Ealing's first at Borehamwood.

The Shiralee
Director: Leslie Norman
Producer: Jack Rix
Cast: Peter Finch (Jim Macauley)
Elisabeth Sellars (Marge Macauley)
Dana Wilson (Buster Macauley)
Rosemary Harris (Lily Parker)
Russell Napier (Mr Parker)
George Rose (Donny)
Niall McGinnis (Beauty Kelly)
Tessie O'Shea (Bella)
Sidney James (Luke)
Charles Tingwell (Jim Muldoon)
Reg Lye (Desmond)
Barbara Archer (Shopgirl)
Alex Mango (Papadoulos)
John Phillips (Doctor)
Script: Leslie Norman, Neil Paterson,
from the novel by Darcy Niland
Photography: Paul Beeson
Art direction: Jim Morahan
Editing: Gordon Stone
Music: John Addison
Opening: July 1957
Running time: 99 mins.

Back to Australia for a story about a
swagman who, finding his wife has a
lover, takes to the road again with his
small daughter. There is much outback
scenery, and a feeling of space and
remoteness, but the film is most
successful in depicting the growth of the
relationship between the little girl and her
itinerant father.

Barnacle Bill
US *All At Sea*
Director: Charles Frend
Associate producer: Dennis von Thal
Cast: Alec Guinness (William Ambrose /
Six Ancestors)
Irene Browne (Arabella Barrington)
Maurice Denham (Mayor)

Victor Maddern (Figg)
Percy Herbert (Tommy)
George Rose (Bullen)
Lionel Jeffries (Garrod)
Harold Goodwin (Duckworth)
Warren Mitchell (Artie White)
Miles Malleson (Angler)
Frederick Piper (Harry)
Richard Wattis (Registrar)
Eric Pohlmann (Consul)
Jackie Collins (June)
Donald Churchill (Teddy Boy)
Donald Pleasance (Teller)
Allan Cuthbertson (Councillor)
Lloyd Lamble (Supt. Browning)
Script: T. E. B. Clarke
Photography: Douglas Slocombe
Art direction: Alan Withy
Editing: Jack Harris
Music: John Addison
Opening: December 1957
Running time: 87 mins.

A promising Tibby Clarke joke, about the last of a line of seadogs who is afflicted with such chronic seasickness that he can only command a seaside pier, fails to take off into the splendid fancies of only a few years earlier, and the portrayal by Alec Guinness of all his ancestors uneasily recalls *Kind Hearts and Coronets*.

Davy
Director: Michael Relph
Producer: Basil Dearden
Cast: Harry Secombe (Davy Morgan)
Ron Randell (George)
George Relph (Uncle Pat)
Susan Shaw (Gwen)
Bill Owen (Eric)
Peter Frampton (Tim)
Alexander Knox (Sir Giles)
Adele Leigh (Joanna)
Isabel Dean (Miss Carstairs)
Gladys Henson (Waitress)
Joan Sims (Waitress)
Elisabeth Fraser (Waitress)
Kenneth Connor (Herbie)
Campbell Singer (Doorkeeper)
Bernard Cribbins (ASM)
George Moon (Jerry)
Clarkson Rose (Mrs MacGillicuddy)
Script: William Rose
Photography: Douglas Slocombe, in Technicolor/Technirama
Art direction: Alan Withy
Editing: Peter Tanner
Music: Wagner, Puccini, Mozart, played by the orchestra of the Royal Opera House, Covent Garden
Opening: December 1957

Running time: 83 mins.
Slapstick and tears behind the scenes with a family variety troupe, when a key member is auditioned at Covent Garden. Will Davy turn to opera, or stay clowning? An uneasy collision of opposed cultures.

Dunkirk
Director: Leslie Norman
Associate producer: Michael Forlong
Cast: John Mills (Corp. Tubby Binns)
Bernard Lee (Charles Foreman)
Maxine Audley (Diana Foreman)
Richard Attenborough (John Holden)
Patricia Plunkett (Grace Holden)
Anthony Nicholls (Spokesman)
Cyril Raymond (Gen. Lord Gort)
Robert Urquhart (Mike)
Ray Jackson (Barlow)
Ronald Hines (Miles)
Sean Barrett (Frankie)
Roland Curram (Harper)
Meredith Edwards (Dave Bellman)
Michael Gwynn (Sheerness Commander)
Kenneth Cope (Lieut. Lumpkin)
Joss Ambler (Small Boat Owner)
Frederick Piper (Small Boat Owner)
Lionel Jeffries (Medical Corps Colonel)
Harry Landis (Dr Levy)
Victor Maddern (Seaman)
Bud Flanagan (Himself)
Chesney Allen (Himself)
Rodney Diak (Pannet)
Michael Shillo (Jouvet)
Eddie Byrne (Commander)
Script: W. P. Lipscomb, David Divine, from *Dunkirk* by Ewan Butler and from the novel *The Big Pick-up* by Elleston Trevor
Photography: Paul Beeson
Art direction: Jim Morahan
Editing: Gordon Stone
Music: Malcolm Arnold
Opening: March 1958
Running time: 135 mins.
The story of the great retreat of the British army in 1940 is told through a handful of characters and their experiences. A respectful war film at the conclusion of Ealing's career under Sir Michael Balcon.

Nowhere to Go
Director: Seth Holt
Associate producer: Eric Williams
Cast: George Nader (Paul Gregory)
Maggie Smith (Bridget Howard)
Bernard Lee (Vic Sloane)

Geoffrey Keen (Insp. Scott)
Bessie Love (Harriet P. Jefferson)
Andrée Melly (Rosa)
Howard Marion Crawford (Cameron)
Arthur Howard (Coin Dealer)
Lionel Jeffries (Pet Shop Man)
Harry H. Corbett (Sullivan)
Harry Locke (Bendel)
Noel Howlett (Mr Howard)
Oliver Johnston (Strongroom Official)
Beckett Bould (Gamekeeper)
Margaret McGrath (Rosemary)
Script: Seth Holt, Kenneth Tynan, from the novel by Donald Mackenzie
Photography: Paul Beeson
Art direction: Alan Withy
Editing: Harry Aldous
Music: Dizzy Reece
Opening: December 1958
Running time: 87 mins.
A stylish action thriller that begins with a jailbreak. A thief is sheltered by a girl socialite, and dies on the run falsely suspecting that she has betrayed him. Maggie Smith makes her film debut.

The Siege of Pinchgut
Director: Harry Watt
Producer: Eric Williams
Cast: Aldo Ray (Matt Kirk)
Neil McCallum (Johnny Kirk)
Heather Sears (Ann Fulton)
Victor Maddern (Bert)
Carlo Justini (Luke)
Gerry Duggan (Pat Fulton)
Barbara Mullen (Mrs Fulton)
Alan Tilvern (Supt. Hanna)
Kenneth J. Warren (Commissioner)
Richard Vernon (Under Secretary)
Martin Boddey (Brigadier)
Grant Taylor (Macey)
Script: Harry Watt, Jon Cleary, from a story by Inman Hunter, Lee Robinson
Additional dialogue: Alexander Baron
Photography: Gordon Dines
Art direction: Alan Withy
Editing: Gordon Stone
Music: Kenneth V. Jones
Opening: August 1959
Running time: 100 mins.
Harry Watt had the doubtful honour of directing the last of all Ealing films, which was set in Australia with interiors filmed at Borehamwood. A prisoner on his way to a long sentence escapes and holds a family hostage on an island in Sydney Harbour, with a gun trained on a nearby ammunition ship to deter the authorities. Several issues are raised and dropped to make way for excitement.

Bibliography

The following books were consulted in the preparation of *Forever Ealing*:

Anderson, Lindsay, *Making a Film* [Secret People] (George Allen & Unwin, 1952)

Armes, Roy, *A Critical History of the British Cinema* (Secker & Warburg, 1978)

Balcon, Michael (Intro.), *Twenty Years of British Films* (Falcon, 1947)

Balcon, Michael, *Michael Balcon Presents . . . A Lifetime of Films* (Hutchinson, 1969)

Barr, Charles, *Ealing Studios* (Cameron & Tayleur/David & Charles, 1977)

Baxter, John, *The Australian Cinema* (Pacific Books, 1970)

Betts, Ernest, *The Film Business* (George Allen & Unwin, 1973)

Clarke, T. E. B., *This is Where I Came In* (Michael Joseph, 1974)

Collier, John W., *A Film in the Making* [It Always Rains on Sunday] (World Film Publications, 1947)

Danischewsky, Monja (ed.), *Michael Balcon's 25 Years In Films* (World Film Publications, 1947)

Danischewsky, Monja, *White Russian, Red Face* (Gollancz, 1966)

Dean, Basil, *Mind's Eye* [vol. 2 of autobiography] (Hutchinson, 1973)

Durgnat, Raymond, *A Mirror for England* (Faber, 1970)

Fisher, John, *George Formby* (Woburn/Futura, 1975)

Frayn, Michael, in *The Age of Austerity*, Michael Sissons, Philip French (eds.) (Hodder & Stoughton, 1963)

Gifford, Denis, *British Cinema: an Illustrated Guide* (Zwemmer, 1968)

Gifford, Denis, *British Film Catalogue 1895–1970* (David & Charles, 1973)

Gifford, Denis, *The Illustrated Who's Who in British Films* (Batsford, 1978)

Halliwell, Leslie, *The Filmgoer's Companion* (7th Edition) (Granada, 1980)

Hawkins, Jack, *Anything for a Quiet Life* (Elm Tree, 1973)

James, David, *Scott of the Antarctic* (Convoy Publications, 1948)

Kelly, Terence; Norton, Graham; Perry, George, *A Competitive Cinema* (Institute of Economic Affairs, 1966)

Low, Rachael, *History of the British Film* (vols. 2, 3) (Allen & Unwin, 1949, 1950)

McCallum, John, *Life with Googie* (Heinemann, 1979)

Manvell, Roger (ed.), *Three British Screenplays* [inc. *Scott of the Antarctic*] (Methuen, 1950)

Manvell, Roger (ed.), *The Cinema 1950, 1951, 1952* (3 vols., Penguin)

Manvell, Roger, *Films and the Second World War* (Dent, 1974)

Mayer, J. P., *British Cinemas and their Audiences, Sociological Studies* (Dennis Dobson, 1948)

Noble, Peter, *British Film Yearbook, 1945–6, 1947–8* (British Yearbooks 1946, 1948)

Oakley, Charles, *Where We Came In* (George Allen & Unwin, 1964)

PEP, *The British Film Industry* (Political & Economic Planning, 1952)

Perry, George, *The Great British Picture Show* (Hart-Davis MacGibbon, 1974)

Reade, Eric, *The Australian Screen* (Lansdowne Press, Melbourne, 1975)

Seaton, Ray and Martin, Roy, *Good Morning Boys: Will Hay Master of Comedy* (Barrie & Jenkins, 1978)

Speed, F. Maurice, *Film Review* 1944 and annually

Taylor, John Russell (Intro.), *Masterworks of British Cinema* [inc. *Kind Hearts and Coronets*] (Lorrimer, 1974)

Tennyson, Charles, *Penrose Tennyson* (Privately published, 1943)

Watt, Harry, *Don't Look at the Camera* (Paul Elek, 1974)

Wood, Alan, *Mr Rank* (Hodder & Stoughton, 1952)

Index

Page numbers in italics indicate illustrations and/or their captions

EALING STUDIOS present

Alec Guinness & Stanley Holloway
with Sidney James & Alfie Bass

THE LAVENDER HILL MOB

The Cruel Sea
BY NICHOLAS MONSARRAT

starring
**JACK HAWKINS
DONALD SINDEN
DENHOLM ELLIOTT
VIRGINIA McKENNA**

CEDRIC HARDWICKE
STANLEY HOLLOWAY
ALFRED DRAYTON
CYRIL FLETCHER
BERNARD MILES

NICHOLAS NICKLEBY

DEREK BOND
SALLY ANN HOWES
FAY COMPTON
SYBIL THORNDIKE
MARY MERRALL
ATHENE SEYLER

Produced by MICHAEL BALCON Directed By CAVALCANTI
Screen Play By JOHN DIGHTON

EALING STUDIOS present
Jack WARNER
Alastair SIM
Valerie WHITE and

The Blood-&-Thunder Boys in

HUE & CRY

Produced by MICHAEL BALCON
Directed by CHARLES CRICHTON
Screenplay by T.E.B. CLARKE

EALING STUDIOS PRESENT
A MICHAEL BALCON PRODUCTION

Stanley HOLLOWAY Naunton WAYNE George RELPH John GREGSON

The Titfield Thunderbolt

with Godfrey TEARLE Hugh GRIFFITH Gabrielle BRUNE Sidney JAMES

TECHNICOLOR

Produced by Michael TRUMAN
Original Screenplay by T.E.B. CLARKE

Ealing Studios present
A MICHAEL BALCON PRODUCTION

GAUMONT HAYMARKET
MARBLE ARCH PAVILION

ERIC PORTMAN
CECIL PARKER
HELEN CHERRY
SUSAN STEPHEN

HIS EXCELLENCY

PRODUCED BY MICHAEL TRUMAN
DIRECTED BY ROBERT HAMER

EALING STUDIOS PRESENT

PINK STRING
and
SEALING WAX

MERVYN JOHNS
GOOGIE WITHERS
GORDON JACKSON
SALLY ANN HOWES

EALING STUDIOS PRESENT
A MICHAEL BALCON PRODUCTION

THE
GENTLE
GUNMAN

PRODUCED AND DIRECTED BY MICHAEL RELPH AND BASIL DEARDEN